WHISKEY

AND

WILD WOMEN

WHISKEY AND

BY CY MARTIN

HART Publishing Company, Inc.
New York City

An Amusing Account of the Saloons and
Bawds of the Old West.

WILD WOMEN

DEDICATED TO
Foster-Harris and Dwight Swain
who taught me how to
get it all together

Copyright © 1974

HART PUBLISHING COMPANY, INC., NEW YORK, N.Y. 10012
ISBN No. 08055-1125-3 (paperback 08055-0185-1)
Library of Congress Catalog Card No. 74-76530

Manufactured in the United States of America

Contents

Acknowledgments

THE AUTHOR WISHES to thank the following for their help in securing photographs: The McBride Museum, Whitehorse, Yukon Territory; the Western History Department, Denver Public Library; the Western History Collections, University of Oklahoma Library, Norman; the Wyoming State Archives and Historical Department, Cheyenne; the Kansas State Historical Society, Topeka; the State Historical Society of Colorado, Denver; the Public Archives of Canada, Ottawa; the Nebraska State Historical Society, Lincoln; the Idaho Historical Society, Boise; the California State Library, Sacramento; the late Graham Hardy of Virginia City, Nevada; the Wells Fargo Bank History Room, San Francisco; the North Dakota State Historical Society, Bismarck; the San Francisco Maritime Museum; the Alaska Travel Division, Juneau; the Provincial Archives of British Columbia, Victoria; the California Division of Beaches and Parks, Sacramento; the Montana Highway Commission, Helena; the Department of Travel Industry, Victoria, British Columbia; and Fort Union National Monument, Watrous, New Mexico. A detailed list of picture credits may be found at the back of the book.

In addition to helping with photographs, James Davis of the Denver Public Library was most kind in making suggestions regarding the text itself. Professor William Egan of the History Department of Southern Colorado State College allowed me to use his excerpts from the early issues of the Pueblo *Star-Journal*. Sam Edelstein was a patient and thor-

7

ough critic of the manuscript. Finally, I must thank my wife for her patience, fortitude, and invaluable assistance in bringing this book to completion.

CY MARTIN
Pueblo, Colorado

The Names of the Dames

THE TENDER FEELINGS many Western men had for their prosti-
tutes is shown in the nicknames they gave their favorites.
"Queen" and "Rose" were popular appellations—Wild Rose,
Texas Rose, Prairie Rose, Irish Queen, Spanish Queen—as
were the more descriptive sobriquets, such as Little Gold
Dollar, Peg-Leg Annie, and Velvet Ass Rose. One of Calamity
Jane's partners for a time in Wyoming was Cotton Tail, who,
of course, was a natural blonde. Some of this sentiment for the
women who helped make the West is expressed in a poem by
Sue Edelstein:

WHAT'S IN A NAME

In the red light districts of boom towns
    Flourished a popular breed.
Heifer-like women plied their trade
    Amongst miners' uncontrollable greed.

The hookers brought humanization
    To the roughness of pioneer life.
The softness and frills of the bawdy house
    Took the edge off o' some o' the strife.

Over hooch in the local casino
    Men would boast of their prowess and strength
With the bawds 'cross the line in the brothel
    Their high praises would be sung at length:

9

"Oh, Velvet Ass Annie's a good un."
  "Don't forget the Oregon Mare!"
"And the Flame of the Yukon's dancin'!"
  "And Cotton Tail's soft golden hair!"

"Why there's Red Mountain Hattie,
  And Scarlet Sister Mattie,
Queen Gertie, 'Short and Dirty,'
  Toothpick Lillie and Two Ton Tillie."

"And you gotta watch Shanghai Kelley,
  And Glass-eyed Nellie,
Whispering Mickey and Cowboy Maggie,
  White Dog Lizzie and Wide-ass Nellie, and more:

"The high class: Madame Bulldog,
  And Josephine Icebod, Lady Jane Grey,
Madame Featherlegs, Madame Butterfly,
  And Madame Gabrielle of the Lively Flea."

Real names are long lost and forgotten
  And these new ones would do in their stead.
You gotta figure few people would use them
  Except in saloons or in bed.

Glossary

Bagnio A house of prostitution. Its first recorded English usage in this sense occurs in 1624. The origin of the word is the Italian *bagno*, or public bathhouse, commonly used for immoral purposes. In England, these houses were also called stews.

Bawd Since about 1700, used in reference to a female who keeps a house of prostitution. The origin is doubtful, but it probably is derived from the Old French word *baud*, or merry.

Bawdyhouse A house run by a bawd.

Boarding House A euphemism used by frontier madams to describe their establishment. Derived from the fact that the girls were furnished room and board.

Broad The word used as a noun comes to us from hobo slang. As an adjective meaning "loose" or "indecent," it dates back to 16th-century England. The origin of the American usage is in the idea that a woman is broadminded if she will sell herself. "Broad" also refers obliquely to the female's wider pelvis.

Brothel A house of prostitution. Its origin is in the Old English word brothern, meaning ruined. The term once referred to the person and not to the place of work.

Bullpen See *cowyard*.

Call Girl A prostitute who does business at a place other than where she lives. She is usually called to work, hence the term.

Celestial Female A Chinese prostitute. The term derives from the high regard in which the oldest trade was held by the Chinese.

Chileano Any Spanish or mestizo prostitute. The term originated with the men who patronized the large number of Chilean women in San Francisco during the gold rush.

Chippy A young girl of loose morals. Originally used as an adjective describing cheap or vulgar physical sensation.

Chola A Spanish or Mexican girl of loose morals.

Courtesan A euphemistic appellation for a prostitute. The origin of the word is French, referring to a woman attracted to the court of a king—hence a high-class prostitute. In English, the word dates back to 1549.

Cowyard A large institution housing prostitutes. The origin is in doubt, but is thought to be from bovine breeding. Sometimes the phrase bullpen, or heifer den, was used instead.

Crib Originally a term which meant a stall for an ox, by 1597 "crib" signified a cabin or hovel. In the American West, a crib was a small dwelling for a prostitute.

Cyprian A prostitute. The origin is, of course, Cyprus, the holy island of the goddess Venus. Cyprus was noted for its temples of love, hence those who practiced Venus' art were called Cyprians.

Daughter of Joy A Chinese slave-prostitute.

Fairy Belle A prostitute. The source of this term is the sexual promiscuity of the legendary fairies.

Gagger Hobo slang for a pimp.

Gooseberry Ranch Hobo slang for a brothel. The origin is from the word goose, meaning to tickle lewdly.

Goosing Ranch   Hobo slang for a brothel.

Harlot   An unchaste woman. In Old English, the word referred exclusively to a man.

Heifer Den   See *cowyard*.

Hog Ranch   A frontier term for a house of prostitution. It probably has the same origin as cowyard.

Hooker   A purely American term referring to a streetwalker. The word probably derives from the habit such women have of hooking arms with their prospects.

Hurdy-Gurdy   A girl who travels with a musical entertainment company. The term comes from the instrument played while she danced.

Kate   A favorite prostitute. The probable origin for the word is the Dutch word *kat*, meaning a wanton woman.

Kimono Girl   A term for prostitute which makes reference to the article of clothing worn during working hours.

Ladies of Joy   Prostitutes.

Line   The prostitution district of a Western town. In the early days, the cribs usually formed a line down a narrow street.

Mac   A pimp; from the French word *maquereau*.

Madam   One who runs a house of prostitution. By 1761, the term was used to describe a kept mistress or a prostitute.

Nymph   A beautiful young lady of actual or imagined immorality. The reference is to the sexually promiscuous nymphs of mythology.

Nymph du Pave   A French term meaning streetwalker or, literally, girl of the pavement.

Old Ladies' Home   A hobo name for a decorous brothel.

Painted Lady   A prostitute. "Good" ladies of the West did not use makeup.

Parlor House A house of prostitution. Customers would wait in the parlor before adjourning to the rooms.

Pimp A man who procures trade for a prostitute and lives on a percentage of her income. The term has been in English since at least the very early seventeenth century. It may be derived from the Old French word *pimpant*, meaning seducing or alluring in outward appearance.

Pretty Waiter Girls Girls who worked in bars and music halls, often prostituting as a source of extra income.

Red-Light District The section of town where houses of prostitution are to be found. Such places customarily advertised by means of a red lantern or light.

Resort A house of prostitution.

Shady Lady A woman of dubious moral fiber. By the mid-nineteenth century, the term was in common use, referring to a woman whose character could not bear any close investigation.

Sister in Law The term used by pimps for their prostitutes.

Sporting Girl An inmate of a sporting house.

Sporting House A house of prostitution. The original meaning of the term was an inn where sporting men gathered.

Strange Woman A prostitute. The origin of the term is in Proverbs 2:16, 18.

Streetwalker A prostitute who makes contact with her clients on the street.

Succubus A prostitute. The term derives from the belief in witchcraft that the Devil has carnal relations with witches through his intermediary, the succubus. Also, the demon succubus had intercourse with mortal men in their sleep.

Tenderloin The red-light district. Originally the term referred to the police district of New York which included the greatest concentration of theaters, hotels, and places of amusement.

Whore   A prostitute. Although the term is now confined to only the coarsest of speech, it is probably the oldest synonym still in use.

Yankedo   A Mexican girl who became a camp follower of the Americans during the Mexican War.

The wild women of the 19th century combined raw sensuality with a maidenly grace that often had to be feigned.

A Little Background

WITH THE END of the Mexican War in 1846 and the discovery of gold at Sutter's Mill in California two years later, the West was opened with a rush. Thousands upon thousands of Easterners—adventurous, avaricious, or discontented—left their homes to try their skill and luck in the wild West. It was not long before the names of such boomtowns as San Francisco, Deadwood, Tombstone, Leadville, and Denver became bywords back East.

Soon after the birth of any new boomtown, it was ready to swing into its first phase of growth. Hustle was the name of the game. Hustle to get the choice town lots. Hustle to get the first shipment of new merchandise. Hustle to build the first saloon, the first gambling palace, the first brothel. There were great profits to be made, but the gamble was equally great. The old warning of "haste makes waste" was never in the thoughts of the boomtown entrepreneurs. Their only object was to dig the gold and silver from the miners' pockets before someone else did, to get a piece of the trail hands' hard-earned cash before it was all spent.

In the rush, all types of people appeared. The first was the prospective saloonkeeper, who knew he was starting a sure thing. Not long after him came the girl of the "line," the row of small houses on the outskirts of town where prostitutes plied their time-honored trade. A successful and ambitious chippy might aspire to become a fancy madam, operating a first-class parlor house.

Typically, the first saloon in a nascent boomtown was a tent in which a board was set across two barrels to form a bar. The saloonkeeper ladled out his whiskey in tin cups to the thirsty men. By the time the proprietor shifted his establishment to a more sturdy structure, he might have procured a few girls to sell their services to the patrons of the bar. The saloonkeeper's next step was the acquisition of a piano, and pianist, both brought into the boomtown at great trouble and expense.

At the time of the Mexican War (or the War of Intervention, as the Mexicans called it), the keyboard virtuosos were playing "Clarin de Campaña" or "The Trumpet of Battle." Then when the California gold rush came along, the favorite was "Hangtown Gals." Through the 1880's and 1890's, saloon music was more quiet and romantic: "Little Annie Roonie," "You're the Flower of My Heart, Sweet Adeline," "She's More to Be Pitied Than Censured," "A Bird in a Gilded Cage." At the turn of the century, after Scott Joplin wrote his "Maple Leaf Rag," the popular songs the "Professor" played all had a ragtime jingle—except when both pianist and patrons were weepily drunk. At such times, usually in the wee hours of the morning, the man at the ivories would play, with many eloquent and fanciful hand gestures, the sentimental and slower-paced songs of Stephen Foster, or perhaps "Genevieve," "After the Ball," or "Only One Girl in the World for Me."

When a preacher invaded the dim precincts of demon whiskey to bring "The Word" before it was too late, he was treated with courtesy, even when his host was assailed as "a fiend in human form." The poker players threw in their cards and pocketed their chips and the bar was closed as the evangelist mounted the Keno platform. The proprietor and the bartenders stood with folded arms during the devotions, then joined heartily in song as the piano played "Jesus, Lover of My Soul."

There was no architectural standard for the early Western saloon. The tent served for a year or so, until it could be replaced by a structure of log or clapboard, or adobe. In short, the saloon was fashioned from whatever was most readily available. Seldom did the exterior have visual appeal, and never did it need it. Visual appeal was to be found inside, at the foundation of the entire business—the bar.

From about 1840 to 1880, bar-making was one of the country's significant crafts, with many a woodsmith reaching the pinnacle of his art in designing the fixtures for a saloon. Crude chairs and tables were good enough for gambling, but the bar and the backbar—the counter space along the wall behind the bar—had to show a richness which would suggest quality to the men who were bending an elbow. As a saloon prospered and acquired tone and class, the decorations grew more elaborate. Not uncommon were such grand features as red plush curtains, thick rugs instead of sawdust, and fancy chandeliers which sprayed a mist of perfume on the sweaty dancers below.

In almost every saloon the major attraction was a nude and nubile girl painted life-size on a canvas which hung just above the eye level of the men at the bar. Many a proprietor would bet that in any given twenty-four-hour period no patron would enter his place without casting a glance at the nude. And no one has heard of a bartender who lost that bet. In the bigger saloons, one might see as many as a dozen examples of Saturday-night art.

Some emporiums would sell beer for a nickel a mug and whiskey for a dime a shot; others would charge as much as two bits for a glass of rotgut. Signs on the Cyrus Noble Saloon in West Texas proudly advertised, "Fire Water and Poor Cigars. Whiskey guaranteed under the National Pure Food Law."

Fancy establishments prided themselves on stocking expensive imported beers. In 1880, Lowenbrau wholesaled out of Chicago at $15.25 for a case of fifty bottles, so the retail price of a bottle must have been upwards of sixty cents— more than it costs today! But it is hard to generalize about the retail price of booze in the Old West. The price depended on the brand, the year, and what the traffic would bear.

Many establishments advertised a "free lunch" to attract customers and, once attracted, keep them thirsting for more refreshment. The food was salted very liberally. Buffet tables filled with sliced bread, hot sausages, beef, pork, crackers, pretzels, and cheese were open to all who invested in a glass of beer.

The saloon was the hub of the Western town. Bar, restaurant, gambling house, town hall, hotel, brothel, and sometimes courtroom or church, the saloon was the first building constructed and the last business to go broke. In the early days of a frontier town, there was no lodge, club, or pool hall where the men might gather. So when our rugged Western individualists felt the need for communal activity, they surged through the only doors available—the bat-wing doors of the saloon.

Often, the leading liquor emporium was also the stagecoach stop. The six-horse stages pulled up to the "Bloody Bucket," "Golden Nugget," or "Mamie's Palace," with a flourish of dust and whip-cracking, because there was no other place to use as a stage depot and good drinking water was scarce. Naturally, it became common to quench one's thirst with the fiery rotgut or a glass of beer. Likely enough, the air the stagecoach passengers had been breathing was biting cold or insufferably hot and dusty; but indoors, in the saloon, it was sure to be relatively comfortable. So even the most timid souls entered, sat at a table with a short glass of beer, and then used the outhouse while waiting for the stage horses to be changed. In time, even the sensitive individuals grew accustomed to the naked lady over the bar and to the stench of bad whiskey and unwashed bodies. Even those few who did not imbibe regarded the saloon as a necessary institution.

Since the leaders of the town hung around at the saloon, people went there to find them. If a miner was shot, his wife rushed to the saloon to get Doc or the sheriff, or the mortician. If there was a nasty accident on the ranch, the injured man's friends stuffed a dirty cloth in the wound, threw him across a horse and galloped into town and the saloon.

Death often visited the saloon. Take the case of Ezra Williams, who got himself badly shot out in California. He was toted inside the local bar and stretched out on a table, under the hanging lamps, while Dr. Thomas D. Hodges removed the bullet.

Ezra groaned in pain.

"He's mighty bad off," said a gambler, "and I'll bet he dies before sun-up."

Doc Hodges, whose pride was deeply touched, angrily snapped back, "Fifty dollars says he don't!"

"You're on," the gambler leered. "Anybody else want to bet?"

Within a few moments, over $14,000 was wagered on Ezra's life or death. Dutch Kate, who later became a stage-coach robber, ambled in and bet a cool $10,000 Ezra would be on his feet before the sun shone again. For hours everybody crowded around to watch the man and the ticking clock. Finally, Ezra obliged Dutch Kate and checked out of the saloon only minutes before sun-up.

Yes, the saloon was a great part of Western history, offering entertainment, food, drink, companionship, and the closest thing to civilization that a frontier town had to offer. Yet even with these attractions, the saloon itself was seldom as impressive as the man behind the bar. In the raw beginnings, the host was sure to be an individual so spike-whiskered and dirty as to frighten all except the boldest. He ladled out his vile diluted whiskey at fantastic prices, thereby netting enough profit to tone up the place and import the girls. When they arrived, some bit of gallantry stirred him: he shaved, cut his hair, washed all over at least once a week, and put on a new suit with a heavy gold chain across his vest. Frequently, this gave him enough respectability to be elected mayor, mar-shal, judge, or some other dignitary of the town. Now the saloonkeeper was affability itself—a glad-handing hypocrite with a broad, gold-toothed smile, his derringer up one sleeve and his sawed-off shotgun hidden just under the bar. Mark Twain described him in *Roughing It*:

> *The cheapest and easiest way to become an in-*
> *fluential man and be looked up to by the com-*
> *munity at large, was to stand behind a bar,*
> *wear a cluster-diamond pin, and sell whiskey.*
> *I am not sure but that the saloon-keeper held a*
> *shade higher rank than any other member of*

*society . . . No great movement could succeed
without the countenance and direction of the
saloon-keeper.*

What about the girls he brought in? Decent folk about
town always nursed an abundance of curiosity about the
soiled doves. Could they actually enjoy their work? No doubt
many of them did, but most were driven to their trade by personal misfortune or financial exigency.

Very few of the saloon girls were truly pretty or
shapely. Yet in any isolated community of 300 or more males,
any female was beautiful. The average saloon girl needed only
two qualifications: she must be friendly, and she must be
willing. Decorum and gentility were prized in the "civilized"
towns, but on the edges of the frontier, directness was the
way to a man's heart, and his wallet. In the real honky-tonk
saloon, the approach was "Hello, Sweetheart," a few moments'
dalliance at the bar, below-the-belt jokes, and hearty laughter, then an arm-in-arm promenade to either her crib out back
or upstairs.

The genial proprietor of the barrelhouse provided the
cribs, small houses hardly the size of an average room, for
which kindness he collected a fee from the girls. For a man
who resisted the strong come-on, dancing—a quick-tempo
routine punctuated with bumps and grinds—often preceded
the bed pressing. Many a lusty man hot off the cattle trail
failed to weather such active foreplay. The girl was prepared
for this, and well coached as to her behavior. So, while the
gambling stopped and everyone whooped it up, trail hand and
"sweetheart" might strip as they danced.

But rowdy and mercenary as these saloon girls might be,
they were not without feelings. Occasionally, a broken-
hearted bar belle would even take the "morphine route,"
leaving behind an incredibly slushy suicide note. One San
Antonio nymph chided her lover in her last letter just as if
she were a convent-bred girl: "The angels in Heaven could
not have been truer to a man than I have been to you."

Suicide was in fact a common end for these poor girls,
though the discernible cause was only rarely a busted ro-

Anyone for racy stereopticon cards? This is half of a 1900 card simply titled "A Dainty Toilet."

mance. The prostitutes labored manfully under a variety of conditions, from rough mining camps to "citified" cattle capitals, from clapboard saloons to the grandest palaces of Tombstone and Fort Worth. They traveled with medicine shows, carnivals, "dramatic" troupes, and in private caravans. As camp followers they rode with the Army, and as Barbary Coast harpies, they helped the "crimps" shanghai their unhappy victims. They sought riches in the saloons and hurdy-gurdy houses from Dodge to San Francisco, Alder Gulch to Tombstone, and from Creede to Silver Heels. Braving the rigors of the trails to reach the gold camps, the bawds hoped that their share of the yellow dust would lead to a better way of life. But it rarely did. Few of them lived long enough to settle into a comfortable retirement.

Why did they pick this way of life? In 1859 William W. Sanger, M.D., questioned 2,000 girls, asking, "What was the cause of your becoming a prostitute?" Their replies he tabulated and published in *The History of Prostitution.*

CAUSES	NUMBERS
Destitution	*525*
Inclination	*513*
Seduced and abandoned	*258*
Drink, and the desire to drink	*181*
Ill-treatment of parents, relatives, or husbands	*164*
As an easy life	*124*
Bad company	*84*
Persuaded by prostitutes	*71*
Too idle to work	*29*
Violated	*27*
Seduced on board emigrant ships	*16*
Seduced in emigrant boarding houses	*8*
Total	*2,000*

The waitresses, dance-hall girls, and professional entertainers were a shade above the common prostitutes, since they were retained by the saloon proprietors to provide dancing partners and "company" for the patrons. It was just no fun bouncing about the room with another bewhiskered male,

24

" 'Going to the Bad'—darlings who take the down slope—a few of the degrees in a rapid descent." This reminder to the virtuous was published in the Illustrated Police News of May 5, 1881.

and no saloon was worth a damn without its stable of nymphs.

The boomtowns were a man's world, but these rough men were romantics too. Deprived of female companionships, they either begged, bought, or stole away an Indian woman, or they spent their spare time sitting around and mooning about the girls back home. Even the most hard-bitten character might finally take the trip "back to the states," to return with "the little woman" beside him on the wagon seat. Men who had no sweethearts back East might decide to make one of the dance-hall girls or flossies respectable by the simple process of a wedding ceremony—especially if the girl were almost pretty. A pretty woman was a rare treat for the eye in the early West, since most respectable women had neither the time nor the energy to groom themselves as well as they did their horses. It took all of a woman's strength of body and mind simply to exist on the frontier, much less be pretty.

Some dance-hall girls and waitresses became caught up in situations they just could not handle. They covered up for vice and crime operations, and they helped their crooked boy friends evade the law. They led men on, causing many a barroom brawl and six-gun showdown in the dusty streets. All too many met their death in a saloon altercation. In Tombstone, Arizona, a grave marker proclaims the fate of one dance-hall girl: "Gold-dollar stuck a knife into Marguerita." Others took their own lives as their fairness began to pall; they were ashamed to go on with life, knowing that from the gambling house and saloon to the red-light district was a short walk.

The girls in the houses and cribs were known by many titles consonant with the Victorian sensibilities of the day: "fair but frail," "fallen angels," "erring sisters." But these were no lost lambs—they were businesswomen who shrewdly pursued the seller's market of the West, always keeping pace with the advancing frontier. San Francisco, mindful of its reputation as the wildest city in the Western world, at one time claimed 10,000 strumpets on its streets and in its parlor houses, cribs, and cow yards. The aged, hard working, flat-footed streetwalker was at the very bottom of the heap, scorned even by the women of the dingy cribs, because she was the ever present reminder of the future. The young and attractive parlor-house girl rated tops in terms of professional prestige, for the luxurious and comparatively soft working conditions enabled her to preserve her charms far longer than could the girls of the street and cribs.

No boomtown more than a few years old was worth its salt unless it could boast of several imposing saloons and gambling palaces, as well as a cathouse or two. These were the epitome of masculine society, and an essential stop for the outlying males on their infrequent visits to town. But in the early years of this century, respectable ladies took up the cause of reform, perhaps because the saloon, dance hall, and parlor house offered too many temptations to the wavering husband. They drove the whiskey and the wild women underground, and though wavering husbands have continued to waver, the open sensuality of the frontier is gone.

Cowboys whoop it up as they ride into town for a hot time at Christmas. An 1889 drawing by Frederic Remington.

— FREDERIC H

Jane Barnes and the Indians

In a 1930 issue of the *Oregon Historical Quarterly*, Kenneth W. Porter describes what most likely was the first white woman on the outermost frontier. Jane Barnes must have been a looker in 1813, for Donald McTavish, a middle-aged Scot, was smitten the moment he set eyes on the vivacious, blue-eyed, flaxen-haired English barmaid. Being a plain, outspoken man, McTavish made Jane Barnes a quasi-indecent business proposition. If she would accompany him to western North America, he would outfit her with a lavish wardrobe of dresses and millinery, and upon their return to England he would assign her a generous annuity. Marriage was definitely not what McTavish had in mind.

At the time McTavish met Jane Barnes, he was residing at a hotel in Portsmouth, England, awaiting embarkation on the *Isaac Todd* for a long sea journey to the mouth of the Columbia River. McTavish was, as one of his acquaintances put it, "of an amorous temperament," with an oft-stated preference for well-rounded blondes. He was also very wealthy, being one of the proprietors of Britain's North West Fur Company. He had come out of retirement only because of the War of 1812, which offered an excellent opportunity for his company to regain its lost power in the West. Shortly before McTavish's scheduled date of departure, his North West Fur Company had captured John Jacob Astor's trading post, Astoria, and renamed it Fort George.

Bound for the Columbia to serve as governor of the company's American empire, McTavish was a man who would sorely miss the comforts of home—fine wines, rich cheese, bottled porter, roast beef, and a comely blonde to share his bed. His ship, the *Isaac Todd*, was loaded with plentiful stores of gustatory treats, but until he met Jane there was no tart on his ship. Such a deficiency would be felt, for the voyage would be a horrendously long one, and no fair but frail would be waiting on the dock. A fur trader in his younger days, McTavish no doubt remembered with nausea the coarse, fish-eating Indian maidens of the North Pacific Coast. To be able to look at Jane's fair hair and pulchritudinous figure in the brave new world of North America was worth all the dresses and finery in England.

One of Jane Barnes' unnamed admirers said, "she consented to become *le compagnon du voyage* of Mr. McTavish in a temporary fit of erratic enthusiasm." Whether her decision was well thought out or not, McTavish's offer was a tempting one, and Jane Barnes must have relished the thought of becoming the first white woman on the northwest coast of America.

The portly McTavish and his pretty mistress were on the high seas for thirteen months before they crossed the bar of the Columbia on April 17, 1814. On Sunday morning, one week later, the *Isaac Todd* lay at anchor in the river off Fort George. At about eight o'clock, a small sloop from the fort came alongside. The craft still bore the name *Dolly* in honor of John Jacob Astor's wife, since the British had not yet rechristened the captured vessel. Among those in the Fort George reception committee was Alexander Henry, Jr., a very proper, prim, and puritanical young man who wrote in his journal with obvious peevishness, "McTavish was just up." He continued tersely, "He met me on deck, and we went into the cabin where I was introduced to Jane Barnes." Henry was surely astonished to discover a young white woman, and a courtesan at that, in the new Governor's cabin.

That evening, McTavish invited Henry and other Fort George officials to dine on board, where they could cast approving eyes on the "Governor's Lady." Jane turned on all her charm, until even the straight-laced Mr. Henry was seeking the reward of her smile. Later that evening, back at his quarters, he wrote rather disapprovingly that "a vile discourse took place in the hearing of Jane on the subject of venereal disease and Chinook ladies." We can see poor Henry was already becoming attached to Jane. When the party went ashore, Jane flounced and flashed her saucy smiles and blonde curls at the rough voyageurs and shy clerks. All gazed hungrily at her, since for many a year the only females any of them had seen were Indian. Jane doubtless felt more like a queen than an ex-barmaid.

The men all agreed that the sloop *Dolly* must be rechristened *Jane* in honor of the Governor's mistress. So the next day, McTavish, as one of his first official acts, chivalrously renamed the vessel. During the next week, Miss Jane, accompanied by Doctor Swan and dear old Donald McTavish, made other visits ashore on the *Jane*. On May 1, the threesome returned Henry's visit by having breakfast with him. McTavish was planning on taking up residence on shore at once, even though the accommodations were far less comfortable than his cabin on the *Isaac Todd*. So, accordingly, two men were put busy on constructing "a room in order for Mr. D. McTavish and Jane." Until it was finished, McTavish preferred keeping Jane aboard the *Isaac Todd*, where he could spend his nights with her in splendid isolation, away from the woman-starved trappers of the fort.

It seems McTavish had intended, after supervising the establishment of the fort, to take Jane with him overland to Montreal. But "on learning the impracticality of her performing such an arduous journey," he abandoned that idea and made arrangements with the captain of the *Isaac Todd* "for her return to England by way of Canton." The *Isaac Todd* was to sail on August 1, and McTavish himself may have expected to leave before that day.

At any rate, the Governor saw that the inevitable break should come at once, and in order to protect Jane from the crowd of clerks and voyageurs at the post, he proposed to turn her over formally to Alexander Henry. Henry, the prude, after a joint conference with McTavish and Miss Barnes, finally consented. He described the arrangement as "more an act of necessity than anything else," and, believe it or not, disclaimed "all emotional considerations save those of humanity."

Henry never did take to the Chinook ladies; he was revolted by their immodesty and sexual looseness. But the blonde barmaid was . . . different. A few days after the agreement with McTavish, Henry offered Jane the use of his room at the fort. On May 8, she accepted. In his journal, he wrote: "The longboat came with Jane, bag and baggage," and "about sunset the jolly-boat took Mr. D. McTavish on board alone. Jane, of course, remained, having taken up her lodging in my room." Why McTavish returned to the *Isaac Todd* has not been explained. Perhaps he preferred his luxuriously furnished cabin to the crude comforts of the fort. Or perhaps he was simply tired of Jane, or she of him.

During the next several weeks, Jane Barnes ruled Fort George like a queen, setting off her natural gifts with many purchased beauty aids. One day she would decorate her head with feathers and flowers; the next, she would braid her hair and wear no bonnet, always displaying her well-proportioned figure to its best advantage, to the delight of all observers. She was the greatest curiosity to the wondering eyes of the Chinooks, arousing mingled feelings of fear, envy, and admiration among the women. The Indians thronged in numbers to the fort for the sole purpose of gazing on and admiring the fair barmaid.

On May 17, the Jane-less McTavish consoled himself with the Chinook ex-wife of the Astorian, Benjamin Clapp. As recompense, he clothed her "in fine black broadcloth which cost 23 shillings sterling a yard," as the thrifty Henry wrote disapprovingly. But five days later, both women were deprived of their protectors—and Jane suffered a double bereavement. While going from Fort George to the *Isaac Todd* in an open boat, Alexander Henry, Jr., Donald McTavish, and all the boatmen but one were drowned. Although deprived at one stroke of both past and present protector, Jane Barnes was not left entirely alone and unwanted. She had captured the heart of a governor; her next admirer was to be no less than a prince—Cassakas, self-styled "Prince of Wales," the son of Comcomly, the wily one-eyed principal chief of the Chinooks.

31

Fur trader weighing pelts brought to the fort by a somewhat bewildered Indian. Twenty-four dollars for the lot, perhaps?

One day, Cassakas bedaubed his face with red paint, smeared his bronzed body with whale oil, and in full courting array appeared at the fort for audience with Miss Barnes. He promised her that if she would become his wife he would "send one hundred sea otters and a huge quantity of dried salmon to her relatives," he would "make her mistress over his other four wives," he would "never ask her to carry wood, draw water, dig for roots or hunt for provisions," and he would "permit her to sit at ease from morning to night," smoking as many pipes of tobacco "as she thought proper." He would even allow her to wear her own clothing instead of the scanty bark garments of the Chinook women, and he would promise "she would always have abundance of fat salmon, anchovies, and elk."

These tempting offers held little appeal for Jane. The thought of pressing against his oily body was just too much. She replied firmly that she did not want a lover with "a flat head, a half-naked body, and copper-colored skin besmeared with whale oil." Her suitor did not give up easily, however, and on several occasions he renewed his offers, but all in vain.

Cassakas' pride was crushed by Jane's refusal. He vowed indignantly that "he would never come near the fort while she remained there." But shortly afterward, rumors reached the fort that Cassakas was planning "with some of the daring young men of his tribe to capture her and carry her off while she was walking on the beach." Warned of the danger, Jane discontinued her nightly walks alone while the men of the fort were finishing dinner.

As she settled into the life of the fort, Jane began holding daily informal salons. And it is not surprising that "Prince" Cassakas became more and more unfriendly to the whites during the next few months. Left with no protector, we must assume Jane found someone among the array eager to console her in her double bereavement. The records show she flatly turned down the fort's surgeon, Dr. Swan, when he offered a semi-permanent arrangement. Perhaps she was tired of the crude accommodations and looked forward to Canton and the Orient.

Many of the men at the fort kept journals, and we are indebted to Ross Cox for the following amusing picture of Jane in action. On a certain occasion, one of the Scottish clerks was chivalrously upholding the native and half-breed women, whose character white sister Jane was violently attacking. The Indians' unconcern over propriety in sexual conduct probably seemed to Jane a frank and unflattering caricature of her own sexual indulgence. Believing a spirited attack is the best defense, the clerk retorted with a vigorous and unflattering appraisal of the conduct of white ladies.

"O, Mr. Mac!" Miss Barnes declared, "I suppose you agree with Shakespeare, that 'every woman is at heart a rake'?"

"Pope, ma'am, if you please," corrected the clerk.

33

"Pope! Pope!" exclaimed the astonished Jane. "Bless me, Sir! You must be wrong; rake is certainly the word. I never heard of but one female Pope."

One such slip might have been pardoned, but, in order to terminate the argument, the would-be literary lady made matters worse by turning away and pretending to read an old newspaper which she snatched up from a table; unfortunately, she was holding the newspaper the wrong side up. With a malicious and triumphant grin on his face, the clerk left abruptly. At the door he explained his encounter to Ross Cox.

"What do you think? I have just had a conversation with that fine looking damsel there, who looks down with such contempt on our women, and may I be damned if she understands B from buffalo!"

After four months in America, Jane boarded the *Isaac Todd* and sailed for Canton, where she went ashore and immediately "captivated an English gentleman of great wealth connected with the East India Company." The gentleman offered her "a splendid establishment." When he finally tired of her, she set sail once more and wound up back in England. She had been around the world on a glorious adventuresome trip. In England she tried to collect back wages and the annuity which she claimed was promised her by Donald McTavish, but failed. So then Jane simply retreated into the shadows of London, and no more was heard of her.

But Jane probably had no trouble finding a place for herself, what with the charms which captivated a governor, an ardent young Chinook, and an English gentleman, to say nothing of an experience which no other barmaid in England could hope to match. In securing another position where she could ply her trade, her tales would undoubtedly bring customers to her employer's public house. One can imagine her telling her story for the hundredth time, each narration accompanied by its own bit of exaggeration, with the oil-smeared, flat-headed Indian being transformed into an East Indian rajah, the wealth of dried salmon and sea otters becoming pearls and diamonds. Nonetheless, she would probably tell her breathless audience, all his entreaties were fruitless. Perhaps she concluded her tale by saying, "Let her who wants 'em have these foreign nobles, but I'll take Old England forever!"

Even before Jane Barnes arrived at Fort George, Alexander Henry, Jr., described in his journal how Donald McTavish had purchased one of Chief Comcomly's daughters. "He gave 5 new guns, and 5 blankets, making a total of 15 guns and 15 blankets, besides a great deal of other property, as the total cost of this precious lady. This Comcomly is a mercenary brute destitute of decency."

Prices were cheaper at times, Henry observed:

> . . . for a few inches of twist tobacco a Gros
> Ventre will barter the person of a wife or
> daughter with as much sangfroid as he would
> bargain for a horse. All those tribes (Blackfoot,
> Blood, or Piegan) are a nuisance when they
> come to the forts with their women. They in-
> trude upon every room and cabin in the place,
> followed by their women, and even though the
> trader may have a family of his own they insist
> upon his doing them the charity of accepting
> of the company of at least one woman for the
> night. It is sometimes with the greatest diffi-
> culty that we shut the gates, they hide in every
> corner, and all for the sake of gain, not from
> any regard for us, though some of the men tell
> us it is with a view of having a white child—
> frequently is the case.

Henry's diary has other, more indelicate comments about the Indian women which bring out the general attitude traders held toward these women:

> At 11 P.M. I went to bed; Mr. McTavish was
> inclined to sit up. Mr. J. Cartier discharged his
> lady, she being so far gone with venereal
> disease that he already has two pimples, and on
> examination the doctor gives it his opinion that
> he is in a very bad way. Mr. Bethune keeps his,
> though he is very dubious about her.

35

Later he wrote about a family burial of a daughter who died from syphilis:

> *They did so, but in a barbarous manner, by dragging it perfectly naked down to the water, tying a cord around the neck, and towing it along the beach for some distance; then they squeezed the body into a hole, pushed it down with a paddle, and covered it over with stones and dirt. The poor girl had died in a horrible condition, in the last stage of venereal disease, discolored and swollen, and not the least care was ever taken to conceal the parts from bystanders.*

There was a high rate of venereal disease among many Indian tribes, but the white men were anxious to forget that V. D. was an unwanted present they themselves had brought to the far West.

Henry was at his priggish best when he wrote:

> *This afternoon I had an opportunity of observing the total want of modesty, or even decency, in the women of this coast. I was walking on the wharf, where several women were washing themselves, as is their daily custom, in the small ponds left on the beach at low water. They were perfectly naked, and my presence did not affect their operations in the least. The disgusting creatures were perfectly composed, and seemed not to notice me. Although they stood naked in different postures, yet so close did they keep their thighs together that nothing could be seen.*

For all his professions of disgust, Mr. Henry seems to have observed the bathers with more than a little prurience.

It was not long after the days of the Columbia River forts that the mountain men and trappers, with their shaggy beards and dirty buckskins, drifted into the Rocky Mountains. For bedfellows they turned to the Indian women, whose affections they bought, bartered, or stole. Sometimes the arrangement was permanent, sometimes it was only temporary. At the Rendezvous, as the trading session was called, things got off to a roaring start. The alcohol kegs were unpacked, watered, and perhaps a few handfuls of tobacco were thrown in for color and flavor. Indian whiskey was all the trappers or Indians could get for years and the formula for it survives to this day: "1 gallon raw alcohol to 3 gallons of water. A pound of tea, or rank black tobacco, some ginger, and a handful of red peppers." The Indians, mindful of the good rum at the river trading posts, were completely fooled by the addition of a quart or so of blackstrap molasses to the vile concoction. Camp kettles were passed around cheerfully, emptied, and refilled with regularity as the party grew ever wilder.

The trappers lied, bragged, challenged each other to horse races, foot races, drinking bouts, card games, shooting contests, knife fights. Every man, to hear him tell it, was the greatest he-man in the entire Rocky Mountains and stood ready to prove it.

All during the week-long excitement, the bucks of the various tribes would wander around from one trapper group to another with their wives, sisters, or daughters in tow, accosting the sex-starved mountain men and reciting at length on the beauty and fleshy excellencies of the particular females being offered. Somehow a price was agreed on, which always went to the man in charge, never the woman involved. The trapper either bundled his squaw into the nearby bushes, or simply laid her down on the ground in front of everyone, to the yells of encouragement and laughter of his friends.

The more independent squaws would be parading around camp on horseback or afoot, dressed in their finest beaded doeskin robes, looking for something more permanent than a quick tumble. They wanted a mountain marriage, with all the wealth and ease it would bring into their lives.

All the while, the pelts disappeared magically into the factors' packs, much, much faster than the beaver came out of the bitter-cold Rocky Mountain streams. As senses dulled, the alcoholic concoction got weaker and weaker and the shooting and shouting got wilder and wilder. It was the mountains' greatest social event of the year, this week of Rendezvous, and everybody who was anybody was "there with bells on."

Many of the great names of western exploration married Indians and thus became "squaw men"—Jim Bridger, Kit Carson, John McLoughlin, William Bent, Joe Meek, Peter Skene Ogden, Milton Sublette—and not all of them limited themselves to one wife. Jim Beckwourth claimed he owned eight wives, all from the Crow tribe. Some early fur trappers swapped, borrowed, or stole each other's squaws. Joe Meek and Milton Sublette, although partners, were rivals for the hand of a beautiful Shoshone girl named Mountain Lamb. Sublette won out because he owned more horses, but when he went back east for the treatment of his ailing leg, Joe Meek "so insinuated himself into the good graces" of Mountain Lamb that she was won over and joined her fortunes with his. Meek later said:

> *She was the most beautiful Indian woman I ever saw and when she was mounted on her dapple gray horse which cost me three hundred dollars, she made a fine show. She wore a skirt of beautiful blue broadcloth, and bodice and leggins of scarlet cloth, of the very finest make. Her hair was braided and fell over her shoulders. A scarlet silk handkerchief, tied on hood fashion, covered her head; and the finest embroidered moccasins on her feet. She rode like all the Indian women, astride, and carried on one side of the saddle the tomahawk for war, and on the other the pipe of peace.*

Mainly because of the trouble caused by alcohol, the government passed some very strict laws about bringing alcohol or liquor to the Western frontier. But in 1833, Kenneth McKenzie of the American Fur Company found a way to beat the government and its pestiferous liquor laws. If it was against the law to import liquor into the mountains, so be it. He would make it for himself.

McKenzie sent the necessary material for the distillery up the Missouri River aboard the two company boats, the *Yellowstone* and *Assiniboine,* in the spring of 1833. McKenzie also planned to test the strict liquor act of the year before by taking up his usual supply of booze in addition to his small still. At Fort Leavenworth, he discovered the government was serious after all. Shortly after being stopped, he wrote to Pierre Choteau, Jr.:

> *I have been robbed of all our liquor, save seven barrels shrub, one of rum, one of wine, and all the fine Men and Sailors' Whiskey which was in two barrels. They knocked about everything they could find and even cut through our bales of blankets which had never been undone since they were put up in England.*

At the mouth of the Iowa River, McKenzie put ashore a small crew to farm Indian corn for the grain he needed for his still. By the time Milton Sublette and others arrived late in August 1833, the distillery was running full blast and producing adequate spirits. McKenzie was happy, and declared, "The Mandan Indian corn yields quite badly, but makes a fine sweet flavored liquor." In a letter to Choteau and Ramsey Crooks, McKenzie said, "It succeeds admirably. I have a good corn mill, a respectable distillery, and can produce as fine a liquor as need be drunk." And so the booze problem for the frontier was solved.

Perhaps the most curious aspect of the relation between the Indian women and the mountain men and traders is that it gave rise to no social reproach until the "puritanical" white girls began arriving. The first contingent had hardly settled before it was considered a disgrace for a white man to live with an Indian and the derisive epithet "squaw man" was born. From now on, the Indian women would have to take a back seat, for the professional tart had arrived with all her paint and finery.

39

Fandangos and Yankedos

IN THE EARLY 1840's, as the wagons neared the end of the old Santa Fe Trail, the spirits of the trail hands soared, for just over the hill was at long last the end of the rainbow. Here, while still curtailed by the hills and evergreens, the caravan pulled to a stop so the small wagons could be dismantled and their parts hidden in the underbrush. The contents of these small vans were heaped upon large vehicles, making them gigantic. At this date, the Southwest was still in Mexican hands, and a tax on imports was assessed by the wagonload; thus, the shrewd Yankee traders made one wagon roll into Santa Fe where two or three had rolled along the trail.

While this operation was going on, the men took time out to wash up and shave. Sunday go-to-meetin' clothes came out of the baggage and everybody put on his best bib and tucker for the grand entry into town. Weapons were cleaned and reloaded, teamsters fastened new crackers to their long whips, and old-timers regaled their juniors with tales of Taos Lightning and the sensual Mexican women.

The wagoners' excitement at nearing Santa Fe was even greater than that of cowboys at the end of a long trail drive, or of storm-tossed sailors making a friendly port. Santa Fe was not just the culmination of 800 miles of danger and deprivation—it had a foreign color, a savor that separated it from all the other towns in the West. Everything was strange, romantic, fascinating.

Finally, the wagons rolled into the city with everyone

merry, intoxicated with anticipation. Greenhorns were no doubt disappointed at their first glimpse of El Dorado—drab square blocks of adobe huts scattered among the green fields of dwarf corn and beans; high adobe walls lining the road. Little did they realize that behind those walls were the gardens and orchards from which they would receive peaches, apples, apricots, grapes, corn, and wine. And under the flat roofs of those unimpressive mud cubes were plump mattresses to lie on, bright fires to sit by, corn-shuck cigarettes to smoke, and women's smiles to enjoy. Like a horde of savages entering a friendly camp, the wagoners emptied their rifles and pistols noisily into the air, whooping until their horses reared.

The citizens shared the enthusiasm, swarming out of their houses into the muddy lanes and calling, "*Los Americanos! Los Carros! La entrada de la caravana!*" Lithe, dark-skinned

The end of the Santa Fe Trail: early-day Santa Fe, New Mexico. The simple adobe dwellings and walls gave little hint of the good whiskey and beautiful women of El Dorado.

young men, somber under their big hats, watched intently as their future rivals for the women's favors rolled into town. Menacing Mexican soldiers lounged about, as did the dragoons with their enormous mustaches and clanking sabers. Shabby rancheros watched from beneath their tattered, faded ponchos and battered wool hats.

And there were the girls!

A young woman—any young woman—would have thrilled the men. But the dashing senoritas of Santa Fe were irresistible in their exotic, colorful skirts and low-cut blouses, with faces bleached under a coat of flour-paste, lips brilliant with smears of scarlet, their blue-black hair and soft brown eyes, their flashing white teeth and inviting manner. They could be haughty and coy, but they also knew how to be engaging and flirtatious. Coquetry with them was an instinct, not a plan. Their smiles said, "Women need men as men need women. There is no use in our quarreling about it!"

The way these Spanish beauties dressed was excitingly different to the men, for they didn't bother themselves with underwear, let alone petticoats, bustles, and bodices. The women wore a skimpy *casima* with loose sleeves, a short red skirt, a gay shawl, and slippers. They made a "prodigal display of their bodily charms," as noted by one American visitor. And when the wagons slid to a stop on the wide sunbaked plaza, the men and women met and mingled together. Their greetings were cordial, with the New Mexican salute as agreeable as it was novel to the greenhorns. The man swept off his hat as the lady extended her right hand. The man grasped it warmly and gently drew her toward him. Then he threw his left arm about her waist, embraced her, and laid his cheek against hers, murmuring his compliments into her ear. Then he released her, and put on his hat again.

The Americanos went into the bar of La Fonda, emptied several glasses of firewater, and understood why the Santa Fe trade was growing by leaps and bounds. Already they may have been invited to attend the first of a series of bailes, or— as they were called by most Americans—fandangos. These men were convinced that the women of Santa Fe went to a dance every night of their lives. Nearly all the householders

The Belle of the Fandango, a Mexican welcome after the long trail ride.

of Santa Fe offered the use of their *salas* for the series of fandangos which invariably celebrated the arrival of a wagon train. This was a profitable event, for the men were generally pretty eager to scatter their wages. The sale of whiskey produced a handsome profit to the fortunate individual whose home was selected for a fandango. For the first baile, the large *sala* of the *alcalde* (mayor) was selected and put in order; a general invitation was sent out; and all the dusky beauties were soon busy getting themselves ready for the celebration.

Off came the coats of makeup and dust which had bedaubed their faces since the last celebration. The women scrubbed their bodies and washed and combed their long black hair, then plastered it behind their ears and plaited it into a long queue which hung down their backs. *Enaguas*, short skirts of gaudy colors (red being the favorite), were put on, fastened around the waist with ornamented belts. Above this a *camiseta* of snow-white linen was the only covering, allowing a bounteous display of their mammary charms. Mas-

The fandango was the highlight of every wagoner's trip down the Trail. This drawing depicts the interior of a Santa Fe sala during a fandango: musicians to the left, refreshments to the right, and revelry all around.

sive gold and silver ornaments of ancient pattern decorated their ears and necks, or large crosses hung between their breasts. The fact that their *enaguas* came down only halfway between the knee and the ankle enabled the women to display their well-turned calves and ankles. Their tiny feet were clad in little silver buckled shoes of Cinderella dimensions. Thus dressed, with rebozos drawn over their heads and faces and a *cigarito* dangling from each pretty mouth, the coquettes entered the fandango hall.

At one end of the *sala*, the musicians were already seated with guitar, *bandolin,* and hand-drum. Gradually, the long room filled with men and women in native costume, all mingling among the American traders and teamsters, who wore

shirts of bright calico and at their belts, long knives and pistols.

Soon, most of the room was filled by the crowd, and only the center of the dirt floor remained open for dancing. At first the Mexicans did most of the prancing, doing such numbers as the close-held waltz or the cradle dance. During a lull in the music, gourds were filled with whiskey which went the rounds—even to the ladies—with appreciative gulps quaffed by the pilgrims from the East. As the gourds were drained and refilled time and again, the spirits of the teamsters became ever more boisterous. And as their attentions to the females became warmer, the jealousy of the local men waxed hotter.

Time passed, and the whiskey took its hold on the teamsters, who horned into the performance. Not knowing the native steps, they interpolated dances of their own learned on the frontier of Missouri or in the camps along the Santa Fe Trail, yelling and whooping and shouldering aside the lithe young men of the town. At that altitude, over seven thousand feet, only a little alcohol became too much, and the rough Americans took command and kept the women to themselves. If a daring Mexican stepped into the ring, he was likely to be shoved back against the wall with a rough warning. Between dances, there was more drinking, making the ladies more flirtatious, the Americans more truculent, and the Mexican men more envious.

The dances in which the teamsters were prominent were without visible form or figure. Grabbing his partner around the waist with the grip of a grizzly bear, each man whirled and twirled, jumped and stomped and whooped, and then raised each foot alternately from the ground, in the jerking step so much in vogue in the Indian camps.

One unnamed American participant in a Santa Fe fandango of the 1840's described the rowdy goings-on in his journal. According to his account, the *sala* was filled with nearly 200 people swearing, smoking, drinking, dancing, and shouting, with the Americans monopolizing the women to the evident chagrin of at least threescore scowling *pelados*. One of these, maddened by whiskey and envy, suddenly seized his girl from the arms of a teamster and pulled her toward him.

For a moment, the rough Missourian stood stock still; then he raised his hand to his mouth and gave a ringing war whoop. He jumped on the rash young man, lifted him over his head as if he were a child, and dashed him against the wall.

At last, the long simmering fight commenced; twenty Mexicans drew their knives and rushed the teamster, who stood his ground. "Howgh-owgh-owgh-owgh-h!" burst from the throats of his friends in the well-known war whoop of the mountain men, and they rushed to his rescue. The women screamed and ran for the door, blocking it in their eagerness to escape the *sala*. The Mexican men were now compelled to stand their ground and fight.

Knives glittered in the lamplight and quick thrusts were given and parried. In the center of the room, the Americans gathered to stand shoulder to shoulder, forming a flying wedge. They surged toward the door, fought their way out, then ran down the lane and across the plaza to their wagons where they had left their rifles. Grabbing these, they rushed on and occupied one of the smaller buildings on the grounds of the *alcalde*. There they bound up their wounds and prepared to defend themselves against the town. Officials came and demanded their surrender, but they were answered by yells of derision from the wagoners. After a day or so, the hot blood cooled a bit, and the Americanos came to terms. They paid the blood money, purchased masses to be said for the injured men, posted a guard, and began trading. They were greeted by scowling, bitter faces, but within a few days the affair blew over.

After a few of these fandangos, the gaiety of Santa Fe palled on the men from the Trail. Now that the trading was completed, they were sick of the place and sick of its people. The wagon boss heaved himself up to a high seat and gave his sage advice, "In the mornin' we're puttin' out back to the prairies whar thar ain't nothin' to bother us but a passel of screechin' Indians! Hurray for the Santa Fe Trail!"

In 1846, U. S. soldiers came down the Trail to invade New Mexico. For the first time, they saw the dark-eyed, raven-haired cholas, the mestizo women of unrivaled beauty.

During the Mexican War, many of these women became camp followers, *Yankedos,* as the villagers called them. They lived with or followed the American soldiers. Until the war, the small sleepy towns of the Spanish-speaking Southwest had maintained an amazing state of moral purity. The Church dominated all aspects of society, and what vice there was in these towns was universally regarded as a crime against God. And just in case God neglected to exact his vengeance, the pillars of the town anticipated his wrath. Witness the report of W. W. Robinson regarding a public punishment in early-day Los Angeles:

> *In its earliest period those who kept close watch on the Plaza might have witnessed there the punishment of offenders against morality and good order. Two women, it is recorded, were forced to expose themselves with shaved heads at the church door—for scandalous conduct.*

Before the Mexican War, the power of the Church was an effective deterrent to prostitution. But the woman-hungry American troops unleashed the erotic energies of the girls who had labored in the cantinas. The American trooper, these girls discovered, offered praise—as well as cash—for a pleasurable service which their own society condemned. Thus many cholas were drawn into the ranks of U. S. Army camp followers.

But when the Mexican campaign ended in 1848, the Army returned home and these girls faced the wrath of their own people. The returning defeated Mexican soldiers poured their resentment and vengeance upon the *Yankedos,* whom they considered traitors of the first magnitude. Some women were branded with the letters "U. S.," others had their hair or ears cut off. Samuel E. Chamberlain, in his memories of the Mexican War, wrote:

48

> *At Saltillo there were a number of such women who had lived with Americans. After General Lombardini's Mexican division reoccupied the*

town the authorities got up a grand celebration
to commemorate the treaty of peace. At mid-
night the Grand Plaza was ablaze with fire-
works, and full of drunken soldiers and la-
drones, when a Dominican monk, one Padre
Olitze, got up on the fountain in the center of
the Plaza and in the most fiery language de-
nounced these poor Yankedos to the mob. Yell-
ing like fiends they searched out the miserable
creatures, dragged them in their night clothes
to the Plaza, where for hours they subjected
them to nameless horrors, had their ears cut off,
and the finishing stroke (a merciful one) given
by cutting their throats. Twenty-three young,
lovely and accomplished senoritas were tor-
tured to death at this time, and no notice was
taken of it by General Lombardini, or anyone
else among the Mexican authorities.

American women who became camp followers fared better than the Mexican girls, for their presence was encouraged
by the Army brass, and there was no postwar backlash. Since
military regulations prohibited single women from joining
marches, temporary or "Scotch" marriages without the benefit of clergy were common, and the ladies suffered no social
stigma. The case of Mrs. Sarah Borginnis, the "Great Western," emphasizes this fact. Early on the morning of July 19,
1848, the American Army in Mexico gathered at Walnut
Springs for its march northward to California and New
Mexico. Applying for permission to leave with the troops was
the Great Western. With the U.S. Army leaving Mexico, there
was nothing to hold her there.

Permission granted, she caught up with the military on
their third day out. She rode straight up to Major Bucker, and
asked whether she could accompany the men. Bucker replied
that if she would marry one of the dragoons and be mustered
in as a laundress, he had no objections to her going along. The
lady gave him a smart military salute, and then rode off
toward the front of the column, bellowing out, "Who wants a

wife with $15,000 and the biggest leg in Mexico? Come on, my beauties, don't all speak at once—who is to be the lucky man?"

Whether the general knowledge that she had had one husband in the Seventh Infantry and another in Harney's Dragoons made the men shy is hard to say. But no one seemed interested in her offer until finally Trooper Davis of Company E said, "I have no objection to making you my wife, if there is a clergyman here to tie the knot."

With a shriek of laughter Sarah whooped, "Bring your blankets to my tent tonight and I will learn you to tie a knot that will satisfy you, I reckon!"

Sarah was probably born in Tennessee sometime in 1813, and it is she and her nameless first husband who enlisted in the 8th Regular Infantry at Jefferson Barracks, Missouri. However, it was as a cook for one of the officers' messes of the Seventh Infantry during the Mexican War that she won her claim to fame. During the bombardment of Fort Texas, Sarah became a center of national attention. The small fort stood on the bank of the Rio Grande, just opposite the Mexican town of Matamoros, and the Yanks clashed with the Mexicans in a heated artillery duel that lasted eighteen hours. During this scorching battle, the Great Western served hot coffee and soup to the worn and weary artillery men.

Historian Arthur Woodward gives us the following description of this remarkable woman:

> In appearance, Sarah was about six feet tall, her hair was reddish, her complexion fair, and she had blue eyes. By nature she was kind-hearted. Apparently she operated a restaurant or hotel in Saltillo, the city five miles north of the Buena Vista battlefield, and according to a Texan in Taylor's Army, "She was a great nurse and . . . would always get up at night at any time to get one something to eat. . . ."
>
> The boys tell about one of the Indianans that when they broke through, two of Minon's cavalry made a dash for them on horseback.

*The Indianan was so scared he rushed right
down to the Great Western's headquarters,
yelling that the army was all cut to pieces and
the Mexicans were under full way for Saltillo.*
*She just flew off and hit him between the
eyes and knocked him sprawling, saying, "You
son-of-a-bitch, there ain't Mexicans enough in
Mexico to whip old Taylor. You just spread
that report and I'll beat you to death!"*

For the rest of the campaign, this giant female ran a series
of saloons for the men as they fought their way through Mexico. The Great Western was loved and admired by the rough-edged, tough-as-nails soldiers for her acts of kindness and for
her sympathetic understanding.

Sarah never seemed to keep a husband for long. She
stayed with Trooper Davis only until the column reached the
border, at the town now known as Juarez. Sarah then moved
to Fort Yuma, bought property in the newly formed town of
Colorado City, built a restaurant there, and went on to become the first American woman to settle in the city of Yuma.
Finally, on December 23, 1866, Mrs. Sarah Borginnis-Bow-man-Phillips-Foyle-Davis, many times married and seldom
divorced, died and was buried in the lonely cemetery at Fort
Yuma. The soldiers from the post gave her a splendid military funeral with a band and full honors. In August 1890, the
Quartermaster's Department removed all the bodies from the
old post graveyard to the San Francisco National Cemetery.
Among the 159 bodies reburied was the remains of the Great
Western. Fittingly, she rests among the rough and ready men
she knew and served from 1841 to 1866.

With the Southwest now captured, Yankee-style prostitution was common in all the villages where the troops were
quartered. The soldiers and dragoons were scattered throughout New Mexico until 1851, when Secretary of War C. N.
Conrad ordered Lieutenant Colonel Edwin Z. Sumner to
"break up the post at Santa Fe, that sink of vice and extravagance." Colonel Sumner examined the moral condition of the
1,300 soldiers in the New Mexico command, and he was ap-

palled. Being a good soldier, he promptly carried out his orders, removing the troops to a spot 100 miles to the northeast, where he supervised the building of Fort Union well away from any village of size. But the Colonel did not reckon with Loma Parda, a small farming hamlet six miles west of the new outpost. Loma Parda was first settled early in the 1830's, for the moderate climate and adequate water produced fine crops of beans and chile. The "Grey Hill" area changed rapidly as the troops built the new fort a few miles away.

Within a month it was apparent that the isolation of Fort Union would not protect the troopers from sin and vice. A band of fallen women set up shop in some caves less than a mile west of the fort, where they did a thriving business until Captain Sykes arrested a pair whom he ordered publicly whipped and shaved of their tresses. The rest fled to a more suitable climate. Yet Captain Sykes could do nothing to stamp out the Sodom of the West, which lay just six miles away, beneath a row of giant cottonwoods on the Mora River.

"La Loma" rocked with riotous revelry every day of the week, as string bands played twelve-hour shifts at Julian Baca's dance hall. Gambling, Loma Lightning, and whores were as plentiful as could be desired by any soldier. Loma Lightning was the same rot-gut known as Taos Lightning. Two drinks would eat a hole in any but a truly cast-iron stomach. Blood spilled by the gallon as shootings and knifings became daily occurrences. This was all to be expected, since the fortunes of Loma Parda depended not only on the vice trade run for the Fort Union troops: the Santa Fe Trail passed by just four miles away, cattle drivers, cowboys, mule skinners, and ox-drivers all came to town and sampled the stock of sin.

As the "blue coats" flocked to town, business boomed, until by the start of the Civil War, Loma Parda was wide open and going full blast. When the First Colorado Regiment of Volunteers moved into Fort Union in 1861, a trooper of that regiment, O. J. Hollister, wrote:

> . . . *drinking, fighting, and carousing with the*
> *whores at Loma, a small "Sodom" about five or*

six miles from Union, was the favorite pastime
of our regiment. . . . Fandangos, Loma Light-
ning, and Pecadoras were the main attraction
and rows of considerable magnitude were of
nightly occurrence. The guard house was filled
with Loma cadets, and the hospital with Loma
patients. The hell-hole was an unmitigated
curse to the soldiers, but was most generously
patronized, nonetheless.

For all his criticism of Loma Parda, Hollister almost surely visited the place, for few, if any, soldiers stationed at Fort Union resisted the temptations of "Sodom on the Mora."

Tracing the history of Loma is trying to catch a will-o-the-wisp, for there are only occasional references to the town in the early newspapers. The best study was one written by Dale F. Giese, park historian at Fort Union National Monument. According to Giese, Loma Parda's greatest boom and most violent period came immediately after the Civil War. At that time, Fort Union was the nerve center and supply depot for all the Indian campaigns throughout the Southwest. Frequently, the fort boasted a population of 3,500 people, both military and civilian. That's a pretty large audience to cater to, but Loma Parda seems to have offered enough diversion to keep any number of customers content.

The biggest attraction was the dance hall and saloon run by Julian Baca. At Baca's dance hall, the sexy senoritas reminded the soldiers that there were things worth fighting for. Baca himself dealt a mean game of three-card monte, and dice and poker games were always going concerns in the back room. Occasionally, Baca had trouble from his customers, but in general, they were satisfied with the bill of fare.

The most popular men in Loma Parda were Sam and Martin McMartin, a pair of Canadians who ran the wagon taxi from Loma Parda to the fort. A dollar for a round trip— a pretty steep price in those days—entitled you to sit on the wagon's crude seats and suffer the bumps. Nevertheless, it did beat walking, and the other option—not going to Loma Parda—was unthinkable.

Julian Baca's fandango dance hall and gambling house, the biggest attraction in Loma Parda, New Mexico. Baca's infamous operation contributed largely to the town's reputation as the "Sodom on the Mora."

It was not the soldiers who proved the undoing of Sam Seaman, the Chief of Police of Loma Parda, and a Loma resident named Toribio Garcia. Instead, it was a band of Texas cowboys with a trail herd. In September of 1872, they entered Loma Parda looking for cattle stolen by the Comancheros further down the trail from Texas. Leading the party was John Hittson, a prominent Texas cattleman. On their first trip to Loma Parda, the Texans confiscated seven steers, but the cowboys gave the cattle back when confronted by a well-armed group of Loma natives. The next day, they returned to Loma Parda with reinforcements—about twenty Texas cowboys in all. The armed Texans descended on the little village en masse, and began the round-up of stolen cattle in earnest.

On reaching the home of Julian Baca, owner of the dance hall and saloon, they found two saddle horses with fresh brands in his corral. The Texans demanded the nags, claiming they were stolen. Julian Baca flatly refused, claiming he had bills of sale for the pair. The cowboys seized him and beat him up on general principles. His wife ran down the street screaming for help. Toribio Garcia quickly ran to Julian's aid with a loaded horse pistol in his hand. The cowboys warned him, "Drop the hogleg!" According to the residents of Loma Parda, Garcia dropped his sixgun and fled, but the Texans shot him in the back while he was running down the middle of the main street. Sam Seaman came tearing out of his home toting a revolver; he was knocked senseless with a rifle butt, then dragged into the horse corral where the cowboys shot him to death as he lay unconscious on the ground.

The *Santa Fe New Mexican* sided with the Loma Pardans, saying:

> *The murderers with their party now moved off down the street, yelling like Indians and shooting up the street and into the houses. The Alcalde came into the street with his gun in his hand and was shot at one hundred and fifty yards by one of the gang, the ball passing through the fleshy parts of both thighs.*

The Texas version was a bit different. The cowboys claimed nearly everyone in Loma Parda had been willing to cooperate in the search for the Texans' lost cattle and horses. The way they saw it, both Seaman and Garcia refused to help in the search because they were part of the gang of thieving Comancheros. The town men allegedly drew first, thus making the killings a matter of self-defense. Exactly where the truth lies has never been stated to the satisfaction of all parties. The only thing for certain was that in Loma Parda trigger fingers got to itching mighty easy.

No matter how rough events might be for the residents of Loma Parda, things were rougher still for the patrons of the town's pleasure palaces. In October of 1871, this notice appeared on the post bulletin board at Fort Union:

> *A report has just come to us that a murder was committed at Loma Parda on Sunday last, the*

*9th day of October, 1871. A man lies dead in
the bushes close by, about one mile from the
village, near the partida. Horses were saddled
and several men were dispatched. A dead man
was found devoid of all clothing which seems
to have been the real motive. What a crime!*

*To kill a man for the clothes on his back!
The dead man was named Bergman. He belonged to the 8th Cavalry Band, stationed here
at Ft. Union. His head was beaten to jelly by
stones and his clothes were sorely wanted by
the murderers.*

Loma Parda was famous throughout the territory as a
hang-out for cutthroats and desperados. In 1888, *The Las
Vegas Optic,* the weekly newspaper of the nearby New Mexican town, reported:

*In Loma Parda, James Lafer is still remem-
bered as the man who picked up a New Mexican woman in the street, placed her across his
horse in front of him and rode into a saloon,
making the bartender set up drinks for the
whole party. And because his horse would not
drink, he shot him through the head, lifted the
woman from the saddle before the horse fell,
and walked out, leaving the dead horse lying
on the floor.*

This same James Lafer was wanted for murder in both Arizona and New Mexico. Wanted posters with his name on
them flooded the towns of the Territory, offering sizable re-
wards—dead or alive. Obviously, Lafer found his sanctuary
in La Loma.

A different side of Loma Parda is recorded in the diary
of Frank Oldsmith, a bugler in a contingent of troops accom-
panying a Congressional Committee and General McCook to
Fort Union. The Committee was investigating the recent out-
breaks of hostility with the Indians, and expected their junket

56

to bring understanding and peace. Oldsmith's description of Loma Parda was certainly different from most others:

> A little village called Loma Parda, within a half hour's ride of the post, was the chief recreation center. The population derived their subsistence largely from catering to the desires of the troops for social entertainment and amusement with wine rooms and restaurants.
>
> Dancing pavilions, most of them with gambling places in connection, were plentiful and for the most part were all patronized from early evening to dewy morn. The music was very good, exclusively of the Spanish type. At the fandangos, as the balls were termed, the New Mexican girls were adept at waltzing. The young fellows of the command found it most enjoyable. For many of them, it was the one place in all that country that they left with a feeling of regret.
>
> The girls were all devout, dedicated to the service of the church. For amusement, they depended chiefly on dancing, music, and gambling. It was this trait, I grieve to say, that made Loma Parda one of the principal resorts for pleasure for our command.
>
> Every night parties were organized with the consent and often the participation of a commanding officer, where we danced, smoked, and indulged in flirtation with the native damsels, over glasses of white Mexican wine, until approach of dawn in the eastern sky. With it all there was little drunkenness and the utmost of good humor.

Regardless of which accounts are true, the undisputed fact remains that Loma Parda was the favorite place of the soldiers at Fort Union, and the soldiers' favorite resident was Vincente C. de Baca, who would call square dances both in

English and Spanish. Two bands rotated shifts at the dance hall during the heyday of Loma Parda. They played twenty-four hours a day, seven days a week, and the enlisted men danced as long as possible. The little village never knew a quiet moment. But with the coming of the Santa Fe Railway in the 1880's, Fort Union and Loma Parda faded, as did the Santa Fe Trail. New Mexican sin shifted to the railroad towns, such as Las Vegas, Albuquerque, and Belen.

Sin for the Argonauts

THERE WERE PROSTITUTES in San Francisco and California before the gold rush and before the "Great Whore Invasion" of 1850-51. The tiny Mexican-Indian settlement of Yerba Buena had a few early *remeras,* for in 1846 when Captain Montgomery led his sex-starved sailors from the sloop *Portsmouth* ashore to raise the Stars and Stripes over the plaza, they were met at the ramshackle wharf by several eager Mexican, Chilean, and Peruvian prostitutes. The same hardy contingent of peso-minded senoritas welcomed the first of the horde of gold-seekers who poured in on the heels of Marshall's discovery of gold at Sutter's Mill in 1848. The "Chileno" women —as the sleazy charmers were called—entertained the new arrivals, sometimes a dozen at a time, on an assembly-line basis, in their waterfront tents and board shanties on the bay side of Telegraph Hill.

References to prostitution are rare in California's pre-gold-rush writings. But in January 1835, a young Bostonian stood on the deck of the brig *Pilgrim* to catch his first glimpse of the coast of California. Richard Henry Dana, Jr., was to spend more than a year calling at the various ports, and later his recollections were published under the title *Two Years Before The Mast.* Young Dana did not leave the women unobserved:

> *They dressed to be noticed, in gowns of various*
> *textures—silks, crepes, calicoes—made after*

The "pleasure palaces" of the old West are rather ramshackle by modern standards. This building in Coulterville, California, housed a saloon on the ground floor and a parlor house upstairs.

the European style, except for the short sleeves, which left the arms bare, and the loose waists, corsets not being in use. They wore shoes of hide or satin, sashes or belts of bright colors, and almost always a necklace and earrings. These styles prevailed except among the Indian women, who wore very little of anything, and often nothing above the waist.

The fondness for dress among women is excessive, and is sometimes their ruin. A present of a fine mantle, or of a necklace or pair of earrings gains the favor of the greater part. . . . If their husbands do not dress them well enough, they will soon receive presents from others.

One can imagine the reception of the following shocker, considering Dana's book was published in 1840:

I have frequently known an Indian to bring his wife, to whom he was lawfully married in the church, down to the beach and carry her back again, dividing with her the money which she had got from the sailors. If any of the girls were discovered by the alcalde to be open livers, they were whipped, and kept at work sweeping the square of the presidio, and carrying the mud and bricks for the buildings, yet a few reals would generally buy them off.

Little has been written of the pioneer prostitutes of the California gold rush, but almost all of them came from Mexico, Central America, and South America—more specifically by ship from Mazatlan, Guaymas, or San Blas. Few had any money for their passage, yet this obstacle was easily overcome, as explained by Spanish-Californian Captain Jose Fernandez:

They did not pay passage on the ships, but when they reached San Francisco the captains sold them to the highest bidder. There were men who, as soon as any ship arrived from Mexican ports with a load of women, took two or three small boats, or a launch, went on board the ship, paid to the captain the passage of ten or twelve unfortunates and took them immediately to their cantinas, where the newcomers were forced to prostitute themselves for half a year, during which the proprietors took the bulk of their earnings.

The Peruvian prostitutes who came to California along about 1849 and 1859 were one of three types: cholas, a cross between the Indians and whites, "often the middle classes"; the mulattoes, again a numerous class, "extremely beautiful and extremely frail (easily broken)"; and the white Creoles, who were noted for their sensuality and dances of "indescribable obscenity." Peru exported not only its native product, for San Francisco's first contingent of French prostitutes was made up of women from Lima and Valparaiso, as well as the French Marquesas and the Hawaiian Islands.

The girls from Chile were dark-complexioned, with florid

cheeks, bright black eyes, and glossy hair which hung down their backs in braids. More than half of those who came to California were in their teens, some as young as thirteen. Their habitat was "Little Chile," the southern slopes of Alta Loma (Telegraph Hill):

> Both sexes lived almost promiscuously in large tents, scattered irregularly upon the hill sides. Their dwellings were dens of infamy, where drunkenness and whoredom, gambling, swindling, cursing, and brawling were constantly going on. . . . The tents were a far remove from the parlor houses to come, as many as a half dozen prostituting themselves under one canvas. . . . Their habits were unclean and their manners base.

It remained for women from the East and from Europe to really make prostitution into big business. During the first six months of 1851, more than 2,000 women, practically all of them "fallen," poured into San Francisco from New York, New Orleans, Paris, Marseilles, South America, Australia, Asia, and the Pacific Islands. French women, the traditional queens of harlotry, were the standard-bearers. The lower part of Jackson and Commercial Streets soon became known as Frenchtown, as the first French *filles de joie* quickly took over from the Chileno remeras.

The massive red-light migration of 1850 to San Francisco was a phenomenon of such world-wide notice that the Paris correspondent of the New York *Herald* reported in August of that year:

> A speculator of Paris has just arranged the departure of two hundred women for California, and these houris of our harems of Paris, Rouen, Lyons, and Havre, will sail for the gold country within a fortnight. . . . Be it understood that these beauties are not diamonds of the first water. But no matter, they leave

France with a strong resolution to be good
girls. I hope they will stick with it.

These French belles who scurried to California had their own gold mines right in their beds. The eager forty-niners—including the sailors who abandoned their ships in the harbors—found the French coquettes irresistible. Prospectors fresh back from the gold country thought nothing of offering the scarlet belles $500 or $1,000 for a single night of love. The

A California forty-niner panning gold from a creek bottom. After a few weeks of such work, the forty-niners roared into town, spending their hard-earned gold on a few nights of pleasure.

free-wheeling, wild-spending miners and sailors did not realize—and had they realized, probably would not have cared—that the imported floozies who made the long voyage to San Francisco usually had been streetwalkers of the lowest class, who could be picked up on any Paris boulevard for a few sous. The horny, newly rich forty-niners saw only the novel, exotic charm of *les nymphes du pave* with "their graceful walk, their supple and easy bearing, their charming freedom of manner."

In 1851, there came a new wave of French girls, spurred on by the fantastic lottery of the Golden Ingots, a scheme devised by the wily Prince Louis Napoleon to help pave his way to the throne. A national lottery was announced in France, with tickets selling at one franc apiece; the prizes were two hundred bars of solid gold. The proceeds would be used to ship 5,000 deserving French citizens of the poorer classes to California, to give them a new start in life. The lottery was rigged so that the gold bars would find their way back into the hands of Louis Napoleon and his cronies. Instead of using the proceeds to ship citizens of the poorer classes to California, the promoters sent several shiploads of undesirables, mostly whores, pimps, thieves, and cutthroats, the dregs of the worst prisons and slums of France. One writer, telling of the arrival of the first shipload of "ingots," reported:

> *Three hundred fallen women, accompanied by men accustomed to the business of conducting houses of gaiety, arrived in California to ply their depraved profession.*

The vice operators now discreetly confined themselves to a section on the edge of North Beach, between Chinatown and the Embarcadero. This sordid district included Frenchtown, and was once called Sydney Town; it was not long before it became known as the Barbary Coast. No one knows who first gave the district the name, derived from the pirate-infested Barbary Coast of North Africa—but the designation was appropriate, and it stuck. For more than half a century, the Barbary Coast, centering along Pacific Street—nicknamed

64

In the eye of the storm: the Barbary Coast, San Francisco, in an 1878 sketch by E. A. Abbey. For more than 50 years, the Barbary Coast was a byword for vice, violence, and depravity in all its forms.

"Terrific Street"—was an international byword for vice, violence, and festering depravity. The French strumpets, madams, and their macs were joined by native American thieves and con men who were known as Rangers. In 1869, the *San Francisco Call*, addressing itself to the respectable citizenry, editorialized:

*The Barbary Coast! That mysterious region
so much talked of; so seldom visited! Of which
so much is heard, but little seen! That sink of
moral pollution, whose reefs are strewn with
human wrecks, and into whose vortex are constantly drifting barks of moral life, while
swiftly down the whirlpool of death go the
sinking hulks of the murdered and the suicide!
The Barbary Coast! The stamping ground of
the Ranger, the last resort of the* blasé *and
ruined* nymphe du pave, *the home of vice and
harbor of destruction! The coast on which no
gentle breezes blow, but where rages one wild
sirocco of sin!*

*Night is the time to visit the Coast. In the
daytime it is dull and unattractive, seeming
but a cesspool of rottenness; the air is impreg-
nated with smells more pungent than polite;
but when night lets fall its dusky curtain, the
Coast brightens into life, and becomes the
wild carnival of crime that has lain in lethargy
during the sunny hours of the day, and now
bursts forth with energy renewed by its siesta.*

Benjamin Estelle Lloyd, in his *Lights and Shades of San
Francisco in 1876*, was roused to similar indignation:

*The Barbary Coast is the haunt of the low and
the vile of every kind. The petty thief, the
house burglar, the tramp, the whoremonger,
lewd women, cutthroats, murderers, all are
found here. Dance halls and concert saloons
where blear-eyed men and faded women
drink vile liquor, smoke offensive tobacco, engage in vulgar conduct, sing obscene songs
and say and do everything to heap upon themselves more degradation, are numerous. Low
gambling houses, thronged with riot-loving
rowdies, in all stages of intoxication are there.*

66

Opium dens, where heathen Chinese and God-forsaken men and women are sprawled in miscellaneous confusion, disgustingly drowsy or completely overcome are there. Licentiousness, debauchery, pollution, loathsome disease, insanity from dissipation, misery, poverty, wealth, profanity, blasphemy, and death are there. And Hell, yawning to receive the putrid mass, is there also.

Of all the Barbary Coast characters, the most famous was Ned "Bull Run" Allen, so named because he claimed to have fought in both battles of Bull Run. He was a huge, coarse, flamboyant thug who operated Hell's Kitchen, rated by the police as the toughest joint in San Francisco. A fashion plate in his frock coat, cream-colored breeches, tile hat, ruffled silk shirt, and cluster of diamonds, Allen spent his days drinking in the saloons of his competitors. He was an ugly-looking character, with a flaming red nose and a handlebar mustache so long that the ends could be tied together while he was being shaved.

Allen's emporium at Pacific Street and Sullivan Alley was housed in a three-story building with a bar and dance hall in the cellar, and another on the street floor. The two upper floors were divided into cribs for the amorous use of his gaudily costumed "pretty waiter girls." These girls were mostly French and Spanish, in keeping with the popular myth that they were more passionate than American women. He also gave his strumpets hard liquor instead of the usual colored-water confections on the theory that a drunken bawd added to the overall excitement.

Though various amusements were available to the restless, gold-hungry men who invaded San Francisco, gambling and girl-watching were their favorite diversions—next to sex, of course. Since digging gold from other's pockets was much simpler than digging it from the ground, gambling and entertainment palaces sprang up everywhere.

The waitresses/prostitutes who worked in these establishments were called "pretty waiter girls," though few were pretty and even fewer were still girls. Their wages usually ranged from fifteen to twenty-five dollars a week, plus a commission on the liquor they sold and half the proceeds of the prostitution. A girl might earn as much as fifty dollars a week.

One of the most notorious of the establishments employing these girls was the Bella Union, an ornate casino which first opened its doors in 1849 and stayed in business despite two devastating fires, until the great earthquake of 1906. The Bella Union had twenty-five or thirty pretty waiter girls working the upper and lower tiers of curtained boxes between their brief onstage appearances. When a girl entered a box, she perched herself on the occupant's lap and induced him to buy drinks. If he demurred at purchasing champagne, she settled for a less expensive wine. Displaying her bodily charms, she aroused the customer's desire for entertainment of a more intimate nature. On drawing the curtains, she was pleased to supply it on the spot, for a price.

In the same class as Bella Union, but with less luxury and less attractive girls, were the Olympic, the Pacific, and Gilbert's Melodeon. The drinks were often drugged, and the man was frequently robbed. One fandango house of the 1870's clad its girls in red slippers, black stockings, fancy garters, short red jackets, and nothing else to interfere with the real business at hand. However, this bottomless innovation in dress was abandoned after a few weeks. Because of the huge crowds, order was impossible to maintain, and the girls complained of the cold.

As prostitution flourished in San Francisco, many of the Cyprians were able to amass great fortunes. One French prostitute is said to have banked $50,000 during her first year of belly bumping.

Prices for a tumble varied, according to the girl's appearance, but the highest fee could be had by a red-haired Jewess, who according to common belief among the Argonauts was the most amorous of all females. One madam called Iodoform Kate made her fortune when she opened a chain of houses with an auburn-haired Jewish girl in each one. If one takes the names of the scarlet sisters as a key to the names most prevalent in young San Francisco, the city was largely populated by Roses, Daisies, Marthas, and Leahs. Other names used by the ladies in red were Rotary Rise, Madame Gabrielle of the Lively Flea, Madame Lazarene of the Red Rooster, Madame Bertha, and Aunt Josie.

Of all the new arrivals to California, only the Chinese refused to adopt the new ways of America. The only thing shared in common by the two cultures was prostitution. Yet even here, the similarity was only on the surface—the Chinese prostitute had nothing in common with her Western sister except the product she was selling. By the latter part of 1854, gambling and prostitution were the principal activities of San Francisco's Chinatown. The importation of Chinese girls to serve as prostitutes began five years earlier under a system of slavery in which the girls were purchased or kidnapped in China by agents of the San Francisco dealers. The *San Francisco Chronicle* of December 5, 1868, reported:

> *The particularly fine portions of the cargo, the fresh and pretty females who come from the interior, are used to fill special orders from wealthy merchants and prosperous tradesmen. A very considerable portion are sent into the interior under charge of special agents, in answer to demands from well-to-do miners and successful vegetable producers. Another lot of the general importation offered to the Chinese public are examined critically by those desiring to purchase, and are sold to the "trade" or to individuals at rates ranging from $500 down to $200 per head, according to their youth, beauty and attractiveness. The refuse, consisting of "boat-girls" and those who come from the seaboard towns, where contact with the white sailor reduces even the low standard of Chinese morals, is sold to the proprietor of the select brothels, or used in the more inferior dens of prostitution under the immediate control of the "swell companies." Those who are*

69

afflicted with disease, who suffer from the in-
curable attacks of Asiatic scrofula, or have the
misfortune of possessing a bad temper, are
used in this last mentioned manner.

In order to satisfy the authorities, a crude contract was drawn up in which the girl promised to prostitute her body. If she was sick one day, two weeks were added to her contract time, and if more than one day at a time, her term of prostitution was extended an additional month. The joker in this deal was, of course, the menstrual period. Since her physiology dictated that the prostitute was unable to work for three or more days each month, she was caught in a vicious cycle from which she could never escape. Although many individuals grew rich by trafficking in these daughters of joy, the largest dealer was the Hip Sing Tong, founded in 1852 for this purpose.

While myths grew up around many of San Francisco's madams—some of whom created their own myths—Ah Toy took a hoary myth about Chinese women—that their vaginal openings were horizontal rather than vertical—and made a great deal of money from it. California's first Chinese settlers, two men and one woman, reached San Francisco in February 1848, aboard the brig *Eagle*. Sometime later that year, or early in 1849, a second Chinese woman arrived—Ah Toy, a twenty-year-old prostitute. Ah Toy's first crib was a small shanty in an alley off Clay Street just above Kearny, in the heart of what is now San Francisco's Chinatown. The line of men waiting outside her shack was often a block long, and some early writers say that whenever a boat from Sacramento docked, the miners would race each other to Ah Toy's house.

Five additional Chinese women arrived in 1850, with two going to work for Ah Toy. Now a madam, she moved to a larger house located off Clay in an alley known as Pike Street. (For the next seventy years, the alley was the location of some of the city's most luxurious brothels, some of its lowest cribs, and some of Chinatown's bloodiest Tong wars.) When, in 1852, several hundred Chinese prostitutes arrived, Ah Toy graduated to an even more elevated position—agent for other

Chinese bordellos. She would attend each new showing of special merchandise at the market, and select the comeliest females for her clients.

A painting of 1852 shows a group of Oriental slave girls newly debarked from a China clipper. They are crowded together in a horse cart on the wharf, overseen by the Portuguese duenna who was hired to keep them under guard during the voyage. Around the cart is a crowd of excited Chinese men, two policemen who are beating back those attempting to handle the merchandise, and the Yankee ship captain standing smugly a short distance away. The destination of carts such as the one depicted in this painting was the basement under a joss house in St. Louis Alley. Here the girls were stripped naked and examined by the prospective buyers, either brothel owners or agents for the wealthy Chinese who sought mistresses. In China, the girls were sold for $30-90, while in California they brought anywhere from $300-3000, depending upon their age and beauty.

In 1854, Ah Toy was arrested, convicted, and fined for keeping a disorderly house. Over the next few years, the law and Ah Toy continued to have their disagreements, until in 1857 she finally had had her fill of harassment. She sold her house, packed her possessions, including her considerable fortune, and sailed for China, announcing to reporters that she had no intention of returning to California. But in March of 1859, she changed her mind. Only weeks after her return, she was again arrested for keeping a disorderly house. In July she was arrested and fined for beating one of her girls, and again in September for running a brothel—three arrests in six months. Now Ah Toy disappeared completely from the scene; some said she had returned to China, and eventually this was accepted as the gospel, but no one knew for sure.

California men remembered "the pioneer of all our fair but frail ones of the soiled doves from Asia," as one Argonaut wrote in 1877. In 1881, Charles P. Duane fondly recalled that Ah Toy "was a tall, well-built woman. In fact, she was the finest-looking woman I have ever seen."

Ah Toy was lucky, for the average life expectancy of a yellow slave in San Francisco was short. In most of the cribs and houses, a girl was never allowed to refuse a customer, even if he was obviously eaten up with disease. Most girls died young, and few ever escaped from bondage until the slave-freeing raids of the Presbyterian missionary ladies in the 1890's.

Mrs. Irene McCready and her companion-lover James McCabe debarked from the *Oregon* in April 1849. McCabe was one of the backers of the El Dorado gambling hall which opened not long after his arrival. It was money wisely invested; no miner's pick and shovel ever earned so much gold. Young Bayard Taylor, reporter for the *New York Tribune*, visited the El Dorado in September 1849 and said:

> *The greatest crowd is about the El Dorado.... We find it difficult to effect an entrance. There are about eight tables in the room, all of which are thronged with copper-hued Kanakas, Mexicans rolled in their serapes and Peruvians thrust through their ponchos, stand[ing] shoulder to shoulder with the brown and bearded American miners. . . . Along the end of the room is a spacious bar, supplied with all kinds of bad liquors, and on a sort of gallery, suspended under the ceiling a female violinist tasks her talent and strength of muscle to administer to the excitement of play.*

The El Dorado was doing well by the time Irene opened her bagnio in the fall of '49, in a one-story frame building not far from the El Dorado. McCabe and his partners were paying $40,000 a year rent for the land under the tent which housed their gambling den, while the rent on Irene's house must also have been high enough to require considerable backing from McCabe. As for the girls and furnishings, neither were plush nor fancy. Irene's may have been the city's first parlor house, but a number of similar bagnios sprung up at about the same time, so it is hard to say. Even the designation "parlor house" might be questioned, for it was one only by comparison to what else was around—the tents and shanties of Little Chile, the backrooms of the dives of Sydney Town and Clark's Point, or the cribs of the French belles. Irene's clientele included some important men—a California governor, a senator, and at least one judge, plus a number of lesser politicians and gamblers. But this did not mean Irene refused the gold of the ordinary miner. Only after California became less of a boom state would parlor houses be noted for their social exclusiveness.

Irene McCready's break with James McCabe finally occurred in the fall of 1859, and it was one of the most memorable lover's quarrels ever. Irene had an unusually fiery temperament, and was always wary lest her man stray from her bed. After making numerous loud and jealous accusations against McCabe, even in front of the customers at the El Dorado, Irene was rewarded with a sound thrashing; thus they parted company. Irene was a real professional when it came to handling men, so she bided her time, letting sly rumors drift back to McCabe of her mortal unhappiness at losing his love. McCabe finally weakened and, attempting a reconciliation, visited her rooms and apologized. Irene forgave him, at the same time handing him a glass of drugged wine. Once poor McCabe was unconscious, Irene did as Delilah did with Samson—except she did not put down her razor after shaving his head, but continued her depilatory labors until McCabe was minus *all* of his hair. If Irene's complaints of infidelity were indeed true, she exacted a phenomenally effective revenge.

In addition to the play-for-pay girls, San Francisco boasted a large group of mistresses who made no secret of their several involvements. One notable example was Belle Cora, or Arabella Ryan, the daughter of a Baltimore clergyman. Though not herself a prostitute, she ran a notorious house on Pike Street where the girls were reputed to be the most beautiful in the trade, and the prices were higher than in any other bagnio in the city (yet lower than the fee of the individual French girls). Belle and her love, Charles Cora, counted among their friends numerous politicians and aristocrats of the gambling world, men such as James McCabe. On the evening of November 15, 1855, she and Charles Cora attended a showing of *Nicodemus or, The Unfortunate Fisherman* at the American Theater. Also in the audience were General W. H. Richardson, United States Marshal for Northern California, and his wife. The Richardsons were outraged that Charles Cora would publicly flaunt his mistress, and they caused a scene and left the theater in a huff. Three days later, Cora shot and killed Richardson outside the Blue Wing Saloon.

Belle mustered all the money and influence she could, and fought Cora's conviction for as long as possible. She retained a lawyer for $30,000, but Richardson was a popular public figure and it became evident that Cora would be hanged for his crime. Just before the Vigilance Committee carried out the sentence at a rope's end, Belle legally married her lover. For a month after the execution, Belle stayed locked in her room. When at last she emerged, it was to sell her brothel and go off into seclusion. By the time of her death in 1862, the bulk of her wealth had been given to charity.

Twenty-five years later, Hubert Howe Bancroft, in *Popular Tribunals*, wrote of her:

> *Belle Cora kept a bagnio on Waverly Place. Like Cleopatra, she was very beautiful, and, beside the power that comes of beauty, rich, but oh, so foul! Flaunting her beauty and wealth on the gayest thoroughfares, and on every gay occasion, with senator, judge, and citizen at her beck and call, and being a woman as proud as she was beautiful and rich, she not infrequently flung back upon her stainless sisters the looks of loathed contempt with which they so often favored her. She was what she was. God only knows how or why; they were what they were, being made so. The homely pure hate the beautiful bad in self-defense so we are told. . . .*

Most California prostitutes preferred to work in the cities and large towns, where conditions were comparatively civilized. Setting up shop in a brush-covered tent was not only a tough way to make a buck, it was sometimes downright dangerous. There are several recorded instances of mountain-camp communities driving out the sisters of sin in distinctly ungentlemanly fashion. Even when moral indignation was not high enough for such forceful steps, the men might just stay away, denying the bawds a profit.

Thus a band of touring doxies were never quite sure of what type of welcome would be waiting for them in a new camp. One party of five girls and their madam, upon approaching Poker Flats on the North Fork of the Yuba River, were shocked to see the entire male population of the camp rush out toward them. One fair but frail maiden fell swooning, convinced the howling mob was bent on lynching them on the spot. As it turned out, a robust welcome was all the men had in mind.

Some years later, in 1860, girl-selling of a different nature aroused indignation throughout the northern California mines. A settler named Ransom Griswold met a westbound emigrant passing through the Honey Lake region. Griswold was so attracted to the man's daughter that he proposed a trade for the girl, offering her father two ten-gallon kegs of whiskey in exchange. His offer was promptly accepted, and Griswold took the girl—who was fourteen—to live with him. Later, having grown tired of the union, he sold the girl to Jim Bradley. However, this all ended happily, for Bradley promptly married the girl and, according to all reports, the two lived happily ever after.

Perhaps the most celebrated of all the *affaires d'amour* which took place in the Sierra gold camps revolved about Juanita, who worked in the Downieville fandango hall. There exist several versions of how Juanita came to her sad end, but all agree on one point—her death was an aftermath of the community celebration on July 4, 1851.

Juanita lived in a tiny cabin with her paramour, a slightly built Mexican named José. Like a good many of his countrymen, José was not allowed to stake out a claim of his own, so he took to gambling for a living. He dealt poker in Craycroft's saloon, where Juanita would meet him early each morning. Hand in hand they would stroll back to their cabin. Many of the miners lusted after the young Mexican girl, but she seemed to be content with her José as a steady lover. Some reports indicate that she may have sold her body, but only to José did she give herself.

Juanita was attractive by all accounts, and was described in one contemporary account as:

> . . . *rather low of stature, stout built, with raven tresses that flowed freely over her neck and shoulders—black eyes, teeth regular and of pearly whiteness. She might be called pretty, so far as the style of swarthy Mexican beauty is considered. She . . . dressed with considerable attention to taste.*

July 4, 1851, dawned bright and clear, and all preparations were made for a grand and glorious celebration. Bunting and flags and speaker's platform were in place; the miners flooded into town, bent on seeing how much tanglefoot they could consume during the parade. By afternoon there was hardly a sober man in camp, as several thousand miners staggered from saloon to saloon.

Most accounts agree that during the afternoon, Jack Cannon, an Australian, and one of his friends tried to break into Juanita's house for the purpose of amour. As she stood in her doorway arguing with Cannon, José tried to get Juanita to go inside, since by now people were gathering around to watch the fracas. Only a few understood what was going on, for Juanita and Cannon were arguing in Spanish. José and several bystanders later claimed that Cannon called Juanita a dirty whore. José finally managed to drag her into the house, but she turned and called out to Cannon, "This is no place to call me bad names. Come into my house and call me that." Cannon stood at the door, continuing to insult Juanita, so she snatched a knife from a table and plunged it deep into his chest.

Cannon staggered back into his friend's arms, crying as he died, "See, the woman has stabbed me!"

In Downieville there was a good deal of sympathy for the hot-blooded Juanita, particularly in view of the fact that Cannon addressed her in abusive and insulting language. Even if it were the truth, one just did not call a woman a "dirty whore." However, the Australian's friends in town refused to let the matter drop. An impromptu court was set up, a judge and jury chosen, and Juanita was charged with murder in cold blood. For the next two days, her trial occupied the undivided attention of the entire area. The counsels for the prosecution and for the defense presented their evidence and made their melodramatic pleas. The spokesman for Juanita admitted she stabbed her victim to death, but he maintained Cannon's behavior made the homicide justifiable. To complicate the whole proceeding, a local physician, C. P. Aiken, took the stand and boldly testified Juanita was pregnant—a statement which she herself indignantly denied.

Despite the pleas on her behalf, the jury found Juanita guilty and the judge sentenced her to be hanged. His decree was promptly carried out by dangling her from the wooden bridge which spanned the Yuba River in the middle of the town.

Sending a woman to the gallows was an unheard-of event in the 1850's, and the news of the sordid affair caused international reverberations. The *London Times* denounced the hanging as a travesty of justice and a shocking testimony to the lawlessness of the California frontier. In vain, the Downieville citizens tried to stem the tide of criticism and abuse by pointing out that Juanita's execution had been no drunken lynching; her trial, conviction, and execution were all in strict accordance with the accepted principles of law. Nevertheless, the little town could not remove the stigma of being the first town along the Mother Lode to hang a woman.

In *Incidents of Land and Water*, Mrs. D. B. Bates related the story of one Lillie Lee, whose widowed mother brought her to California to seek a home for both of them. Mrs. Bates shudders to report that Lillie's thoughtless mother brought a

Downieville, California, as it appeared in 1852, a few months after Juanita was lynched. One of the wooden bridges spanning the Yuba River served as the gallows.

young, lovely girl to "a country where virtue was regarded by the masses only as a name." Lillie Lee was far too captivating to remain long in obscurity, so in spite of her mother's vigilance, she succumbed to the oily wiles of a gambler and fled with him to one of the gold camps. After a day or so of soul searching, the mother armed herself with a Colt revolver and started in angry pursuit. When she arrived at the gold-field town, she wandered from one house of sin to the next where, Mrs. Bates writes, "elegantly attired women within whose natures long since had expired the last flickering spark of feminine modesty, were seated, dealing cards at a game of faro or Lansquenet, and by their winning smile and enticing manner, inducing hundreds of men to stake their all upon their tables."

At last, the mother found the place where Lillie and the gambler were living, and when the villain answered her knock the mother leveled the revolver at his breast. But lovestruck little Lillie pushed between them, and the gambler promised a speedy marriage. The rest of Lillie Lee's story is vintage soap opera, for the man already was married to another, a woman soon to arrive on a ship from back east. Was Lillie taught a bitter lesson by her misfortune? Did she reform and repent of her sins? No, she rushed recklessly into a life of abandon.

At this point in *Incidents of Land and Water*, Mrs. Bates makes Lillie's career so attractive that one can only wonder what the sheltered young ladies who read the book a century ago thought about this paragraph:

> *Lillie Lee would appear in a splendid Turkish costume which admirably displayed her tiny little foot encased in richly embroidered satin slippers. Thus she would promenade the thronged thorofares of the city, the observed of all observers . . . on other days she would mount her glossy, lithe-limbed race horse, habited in a closely fitting riding-dress of black velvet, ornamented with a hundred and fifty gold buttons, a hat from which depended magnifi-*

cent sable plumes, and over her face, a short
white lace veil of the richest texture. . . . The
fire of passion flashing from the depths of her
dark, lustrous eyes . . . she took all men captive.
. . . Gold and diamonds were showered upon
her.

While few Argonauts wrote much in their journals about
the camp harlots, William Perkins, a Canadian, was not so
hypocritical. In his journal he analyzed the girls of Sonora:

The Spaniard in circumstance [a prostitute]
remains a "woman" with all the feminine qual-
ities pertaining to her sex: warm hearted, gen-
erous and unartificial. Frenchwoman is made
up of artificiality; profligate, shameless, avari-
cious, and vain, she studiously covers these de-
fects with a charming manner, fascinating con-
versation and a deportment before the world
which is unexceptionable. She is the apple of
the shore of the Dead Sea—enchanting on the
exterior, within a mass of filth.

While only a few miners so candidly discussed their prefer-
ences in prostitutes, most implied that they rated the French
at the top, the Spanish second, then the Americans and English. Chinese women, the cheapest-priced harridans, were
ranked as their last choice. But by and large, the Argonauts of
the 1850's respected their soiled doves of whatever nationality, for these women shared with their men the dynamic,
independent, and forceful flair of California's golden era.

Some Glamour Girls

IN THE EARLY bonanza days of San Francisco, money flowed as if it came out of a tap. In May of 1853, Lola Montez arrived in San Francisco to get her share of the windfall. The "Countess of Landsfeld," as she was named by Ludwig I of Bavaria, was the most widely known and discussed wicked woman of the times. When Lola signed a contract with John Lewis Baker, manager of the American Theater, to play Lady Teazle in *The School for Scandal*, the demand for tickets was so large that they had to be sold at auction. The best seats went for sixty-five dollars.

Although she was born Marie Delores Eliza Rosanna Gilbert, in Limerick, Ireland, in 1818, the stage name of Lola Montez fitted her perfectly, for she had the dark, sultry beauty and exquisitely molded features of the women of Spain. She even invented a line of Spanish ancestors and a girlhood spent in Seville. Lola was largely unknown during her third tour of Europe, but in Munich, Franz Liszt, the romantic Hungarian composer, was smitten with Lola. He presented himself, arranged a small supper party in her honor, and soon shared her bed. Liszt persuaded her to let him take her to Paris, where he introduced her to the brilliant art, music, and literary circles of Paris.

Lola Montez, in her more glamorous days. The mistress of a writer, a composer, and a king, "The Countess of Landsfeld" was the most widely known wicked woman of her time.

Here she fell desperately in love with Henri Dujarier, the penniless literary editor of *La Presse*. Their relations were most intense until he fought a duel in defense of her honor and was killed. For the rest of her life, Lola said Dujarier was the only man she ever truly loved. She shut herself away from her friends and moved to a country retreat at Fontainebleu, where agents of King Ludwig of Bavaria found her. They presented her with letters from the king and a casket of jewels, which amounted to a royal summons. She promptly departed for Munich, where a completely staffed castle was waiting for her. The king's infatuation became a scandal, but to the day of her death, fifteen years later, Lola clung to the preposterous fiction that her relations with Ludwig were only those of friend and advisor.

After several weeks of public rioting in Bavaria, with the angry mobs marching up and down shouting: "Down with the whore!" Lola escaped to Switzerland, in time to miss the Revolution of 1848 that she had helped to ignite. She returned to Paris, where she received reams of sensational newspaper publicity, favorable and unfavorable, all of which was exploited at the box office. Although her acting and dancing won no acclaim from the critics, her appearances were invariably a tremendous financial success. What the public wanted was to see the beautiful woman for whose favors King Ludwig lost his throne.

With the discovery of gold in California, Lola purchased stock in the Eureka Mine, located at a small settlement named Grass Valley. Most likely this was the first time she had ever given thought to America. Edward Willis, an enterprising and successful theatrical agent and manager, arrived in Paris and sold Lola on America. In November 1851, she and Willis sailed for New York. With great ingenuity, Willis managed to keep Lola's name in the American newspapers daily, continually whetting the public's appetite to see Lola. Packed houses greeted her all along the Eastern seaboard.

Flushed with her initial successes, Lola became convinced she must go to California, since some of the foremost American actors had already appeared in San Francisco and

Sacramento. Accompanied by her new maid—a tall New Orleans mulatto named Hyacinthe Phlery, whom Lola renamed Periwinkle—crossed the isthmus of Panama and arrived safely in San Francisco.

Lola's sensational Spider Dance was a smash, stunning the spectators who had been drawn to the theater by Lola's flamboyant claims, among them the whopper that she was the illegitimate daughter of Lord Byron. She dressed in the Byronic mode, wearing a black jacket and a blouse with a wide rolling collar, and frequently strolled along the San Francisco streets with her two greyhounds on a leash and an enormous parrot upon her shoulder.

On the voyage to California, Lola met Patrick Purdy Hull, a tall, affable, witty writer and part owner of the *San Francisco Whig*. A few days after reaching San Francisco, she married him. Her marriage incensed her manager, who did not care how many lovers Lola took—the more the merrier—but wanted no part of the sanctity that was attached to marriage even in bawdy San Francisco. The audiences wanted to see Lola Montez, the mistress of a king, not Lola Hull, housewife.

Lola's famous Spider Dance was performed in Spanish costume, with full, short skirts and flesh-colored tights. The dance began with Lola wandering onto the stage, then becoming entangled in a spider's web. Suddenly she discovered a spider (made of rubber, cork, and whalebone) on her petticoat and, attempting to dislodge the repellent bug, she shook her petticoat furiously. On examining her skirts, she discovered other spiders and she shook her skirts with similar fury, revealing her tights. Finally she succeeded in shaking off all the spiders and stamped them to death on the floor. Thunderous applause greeted her as she took her bows. This may sound pretty tame, but in the 1850's it was daring enough to make the rowdy San Francisco audiences stand and shout, "Higher! Higher!" as Lola searched beneath her skirts for the evasive spiders.

At the conclusion of the Spider Dance, Lola stripped a silken garter off a shapely leg and tossed it into the audience.

The winner of the ensuing scramble triumphantly waved his prize, which he would treasure forever. One newspaper writer termed Lola "a tigress, the very comet of her sex."

One newspaper ran the following tongue-in-cheek review of Lola's Spider Dance:

> *Spriggins told me there was something peculiar about the Countess' dancing. There is . . . Spriggins said the Spider Dance was to represent a girl that commences dancing and finds a spider on her clothes and jumps about to shake it off. If that's it, Mr. Editor, then the first part of the dance I guess she must see the spider on the ceiling, and that it's in trying to kick the cobwebs down that she gets the spider upon her clothes. She kicked up and she kicked around in all directions, and first it was this leg and then it was the other and her petticoats were precious short, Mr. Editor, on purpose to give her a fair chance. (The kicking match between Lola and the spiders caused this bashful observer to put his hat over his eyes and just peep over the brim, and then a man upstairs began hollering "Hey!" Hey!" and soon everybody was yelling, and I took my hat down from [my] eyes to see what was up.) If the Countess wasn't crazy, I don't know what on earth was the matter with her. She seemed to get so excited like, that she forgot that there was any man at all about there. . . . At this point the audience began stamping on the floor and the shy observer ran out of the theater, frightened . . . the house would come down or she'd take her dress right off, and I couldn't stand it.*
>
> *"Why it is nothing to be afraid of when you get used to it," says Spriggins, "and you went away before you saw it all."*
>
> *But Mr. Editor, I saw more than I wanted to, and I ain't used to it—that's a fact.*

This review was not the only one to be unkind to Miss Montez's entomological hi-jinks. In cultured circles, she was viewed as nothing more than a high-priced hurdy-gurdy dancer. Eventually Lola could bear the ridicule no longer; she left San Francisco in a peevish fit and headed for the mining towns of California. Her tour was a flop. She became increasingly temperamental, refusing to play out a scene when she heard a miner laugh. Lola was shocked and repelled by the crude, woman-starved miners, and the men expected something different from the solemn, haughty Lola. At one camp, Lola is said to have challenged the whole audience in these words: "Apes, give me your pants and take my petticoats. You're not fit to be called men. Lola Montez is proud to be what she is. But you, who have not the courage to fight with her—yes, this woman, who has no fear of you all, despises you!" For this she was showered with vegetables and fruit. Lola had to be escorted to her hotel by a group of gallants with drawn pistols, for it seemed the Countess of Landsfeld was about to be lynched.

Deeply depressed by the precipitous decline of her popularity, Lola retired to Grass Valley, took a small cottage surrounded by a white picket fence, and passed her time tending a flower garden. So delighted were the miners of the area to have even a waning star in their midst, they named the highest peak in the area Mount Lola. Legends followed, one story claiming that when the local minister inveighed against Lola from the pulpit, she donned her stage costume, knocked at his door, and performed her Spider Dance on the good man's front porch. Afterward, the story goes, the remorseful dancer sent the minister a large donation for his church.

In 1855, Lola packed her costumes and sailed for Australia. After a series of appearances there, she returned to San Francisco, gave several farewell performances of the Spider Dance, and then went to New York. She later made a lecture tour telling the story of her life, and wrote a book called *The Arts of Beauty or Secrets of a Lady's Toilet, with Hints to Gentlemen on the Art of Fascination*. But gradually she dropped from public notice and on January 17, 1861, died destitute in New York. She lies in an unmarked grave in Brooklyn's Greenwood Cemetery.

During the time Lola Montez was living in Grass Valley, only one woman in town was friendly to her—Mary Ann Crabtree, who ran a boarding house while her husband, John Crabtree, was out searching for the gold strike he never made. Although always struggling to make ends meet, Mary Ann dreamed of gold, too—not from a creek bed, but in her red-haired daughter who was then an impish seven-year-old. Charlotte, or Lotta, as she was generally called, was an appealing child with her black eyes and easy laughter. Lola liked the little girl, and taught her to ride horseback, to dance, and to sing a few tender ballads.

Lotta Crabtree, a protegée of Lola Montez and for 35 years the perennial pet of the Western theater. Her lachrymose ballads took the miners' hearts and dollars; but Lotta's millions went unspent.

Lotta got her start in show biz when she was eight years old. Theater-owner Mart Taylor needed a child actress to meet the competition from a rival impresario who was featuring his small daughter. Taylor had seen Lotta's amateur efforts, so with her mother's permission, he taught little Lotta an Irish jig and reel. Her singing and dancing won loud acclaim from her audiences of miners, especially the closing number in which Lotta, clad in angelic white, sang a tear-jerking ballad of innocence. Gold and silver coins showered the stage. This rain of wealth frightened the shy child, but Mother rushed out with a basket to carefully collect every coin.

Two patterns were set at this performance: always Lotta Crabtree's trademark would be a lachrymose ballad delivered in a virginal white costume; and always Mother would take in the money. Mary Ann and Lotta, with Mart Taylor as manager, set out on a tour of the mining camps. Taylor played a guitar and Mary Ann a triangle, while Lotta danced and sang the ballads. Their luck was phenomenal. "The singing and dancing of little Lotta was admirable," one miner reported, "and took our hearts by storm." By 1859, Mother decided little Lotta was ready for San Francisco.

The secret of Lotta's success was her girlish innocence. Whatever she lacked in dramatic ability she made up in image—a lamb among wolves, pure as new snow. The only impure element in her show was the filthy lucre which her admirers showered upon her, to Mother's delight.

As Lotta grew older, she took a fancy to smoking cigarillos, and introduced gaminelike bits into her performances—showing her knees by pulling up her stockings, rolling off divans with a flurry of lifted petticoats, and wearing the briefest skirts.

For thirty-five years, Lotta was the perennial little pet of the Western theater, and when she retired at the age of forty-four she still wore her red curls. She lived alone with Mother, who had saved most of Lotta's enormous earnings. And after Mother died, it was too late for any romance in Lotta's life, so her 4 million dollars went to charity when Lotta died in 1924.

Not all the show-women of California were content to cash in on a passing craze or gimmick. One of the first real actresses to come West was vivacious Caroline Chapman. The Chapmans were a famed theatrical family who got their start on the showboats of the Ohio and the Mississippi. In 1852, they trouped to California and were an immediate success. Caroline always played with her father, William Chapman, and they looked so much alike people assumed they were brother and sister. At the end of their first performance in San Francisco, the audience tossed so many sacks of gold dust to the Chapmans that the stage appeared to be carpeted with gold.

Mobs began following Caroline to and from the theater, calling for "our Caroline" to give them a smile. When the Chapmans traveled to Sonora to open the theater there with *She Stoops to Conquer,* a thousand miners formed an escort of honor as they came into town. One reason for the Chapmans' extraordinary popularity was their willingness to play anytime, anywhere, under any conditions. At one mining camp, they played with verve and spirit upon the sawed-off trunk of a large redwood tree. In the mid-1850's, Caroline Chapman became annoyed by all the attention Lola Montez was receiving, along with the corresponding decrease in the size of her audiences. Caroline decided to burlesque the famous Spider Dance, and according to the press, her uproarious performances transformed Lola's act from high sensuality to low comedy.

One of the most glamourous and perhaps the most tragic of the "glamour girls" of the West was the beautiful Pauline Cushman, who during the Civil War served as a Union spy. Her pictures show she possessed a gypsylike beauty, with long black hair, and her voice was likened to that of a lark. Pauline was born in New Orleans on June 10, 1833, but in the 1840's the family moved to Michigan, where Pauline's father opened a frontier trading post. Her youth was spent in the forest among the Chippewas, who called her Laughing Breeze.

At eighteen, Pauline ran away to join a theatrical troupe; within a year, she was playing the leading role. In 1863, while starring in Wood's Theater in Louisville, Tennessee, she agreed to become a Union agent for William Truesdail, chief of the secret police of the Army of the Cumberland. On the way to Nashville, she was picked up by a Rebel scouting party belonging to John Hunt Morgan's command, but Morgan freed her. Not long thereafter, she was recaptured by some of Nathan Bedford Forrest's men, who found in her boots some sketches of the fortifications of Shelbyville. She was court-martialed and found guilty. While she was awaiting sentence, William Starke Rosecrans launched his attack on Shelbyville and the Rebels evacuated the town. Pauline was transferred from the prison to a boarding house where she was given the best of care.

In 1864, Pauline Cushman embarked on a triumphant theatrical career, reciting a dramatic version of her adventures and making the newspaper headlines as she moved from town to town. Pauline and her troupe toured the country from New York to San Francisco, playing to the wildest audiences on the frontier. Many fired sixshooters at the ceiling to signal their appreciation of the performance.

In a town south of San Francisco, Pauline made headlines of another sort. She was part owner of a hotel called La Honda, and had stopped off to manage it for a while between engagements. When she heard another hotel manager make remarks questioning her virtue, she grabbed a stagecoach driver's whip and flogged the slanderer unmercifully.

In 1879, she married Jere Fryer and settled in Casa Grande, Arizona, where she became unofficial referee of six-gun battles. On one occasion she stood in the center of the dirt street, sixshooter in hand, while the leaders of two rival factions fought it out. One fighter had drawn too slow and died on his feet, so Pauline dressed his corpse, said the prayers for the dead, and buried him. On another occasion, armed with a rifle, she climbed to the top of a corral fence next to the hotel she owned and ordered one of the mule skinners to "cut out" a sick animal in his team. The skinner promptly told her to go to hell, so Pauline aimed her rifle directly at his heart and told him she was only counting to three. At the count of two, the skinner relented.

But all these adventures did not make for a happy life in Casa Grande, for her husband, handsome and wild, had a roving eye and broke Pauline's heart. She loved him dearly and tried to overlook his wandering affections, even attempting to hold Fryer by claiming the infant of a prostitute as her own. Her husband was proud of his fatherhood, and for a while stopped his roving. But the child died during a convulsion before it was two, the real mother spoke up, and Pauline's plot was exposed. Broken-hearted and ashamed, Pauline left town to return to the stage. Nobody was interested in the Civil War, the producers told her, and she was already a legend which could not be improved upon.

By this time, Pauline Cushman was an old woman who dressed in a fashion twenty years out of date. Her voice was hoarse, her hair streaked with gray, and her skin dried by the hot desert sun. She was reduced to scrubbing floors in the San Francisco theaters where men had once fired their sixshooters in tribute to her. On December 7, 1893, her landlady forced in the door of her tiny flat and found Pauline Cushman—Union spy, theatrical agent, frontier woman—dead, an apparent suicide. She was saved from burial in potters' field by the Grand Army of the Republic. The plaque they mounted above her grave reads, "Pauline Cushman, Federal Spy and Scout of the Cumberland."

The manager of the Melodeon Theatre in Virginia City, Nevada, placarded every cliff and signboard on Sun Mountain with posters announcing the coming of Antoinette Adams, the first actress to appear in the town. Enthusiasm was boundless as the red-letter day approached, and on opening night, every bench, corner, and windowsill of the Melodeon was filled. After what seemed like ages, the curtain went up and Antoinette Adams strode to the footlights. Ugly as a snaggletoothed dog, she stood nearly six feet tall, with a decided stoop to her shoulders, a long goose neck, watery blue eyes, a large Roman nose, crooked mouth, and faded frizzed "blonde" hair. This Antoinette was old enough to be their aunt, one man protested, and the laughing audience dubbed her "Aunty" on the spot.

*An old view of Virginia City, Nevada, the scene of "Aunty" Adams' famous debut.
Mount Davidson is in the background.*

Miss Adams' opening song was "Under the Willow," a ballad dear to the miners' hearts. Folding her hands on her breast, she began, but even the Washoe "canaries" sang better. Consternation, disappointment, chagrin was on every face. The miners wanted to laugh, they wanted to cry, for they had been taken in and good. As soon as Aunty finished her melody, Hank Blanchard jumped to his feet.

"Now, boys, three cheers for 'Aunty,'" he yelled.

The miners rose as a single man. Cheer after cheer shook the Melodeon. When they sat down, not one of them cracked a smile. The braying songstress was so flustered she could not catch her breath.

Finally, she started again on "the Willow." Again they listened until her last cracked note died upon the air. Again, Hank Blanchard rose from his seat. "I, for one," he declared, "think it's time to retire 'Aunty' from the stage. Let's pension her and let her go!"

The applause swelled, the miners hollered and whooped, stamped and pounded upon the floor. Half-dollars fell on the stage like a hail storm. When order was restored, Miss Adams, all smiles and blushes, again sang "Under the Willow." Once more there was wild applause followed by more half-dollars raining upon the platform. Aunty looked out over the coal-oil lamps at her feet and tried to sing, but exertion and the light mountain air were telling on her voice and lungs.

Even so, thunders of applause greeted her silent song. But Aunty was forced to retire backstage. The foot-stamping was redoubled when the manager came out and tried to speak. "Miss Adams thanks her admirers for their appreciation of her talent as a vocalist, but . . ."

"Aunty! Aunty! Give us Aunty!" the miners yelled.

Miss Adams came out panting, beaten but determined to requite her admirers' passion. She tried to sing, but was so short of breath that all she could manage was a high-pitched wheeze. Out she backed, smiling and throwing kisses, while yet more half-dollars flooded the stage as the curtain fell.

The manager of the Melodeon came before the curtain. "Miss Adams begs me to say," he began, "that she cannot sing any more tonight, but she thanks you for all your courtesy."

The men still clamored for Aunty. The manager shook his head. At last, the miners stood up and filed out into the night. Next morning's stage carried their Aunty and two sacks of half-dollars down Sun Mountain. It was enough to last the rest of her natural life even if she never sang "Under the Willow" again.

The Western masculine audience was ordinarily far more critical than were the tolerant gentlemen of Virginia City, Nevada. The customary expression of their displeasure was to snatch the actors off the stage and toss them up and down in blankets, or send them packing on a rail.

Emma Wixom rose from the obscurity of a small Nevada mining town to win acclaim as Emma Nevada. Born in the California mining camp of Alpha Diggin's in 1859, Emma and her parents joined the rush east to the silver boom at Austin, Nevada. There, her fine voice was recognized by Mrs. S. Prisk, one of her teachers, who encouraged Emma's friends to send her to Mills Seminary in California to study music. At Mills, Dr. Adrian Ebell and his wife were so impressed with her talent that in 1877 they took her to Paris to study voice. As a pupil of the noted Madame Marchesi, Emma progressed rapidly, and in a few years was ready for the stage.

Showing just pride in her Austin background, Emma changed her last name to Nevada in 1880, just before her London debut. From then on, Europe was hers. In the spring of 1885, "the Comstock Nightingale" began her first American tour. She appeared at San Francisco's Grand Opera House on the evening of March 23, and the next morning's papers reported "enthusiasm bordering on lunacy." Her manager, Dr. Raymond Palmer, fell victim to her charms and they were married the same year. Following her American debut, she sang many times in the mining towns of her childhood. In 1902, she gave her last American concert in Nevada City, not far from the place of her birth, and retired to private life. Emma Nevada died near Liverpool, England, in 1940.

Another favorite of the West was Ada Isaacs Menken, who made her stage debut after the triumphs of Lola Montez

Emma Wixom, the Nevada song-
stress who performed under the
stage name of Emma Nevada. Her
San Francisco debut brought "en-
thusiasm bordering on lunacy."

and Lotta Crabtree. "The Menken," as she was called, was not
a dancer like Lola or a variety performer like Lotta; she preferred exciting melodramas. Although privately she lived in
the "wicked" tradition of Lola, The Menken was prompt to
deny any kinship with the Spider Dancer. "Lola Montez began
with a king," she once said, "and ran down the scale through a
newspaper man to a miner. I began with a prizefighter, and I
will end with a prince!" Ada knew the value of a mysterious

background, and she dropped hints that she once lived with Sam Houston in Texas, after the Ranger saved her from Indians. But there was no proof to substantiate this dime-novel tale.

Ada was born in New Orleans, and she enshrouded the identity of her parents in mystery for years. From time to time she changed fathers: James McCord, Richard Irving Spencer, Ricardo La Fuentes, and James Campbell each held the honor at one time or another. Her mother was sometimes a Creole, sometimes a Jewess of Franco-Spanish origin. Ada's other fibs were of truly Munchausen proportion. Though her

Ada Isaacs Menken, the "frenzy of Frisco," in stage costume. During a trip to Europe, "The Menken" became the paramour of both Alexandre Dumas and the poet Swinburne.

education had been at best a haphazard exercise in self-help, The Menken unabashedly stated that she had translated the *Iliad* from Greek to French at the age of twelve.

In fact, she was born in 1835, and her given name was Adelaide. Her father was Auguste Theodore, a "free man of color," and her mother was a Creole. This mixed heritage explains why Adah invented fantastic tales about her ancestry, and it accounts for her dark beauty which made her known as a Jewess, a faith she embraced only after marrying Alexander Isaac Menken.

Adelaide Theodore learned to dance with her sister Josephine, and the two girls became part of the ballet at the French Opera House in New Orleans. She also mastered French and Spanish, speaking both with such ease that no stranger could fix her nationality. From New Orleans to Havana, Adelaide danced through many successful engagements and emerged as "Queen of the Plaza." In 1853, she went to Texas, where three years later she married Menken, a handsome Jewish musician and the son of a prosperous Cincinnati merchant. At the same time as she embraced the Jewish faith, she took the name Ada.

The Menken's marriage was brief. Immediately after divorcing her first husband she hitched on with her second— a prizefighter named John Carmel "Benecia Boy" Heenan. These marriage bonds were no more binding than her first, for she divorced Heenan in 1861 and promptly married Robert Henry Newall. This union lasted five years, a record. Later, while in Paris, she became the mistress of Alexandre Dumas, Fils; in London, she became the paramour of the poet Swinburne.

The Menken's fame preceded her to California, so that her first appearance at Maguire's Opera House, San Francisco, on August 24, 1862, was received with savage acclaim. San Francisco's Bohemian colony recognized her as a kindred spirit. The press called her "the Frenzy of Frisco," and copiously reported her well-cultivated eccentricities. The Menken spread a large Confederate flag across one wall of her hotel room, and walked the streets clad only in a single yellow silk garment. Yellow, she said, was her mystical color.

But America was beginning to pall on Adah, so when in 1863 Astley's Amphitheatre in London offered her the lead in *Mazeppa,* she accepted. *Mazeppa* was a banal dramatization of one of Byron's poems, presented rapid-fire like a three-ring circus. The high point of the performance occurred when the Menken, in an extremely daring costume, was strapped to a horse's back and rode up a narrow runway between two cardboard mountain crags.

The Menken's hit in London led her back to the States, and superheated fans like those in Virginia City. Colorful posters displaying Ada's half-naked form upon the back of the black stallion were hanging in all the bars of the town, and the imagination of every miner was set racing. On opening night, the theater was packed with tense, excited males, all waiting for the ride up the mountain peak. Suspense gripped the miners as stage hands began to bring on the horse. At last, Mazeppa's form was in full view. The miners gaped in astonishment. She was stripped of all but a gauzy maillot! This wealth of lovely flesh exceeded their fondest hopes.

Apparently the only male in all of Nevada not captivated by The Menken's "performance" was a hypercritical news writer from the *Carson City Independent* who wrote:

> *We hope there were no butchers in the audience, for they must have been lost to the play and thought of nothing but veal. Such calves! They were never reared on milk! The acting consisted of sneezing, smoking, and coughing on the part of the supes (viz. supernumerary actors) and some elegant posturing on the part of The Menken.*

The excitement and whirl of life on the Comstock delighted The Menken. She even showed those miners a thing or two. "Benecia Boy," The Menken's pugilist husband, had taught her to box, so one night at the Sazerac Saloon she put on the gloves with "Joggles" Wright, a Washoe Bohemian with a keen zest for sport. In a couple of rounds, she knocked him down several times. She followed up this victory by defeating two more men with ring aspirations.

99

A sketch of The Menken strapped to a horse for her "Mazeppa gallop." Her display of fleshly beauty was the height of theatrical eroticism.

Kings, poets, buffoons, prizefighters—all fell under The Menken's spell, for her appeal was elemental. Directly over the bar of the Sazerac, in the place of honor, hung a picture of The Menken, "naked to the pitiless storm."

Soon, Ada began longing for Europe again, and off she went to seek more fame and notoriety. She finally died in Paris in 1868, at the age of 33. Her death resulted indirectly from her wild ride up and down the stage, for during a performance of *Mazeppa*, her leg was gashed as the confused horse ran into the scenery. The wound never healed properly, and it developed a cancerous growth which proved fatal.

Seven of the most popular entertainers on the Barbary Coast during the 1870's were the Waddling Duck, Lady Jane Grey, the Dancing Heifer, the Galloping Cow, the Roaring Gimlet, The Little Lost Chicken, and Big Bertha. Although these women were called entertainers, their lack of talent was so obvious that they were comical, which of course accounted for their great popularity.

The Waddling Duck, a sickeningly fat singer, was billed as the only female in the world who could sing in two keys at once, which translated to mean that she could not sing in any key. She simply screeched out what she called the scales.

Lady Jane Grey, a middle-aged star, was slightly demented. She believed herself to be the illegitimate daughter of an English Earl, and wore a coronet of cardboard decorated with little bits of glass. The Dancing Heifer and the Galloping Cow were two ex-washerwomen who lumbered across the stage like a pair of hippopotomi performing a classical dance. The Roaring Gimlet, a tall, thin, and wispy creature, sang in a voice which would have put a rutting bull moose to shame.

The Little Lost Chicken was a tiny girl who was known for her talent as a pickpocket as well as her quavering falsetto. She knew only one song, "The boat lies high, the boat hands low; She lies high and dry on the Ohio," and always burst into tears on the last note of the ballad.

Big Bertha was billed at the Bella Union as "the Queen of the Confidence Women." Bertha arrived in the 1880's, posing as a wealthy Jewess who was in search of a man to help her manage her fortune. Naturally, many gentlemen volunteered, but Bertha required each suitor to give her a sum of money as a show of good faith. This would be invested in a manner known only to her. It was not long before she had swindled her "suitors" of several thousand dollars, but Big Bertha was never prosecuted; none of her victims cared to face the publicity.

Later Big Bertha played the boards at the Bella Union as a dancer who could not dance, a singer who could not sing, and an actress who could not act. The only two songs she knew were "A Flower from My Angel Mother's Grave," and

"The Cabin Where the Old Folks Died." Her greatest acting triumph was in a condensed version of *Mazeppa*. Big Bertha wanted a stamp of her personality on the production, so she made a few changes, such as strapping herself to the back of a small burro. One night the poor overburdened animal fell over the footlights, carrying Big Bertha with him. This was the end of Bertha's acting career, and nearly the end of those in the pit orchestra.

No melodrama of the 1870's could ever equal the drama of one unusual performance at the Melodeon in Deadwood, South Dakota. "Handsome Banjo Dick" Brown and his partner, Fanny Garrettson, were doing their act when a dim figure staggered to the footlights, muttered incoherently, and hurled an ax at the players. "Handsome Dick" ducked, then coolly drew his pistol and shot the man dead. The unsuccessful assassin proved to be Ed Shaunessey of Laramie, Wyoming, Miss Garrettson's recently discarded lover, who had come to Deadwood with the hope of winning back her affections. Miss Garrettson wrote to the local paper to stifle the malicious rumor that she had once been Shaunessey's wife. Even though she had lived with Shaunessey for three years, Miss Garrettson avowed, they had never actually married. So there was certainly nothing immoral about her having run away with Mr. Brown, the actor.

Female performers in the cow towns and mining centers knew what their rowdy male audiences wanted and gave it to them. Entertainment, drinking, and women all combined to create a rollicking good time at the Western variety theater. This forerunner of vaudeville made no pretenses of art; all types of acts appeared, including comedians, acrobats, India rubbermen, and singers. The program was geared to please an audience unused to genteel diversion. Between acts, the actresses and painted darlings of the chorus left the stage to lure the customers to purchase refreshments. As the evening wore on, the nature of these lures became bolder, and the last show of the night was invariably the wildest.

Many of the female performers were prostitutes as well, and this last performance served as their come-on. An upstairs seat for the show cost a patron one dollar, with the buck entitling the bearer to hug the girls who came around selling liquid refreshments. During the evening, ten to twenty gaudy angels periodically appeared on the stage, a few at a time. The rest were at work upstairs, beguiling the patrons in the private boxes. One of the "extra added attractions" of attending a cow town variety theater was a visit to the "green room," a secluded place where for the price the cowboys could drink in cozy surroundings and indulge in pleasantries with the actresses.

Much has been written about Lily Langtry and Judge Roy Bean, more than their "relationship" would seem to warrant. Miss Langtry toured the United States in 1882, and in 1888 played in San Antonio, Texas. Bean supposedly purchased a front-row seat to see his dream girl in the flesh, but apparently never exchanged words with her. After the judge died in 1903, "the Jersey Lily" visited Judge Bean's Vinegaroon Saloon as a publicity stunt. She was given the old horse pistol of her strange admirer, which she hung in "a place of honor" in her home in England.

The whore with a heart of gold is a stock character in thousands of stories about the Old West, and Idaho had such a character. "Diamond-tooth Lil" was her name, and she was more famous for her tooth of gold than for her heart of gold. Like most characters in western lore, Lil devoted her lifetime to perfecting her own legend and image. Her gold tooth, prominent in the middle of her smile, was set with a large diamond to gain Lil instant recognition in any company. And Lil loved it. From childhood she had thirsted for fame.

All we know about Lil's colorful life comes from her own stories, recounted through the years to just about anyone who would listen. Whether her stories were true or not does not seem too important, for they make good telling. Mae West's characterization of "Diamond Lil" was based on the life of Idaho's Lil, and in all accounts of her life, the stress lay on Diamond-tooth Lil's beauty and glamor. Words like "fabulous and exciting" are regularly used to describe her, although it

Lily Langtry, "The Jersey Lily," in her concert costume. She was the apple of Judge Roy Bean's eye.

"Judge" Roy Bean in front of the Jersey Lily Saloon in Langtry, Texas, about 1902. The Judge was hardly the spitting image of Paul Newman, Hollywood's Roy Bean.

"Diamond-tooth Lil," the whore with the golden heart. Mae West's characterization of "Diamond Lil" in the 1933 movie of the same name was based on the life of this Idaho madam.

was not Lil's looks but her vitality and sense of showmanship which evoked such adjectives.

Evelyn Hildegarde was born Katie Prado near Vienna, Austria, about 1880. It appears that she and her parents—an Austrian father and a Bohemian mother—came to America when Katie was six years old. When Katie ran away from home, she was only thirteen, but she was quite mature for her age and looked sixteen. She had eloped with nineteen-year-old Percy Hildegarde and used his last name the rest of her life.

105

By her own account, Lil had a total of eight husbands, never worrying about ridding herself of a husband, but just taking another when the mood struck.

Among the men in her life were some pretty colorful characters: prizefighter Kid McCoy, Spider Kelly, Diamondfield Jack Davis, Tex Rickard, and Tom Sharkey. Diamondtooth Lil's friendship with Diamondfield Jack was a natural. The swaggering Jack had plenty of color all his own; although notorious as a gunman, his chief claim to fame was that he was almost hung for a murder he did not commit. Perhaps Jack was the inspiration for Lil's famous tooth, for she did not

"Diamond-tooth Lil," a few years before her death, reminiscing about her bawdy days.

have one when they met in 1907 in the boomtown of Golden-field, Nevada.

Lil had been singing and dancing in music halls and gambling palaces for several years before she ran up against Jack. She was the "toast of the Barbary Coast," and a star at the St. Louis World's Fair in 1904, singing at the Anheuser-Busch Pavilion. But somewhere along the way she got in on the gold rush to Alaska, then came back south to Silver City, Idaho. Boise was her home from 1909 until 1943, during which time she ran rooming houses and opened the Depot Inn in 1933. Diamond-tooth Lil's experience as a "business-woman" began years before, for she claimed she was a madam from the time she was thirteen, and ran large houses in Chicago, St. Louis, New York, and Seattle.

One of her "bosses" in Chicago was said to be Al Capone, and it is no surprise that Lil was not repelled by the violence of the gangster era. Lil herself had had a taste of violence years before, when she was shot at by an ex-husband in El Paso, Texas. Charitable and generous, Lil felt a special sympathy for orphans, and when she left Boise for the warmer climate of California, she promised to will her famous tooth to the Boise Children's Home. But she died in California at age eighty-nine, and the tooth which made her famous was buried with her.

There were other "glamour girls," of course, since sooner or later every Western town built a theater of sorts. But these girls are the standouts in the legends of the frontier.

Guns for Love

IN THE SPRING of 1901, the Wild Bunch, led by Butch Cassidy with cold-blooded Kid Curry second in command, could be seen riding bicycles in the dusty streets of Fort Worth. Past Fannie Porter's bordello they pedaled, to the delighted cheers of the girls and their customers. For the Wild Bunch, Fannie's house was a home, the place where the gang would come back for fun after pulling a caper. Kid Curry, whose given name was Harvey Logan, drank with Fannie after hours; actually, he would sit drinking and she would sit pouring in silence. Fannie was the closest thing to a girl friend the Kid ever had, for he was not known for his good looks. Yet when he needed a woman's company, Fannie never refused, for the Kid was the one man who treated her like a lady. Eventually, the two became sweethearts, and Fannie gave up other men.

One night when dead drunk, the Kid staggered inside Fannie's place and announced he was moving in. Her bordello was the red-velvet, crystal-chandelier type, and the Kid made quite a sight stretched out on satin sheets, wearing his boots and black derby and holding his pearl-handled Colt Peacemaker in his hand. Later that same night, Butch was tipped off that the Pinkerton detectives were on their trail, so Butch ran over to Fannie's, revived Kid Curry, and the gang headed out of town.

Fannie told her friends the Kid would be back just as soon as the Pinkertons left town. She waited for him, but time passed slowly and she took to drinking. Then news came that the Wild Bunch had broken up, and the Kid had gone to New York. Fannie refused to believe the news, and continued her vigil. The newspapers reported that the Kid had been seen traveling in Tennessee with a girl called Annie Rogers, but Fannie still waited. In the fall of 1901, however, came news that Kid Curry had been shot and captured in a pool hall in Knoxville. At last Fannie packed her bags and headed for Tennessee.

The Kid's trial was not held until mid-1902. All during the Kid's long stay in court awaiting the prosecution's presentation, Fannie visited him. Over many a bottle of Mount Vernon, which she smuggled in and the jailer overlooked, they sat together silently. In November 1902, the jury convicted Curry, who received the sentence with a smile on his face. Fannie continued to see Curry as he awaited the results of an appeal, supporting herself by working in a Knoxville restaurant.

Then on June 27, 1903, Curry, using a piece of wire that Fannie may have smuggled in to him, picked the lock of his

Butch Cassidy as a young man. Interest in his escapades soared in the 1970's with the making of the film, Butch Cassidy and the Sundance Kid.

cell and overpowered a guard. As he emerged from the jail, Fannie was there with two horses. With a wink and a smile, the Kid jumped on one and slapped the other, which bolted, knocking poor Fannie down as the Kid sped out of town.

By the time the Kid resumed his career, Annie Rogers was with him once again. Fannie was back in her house in Fort Worth when she read in the newspaper that the Kid had been killed while trying to rob a train. She locked herself in her room for three days, then left the city—to claim his body, some said. But the movements of Fannie Porter were never again recorded in Western history.

A better-known associate of the Wild Bunch, Etta Place, was as tough as she was beautiful. She was the long-time sweetheart of Harry Longbaugh, The Sun-Dance Kid, whom she fell for at a community dance. Etta wore a revolver and men's clothes and supposedly participated in the robbery of Union Pacific Train #3 on August 29, 1900, outside Tipton, Wyoming. When the gang discovered that this effort netted only $50.00, Etta, who was far from stupid, took over the planning for future escapades.

One day, on the way to a bank holdup, Bill Carver, a member of the gang, found a skunk and brought it along. While Etta stood outside holding the horses, Bill and the boys took their stink bomb inside the bank and gassed out the tellers. The take this time was $30,000. Butch, Harry, and Etta went to New York with their share of the money, and, after posing for photographs in the famous De Young photo studio, they headed for South America. For the next seven years, they carved a place in history for themselves as *bandido Yanquis*. As they traveled from Argentina to Chile to Bolivia, they held up bank after bank.

Butch and the Sun-Dance Kid made their big mistake in 1909 when they allowed themselves to be trapped by soldiers in a Bolivia saloon. They were killed, but no one knows what happened to the beautiful Etta Place. After enduring the hardships of outlaw life in South America for five years, Etta left Butch and Sun-Dance in 1907 and was not heard from again.

Butch Cassidy and the Sundance Kid, and friends. Butch is seated right, the Kid is seated left, with Ben Kilpatrick in the center. Their exploits took them up and down the Americas.

The legendary Calamity Jane is almost entirely the creation of the romanticists in need of a tragic Western heroine. These writers paid little attention to the known facts, but in this they had the full-hearted encouragement of Calamity Jane herself.

Yet even after one subtracts the 90 per cent of her life's story that was fabricated, Calamity Jane is still a fascinating figure. Few other Western women could brag about having both worked in and patronized brothels. One of Calamity's claims was that, in male garb and with the aid of a dildo, she could deceive any prostitute she visited. (In the old days, coitus was performed in total darkness even in a whorehouse,

111

and neither the prostitute nor her client removed any more clothing than absolutely necessary.) She also boasted that she was once thrown out of a bagnio in Bozeman, Montana, for exerting a low influence on the harlots!

Many stories are told about how Calamity Jane got her name, but the one most logical is that her paramours were visited by some venereal calamity. One thing for sure, Jane loved the men. But as time went on, her affections switched to booze. When she was twenty-four, she was already an alcoholic who could out-curse, out-shoot, out-shout, and out-drink most men.

Little is known about Calamity Jane's origins. She was born in 1852 or 1853 in Missouri or in Illinois, and her name was Mary Jane Conarry or Martha Jane Canary. Her mother most likely was a prostitute and, around 1866, became the madam of a house called the Bird Cage in Blackfoot, Montana.

The stories say Jane was about thirteen when she herself became a prostitute in Montana. At seventeen, wearing men's clothes, she was a harlot for the railroad section hands of Wyoming. When she was twenty, she made a cowboy crooner named Darling Bob Mackay dance about like a tenderfoot by firing bullets at his feet in a Dodge City saloon—Mackay had had the temerity to say something indelicate about her underwear. At twenty-three, she was the only female member of a geological expedition into the Black Hills. At twenty-four, she was the only woman among the 1,500 men leaving Fort Laramie with a bull train of supplies for General Crook's expedition against the Sioux. It was on this expedition that she was caught swimming naked with some of her buddies in Hat Creek near Sheridan, Wyoming.

Jane was invariably ready for any man's use, if he would only buy her a drink. Greedy showmen hired her for appearances in dime museums. Her ghost-written memoirs were printed as a cheap pamphlet which she herself hawked for whatever she could get for a copy.

But no matter how much one chips away at the myths and legends, Calamity Jane's place in Western history is assured—the main reason being that her name is always coupled with that of Wild Bill Hickok. During the twenty-seven years which elapsed between his death and hers, she never missed the opportunity to join their fortunes. When Calamity Jane died in 1903, she was buried in a grave adjoining Hickok's. One oldtimer at the burial sadly shook his head and said, "It's a good thing Bill is dead—he'd never 'a stood for this." Bill was a rather fastidious sort who would have had nothing to do with so notorious a bawd.

Calamity was married once—to Clinton (Charley) Burke on September 25, 1891, in Deadwood. Charley had lost a leg in the Civil War, and at the time of his union with Jane, he was a widower with a daughter of about ten. Charley was sober, industrious, and patient; he put up with Calamity's tantrums and long absences for ten years, until in the fall of 1901, he decided he had had enough and left for parts unknown.

Calamity was viewed as part of the overhead in bars from Billings to the Rio Grande. She built up a pile of I.O.U.'s wherever she went, and often provoked fights which ended with no damage to the combatants, but plenty to the saloon. Yet, there is no record of any man throwing Calamity from the premises of any public place. It was left to one strong woman, built like an elephant, to throw her out and make it stick! Kitty O'Leary, otherwise known as Madam Bulldog, was the proprietor of the Bucket of Blood Saloon in Livingston, Montana. One day, she took offense at Jane's remarks, and promptly and bodily ejected her from the saloon.

Years before, when Kitty O'Leary took over the establishment, she announced it would be a decent place as long as she ran it, and that she would stand for "no damn foolishment!" She was her own bouncer and believed in conveying her thoughts in the fewest words possible. The most economical of all her messages was "Git," which she backed up with

Calamity Jane's story has come down to us in a somewhat romanticized version. Bawd, scout, Indian fighter, and barroom brawler, Jane was hardly the Western beauty of later-day legend, as this picture of Jane shows.

114

190 pounds of solid muscle and wildcat fury. Kitty could not tolerate a loud, blustery, and bragging type, and when one of them showed his face in the Bucket of Blood, the regulars would back away from the bar to witness the mayhem Kitty was about to unleash. The oldtimers would elbow any nearby newcomers and whisper, "She's on her ear again about something or other. Now watch this."

When Cole Younger hid out in Texas in 1869, he found an old acquaintance for company, Myra Belle Shirley. The Myra Belle he knew back in Jasper County, Texas, was just a scrawny kid in pigtails, but now she was different. In only nine months, she gave birth to Younger's illegitimate daughter, a girl Belle named Pearl Younger (more about her later). Younger left, but in 1870, Jim Reed came south on the lam. Myra Belle took him in, and it wasn't long before she presented him with a boy she named Ed Reed.

By 1881, Myra Belle moved her resort for criminals to the Canadian River in Oklahoma, which she called Younger's Bend. Outlaw lovers came and went, such as Jack Spaniard, Jim French, Jim July, John Middleton, and a flat-nosed Indian known as Blue Duck. Somewhere along the line, Myra Belle had married a Cherokee named Sam Starr, and became known as Belle Starr. When Belle was in residence at Dodge City, her husband, Sam, lost $2,000 at faro. She promptly held up the gambling palace and took $7,000 at gunpoint, once again proving that it is easier to take money from a gambling house with a pair of sixshooters than with a deck of cards.

Myra Belle Shirley Starr, horse thief and cattle thief, suspected stage-robber, prostitute, concubine, and protector of criminals, was shot in the back and killed near Eufaula, Oklahoma, on February 3, 1889. Her nearest neighbor, Edgar Watson, was accused of the murder, but the charges were dismissed. It was rumored she was slain by her own son, Ed Reed, who was known to be angry at his mother for whipping him just because he rode her favorite horse without permission. A few months after their mother's death, Pearl and Ed found themselves in financial straits, so Pearl went to Fort Smith, Arkansas, to open a bawdy house.

A rustler, a prostitute, and a lover of famous outlaws, Belle Starr once robbed a Dodge City gambling palace at gunpoint. Belle is shown here with the Blue Duck, an Indian outlaw she sheltered at her resort for criminals in Younger's Bend, Oklahoma.

Jennie Stevens was sixteen and Annie McDougal was seventeen when the two Oklahoma girls decided to join the dashing outlaws of the Doolin gang. It all started, *The Guthrie Daily Leader* said, after a cowhand at a dance spotted some members of the gang stamping about in their high-heeled boots, and pointed them out to the girls. To young Jennie and Annie, Red Buck, Charley Pierce, and Bill Doolin had an air of the glamor they longed for. Red Buck swung them about the dance floor so excitingly that the girls decided to leave home and become famous outlaws.

But when Annie, wearing pants belonging to the hired man, rode off to join the gang, her horse bucked and threw her. Her hero, Red Buck, was ready to take on Annie as his light o' love, but this exhibition disgusted him so much he

116

rode off and made Annie walk the ten miles to the nearest farmhouse. A few nights later, she again stole the hired man's pants, saddled up, and rode to the town of Ingalls, where her outlaw lover agreed to give her another chance. Soon Jennie came along, and both girls rode with the Doolin boys until the gang broke up. Then they traveled with a "rounder from Pawnee" named Wilson.

Annie was now "Cattle Annie" and Jennie was dubbed "Little Britches." Wilson had been in trouble several times for selling whiskey to the Indian tribes and stealing a cow or two. Marshals Burke and Tilghman located the two girls in a farmhouse near Pawnee. Little Britches leaped out a rear window onto her horse and galloped across the prairie.

Tilghman started out after Little Britches. He did not want to shoot the girl, although he carried a Federal arrest warrant in his pocket. But Little Britches pulled out her Win-

An unlikely pair of outlaws: "Cattle Annie" McDougal and Jennie "Little Britches" Stevens, two young girls who rode with the Doolin gang in the Oklahoma Territory.

117

chester, turned in her saddle, and took some shots at the marshal. Now Tilghman decided to end the chase, so he fired his rifle and brought the girl's horse down. Little Britches tried to leap clear, but her boot caught in a stirrup, pinning her under the horse.

When Tilghman pulled Little Britches free of the dead horse, that's when the battle started. She clawed, kicked and bit, and raked his face with her long and dirty fingernails. Finally, the marshal simply turned Little Britches over his knee and paddled her fat bottom where her Levi's were stretched the tightest. This took all the fight out of her. Now she was a weeping adolescent who wanted to be home with Mother. Tilghman rode back to the farmhouse with Little Britches. There, Burke was having his own troubles, for Cattle Annie, older and tougher, was a good shot and had a rifle. Burke reached up to a window and grabbed her. He soon found he had a wildcat on his hands as Annie clawed, kicked, and bit. When Tilghman rode up, he found Burke holding the girl in a bear hug. He was hatless, minus some hair, and his face was well scratched.

At Perry, a matron scrubbed the girls and dressed them in presentable clothes for their trial. Tilghman made a plea for the now demure and rather attractive girls before Judge Brierer. But the judge sentenced the girls to short terms in the penitentiary at Framingham, Massachusetts. Cattle Annie and Little Britches were celebrities back east, and when they arrived in Boston a huge crowd jammed the railway station to see "Oklahoma's Girl Bandits." After serving two years, they were released. Cattle Annie, older and wiser, married and settled down. Little Britches remained in Boston for a while, then went to New York City "to do Settlement work." She died of consumption in Bellevue Hospital two years later.

More confused is the story of another girl associated with the Doolin gang—Rose Dunn, the "Rose of the Cimarron" who loved "Bitter Creek" George Newcomb, a member of the Doolin gang. One night in the spring of 1893, Bill Doolin and his boys robbed the National Bank of Cimarron, Kansas, and then went into hiding at a robber's roost in Ingalls, Oklahoma.

At the time, Rose was being wooed by Doolin's lieutenant, "Bitter Creek," described as a "fine specimen of young manhood."

Five months later, Federal Marshals converged on Mrs. Pierce's Hotel in Ingalls with about fifteen heavily armed associates, and waged one of the epic encounters of the Old West.

Doolin, "Bitter Creek," Bob Dalton, Tulsa Jack Blake, and Dynamite Dick Clifton were driven from the saloon by the marshals. Seeking refuge, they crouched and ran toward the stable, firing with rifles and revolvers all the way. Laden with extra cartridge belts and spare Colts, Rose of the Cimarron led the pack. When "Bitter Creek," downed in the inn yard with a bullet in his leg, lost his gun, Rose rushed out with a fresh gun and cartridge belt.

Rose, Doolin, and the severely wounded "Bitter Creek" made their escape at twilight. For weeks Rose nursed her lover while the trio hid out in the Creek Nation. For almost four years, they lived in bandit hideaways, emerging only to make occasional raids on remote banks and ranches. The marshals finally closed in one winter afternoon, and "Bitter Creek" was ambushed and shot out of his saddle. Rose of the Cimarron later married a blacksmith and retreated from public notice, but not before she etched her name in Western legend as the most authentic pistol-packing woman of the frontier.

The traditional picture of Rose of the Cimarron, the one used in a score of Western histories, shows her wearing a dark striped dress, and holding a Winchester and a sixshooter. But the woman in this photo is not the real Rose. The woman in the picture was an inmate of a Federal penitentiary at the time of Rose's escapades, and the picture was used by Marshal Tilghman in his attempts to shield Rose's true identity.

Legend has it that "Cattle Kate" (Ella Watson), who was twenty-seven and beginning to show a few signs of wear and tear, told friends she was going to pull up stakes and set up a crib in another town, since Cheyenne was no longer easy pickings. "There's no use pulling the wool over my own eyes, for the sad fact is, I'm not a young chicken any more," she is supposed to have said. Her customers were beginning to throw their business to floozies who had come into the wide-open railroad town. So Cattle Kate moved to Rawlings, a cow town in the Haystack Hills where, except for a few chorus girls who also showed mileage and several squaws who smelled mighty powerful, a favor-selling lady on the decline might still have a chance. Soon Kate, who was a bosomy brunette with a handsome face, quickly had all the customers she could manage.

There was a hitch, for the cattle market was in a slump and cash money was scarce as hen's teeth. But this did not worry Kate. She would simply homestead a grassland quarter-section, and stock it with mavericks which she would accept from her men in place of cash. "When those little critters fat-

This photo has traditionally been identified as Rose Dunn, "Rose of the Cimarron," but the woman is in fact Jennie Metcalf, an Oklahoma outlaw who rode with the Doolin Gang.

ten up, I'll get a nice price for them, you can bet on that," she is reported to have said. It was a sound idea, though in the end Kate paid for her actions with her life.

But the legend of Cattle Kate was created in the editorial room of the *Cheyenne Leader* for the benefit of the Wyoming Stock Growers' Association. Almost overnight, they transformed the real Ella Watson into the infamous woman bandit who killed one husband plus various other men, and had stolen more cattle than any man in the West.

Ella Watson was just one of the many girls who became harlots to escape poverty in the 1880's. At the age of twenty-seven, she was indeed nearly finished after years of whoring in towns such as Dodge City, Ogallala, and Cheyenne. In another year or two, even the men of Rawlins would find her too old for their tastes. So when Ella was invited to join Jim Averill at his combination saloon, grocery store, and post office in Sweetwater, she accepted. The cowhands in the area welcomed her to the desolate country, even though she was no longer young and beautiful. To the contrary, she was short and inclined to weight. Ella was also reported to be handy with a sixshooter and a Winchester, as well as with a branding iron.

In the spring of 1888, Ella filed on the land which adjoined Averill's, brought her meager belongings along, and set up shop in a one-room cabin about a mile from the combination saloon-store. She had a small corral where she kept a few head of cattle. Jim was an enterprising sort, so in addition to his store and Ella's place he most likely dealt in stolen cattle. Hard feelings had already developed between the big owners and the small rancher. The Stock Growers Association was powerful, and had passed through the Legislature the Maverick Bill, which decreed that all unbranded cattle were the property of the Association. Averill wrote many letters to the Casper paper decrying the injustice of the cattle barons, hurling insults, and incurring their anger. He was rapidly becoming the spokesman for the small ranchers of the area.

Ella, reared on a dirt-scrabble farm near Lebanon, Kansas, was the oldest of nine children of a strict Bible Belt family. She fled from the rigidity and poverty of her parents' miser-

121

Ella Watson's career as harlot, rustler, and rancher came to an end in 1889 when she was lynched near the Sweetwater River, Wyoming.

able farm at a tender age, finding employment as a domestic for the town banker. When she discovered that she could earn a week's pay in a single evening out tumbling in the grass, she quit her job and left Lebanon for Concordia, Kansas, a small city but a comparative metropolis. As time went on, Ella plied her trade in St. Joseph, Missouri; Dodge City, Kansas; Ogallala and Omaha, Nebraska; Cheyenne and Rawlins, Wyoming. Then, at Averill's invitation, she opened up shop in Wyoming's Sweetwater Valley.

The big stockmen called Ella's place a "hog ranch." The first hog ranchers were associated with Western military operations, for the hog raisers who supplied pork for the post were forced to set up their pigpens at a distance, so that the strong smell would not reach camp. When any camp follower was not allowed to stay on the post, she would go to the hog ranch to set up her house of prostitution. Sometimes the hog ranchers included a saloon and tables for gambling.

Ella's "hog ranch" did not house pigs, but she did have a few head of cattle on the place. Cowpunchers would ride a considerable distance for the company of a woman, and when they were low on cash, Ella would take a steer or two in trade for her favors. Averill and his new neighbor got on well, as Ella fixed his meals, and came over to sleep with him after her customers were satisfied. He pimped for her in his store-saloon, making sure that everyone who was interested in fleshly delights knew that Ella's were for sale.

Averill was obviously fond of Ella, but had no qualms about other men enjoying her body. This seemed somewhat unusual to the community, but they passed it off by saying Averill was an educated dude from the East, which explained away everything. Within a few months, the combined home-steads of Averill and Ella became a ranch on which many yearlings were fattening. Around this time, someone referred to the hard-working trull as "Cattle Kate," and soon everyone was calling her that name. Averill would take her cattle and ship them to market; from time to time, he would add a few extra mavericks, burning Kate's brand on their hides. Kate kept only a few head in her corral at any one time—too many would look very suspicious. So as the cattle were gathered at the relay point, a man named Frank Buchanan helped out in various ways.

The blizzards of 1888 were hard on the cattlemen. When spring came and the new calves arrived, Averill and Buchanan rounded up any unbranded strays and ran them through Kate's corral. The cattlemen suspected the operation at Kate's corral, and began to keep closer watch. In July of 1889, Averill and Buchanan were weeding out unbranded calves, and supposedly shot the mother cows to keep them from following the calves. Times were bad, and Averill was not a popular man among the cattle owners. When they found out that their calves were in Kate's corral, they organized a posse to take care of the problem.

Kate was captured first, for she was outside when the posse pulled up to her cabin. The men were going to take her in to Rawlins, they said. Kate wanted to change her dress, but they refused to let her near the house for fear she would get her rifle. She was forced into a wagon, and the party drove over to Averill's place. He was also told the posse was going to take him to Rawlins, and the men even claimed they held a warrant for his arrest. They did not show him the warrant, but persuaded him with their rifles that he ought to get in the wagon with Kate. The posse drove off with the pair, but a fourteen-year-old boy named Gene Crowder saw the capture, then ran off to find Frank Buchanan.

Buchanan headed out after the posse which by now had unloaded Jim and Kate in a canyon. When he saw the group, they were standing near some scrub trees. Ropes had been wound around the limbs and the nooses were on Averill's and Kate's necks. Buchanan could hear the man trying to get Jim to jump off a boulder, so he fired at the posse. They returned the fire, but he was completely outmatched and forced to retreat for help. Jim would not jump from the boulder, so he was pushed. Poor Kate got the same treatment. The drop was too short to break their necks and they struggled through a dance of death at the end of their ropes until they finally choked to death. As soon as the bodies had stopped moving, the posse left, leaving them to hang in the sun.

Help arrived from Casper three days later in the form of the sheriff. He cut down the bodies and buried them. The men who had hung Kate and Averill were arrested and a preliminary hearing was held in Rawlins a short time later. Each of the men was freed on $5,000 bail; they were allowed to sign each other's bail bonds. Before the trial in October, Frank Buchanan disappeared mysteriously, and the boy, Gene Crowder, was taken into "protective custody" by the cattlemen. He died before the trial date. There was some evidence he was poisoned.

At the trial, no witnesses came forward to testify against the men, so they were released as not guilty. The powerful Stock Growers Association triumphed; justice had lost. But several months after the trial, one of the men involved in the lynching was mysteriously shot and killed. Most people felt the score was evened up a little by his death.

124

In 1885, Elizabeth Taylor was lynched in Nebraska as hatred and suspicion usurped the rule of reason. But Elizabeth's story begins in 1879, when she was twenty-five. For seven years, she had lived on the Little Blue River in Clay County, Nebraska, with her husband, children, three brothers, father, and mother. As settlers, they were far better off than most of their neighbors. Elizabeth was described as a plump, pretty blonde, with a driving ambition to improve her lot in life. Perhaps this was what made people suspicious of her. Ambition in a man was admired, but in a woman—it was a questionable quality. Across the road from the Taylor soddy lived Rees T. Rees, a bachelor of some importance. He had his eye out for Elizabeth, and made no secret of his feeling toward her.

On May 27, 1882, Elizabeth's husband, Jim, died under unusual circumstances. A neighbor saw him come galloping up to the river bank in the late afternoon, fling himself from his horse, and rush to the river to gulp up the water while gasping for breath. A minute later he was dead, lying face down in the Little Blue. At the inquest, the coroner attributed the death to natural causes. But one of Elizabeth's neighbors said that a few days before Jim Taylor's death, he had seen her purchase a bag of Paris Green poison at the general store in Clay Center. The tale quickly spread that she bought the Paris Green for a purpose other than to de-bug her potato plants.

When Elizabeth's father became ill a few weeks later, it was rumored she had poisoned him, as well. Her nosy neighbors visited the sick man and the doctor was called. He said the old man was dying of cancer. This put to rest—for a while—the rumor that Elizabeth had poisoned her husband and her father. But trouble visited poor Liz again when her line rider, Ed Proust, caught two of John Llewelyn's sons tearing down a piece of their own father's fence. When Llewelyn came storming up to the Taylor house to claim payment for missing cattle, Elizabeth plainly told him to file a legal complaint, for she had a witness to what had actually happened. Llewelyn called her ugly names, but did not file a complaint.

Rees T. Rees, the bachelor from across the road, came calling. Elizabeth knew he was about to ask her to marry him. But his eagerness defeated him, for a decent interval had not yet passed since she buried her husband and father. She flatly

125

said no, and in so doing she created a bitter enemy who would not be satisfied until he saw her dead.

Two years later, Rees learned that Old Ben Bethlemer, Elizabeth's hired hand, had disappeared. Still bitter, he started the tale that Old Ben was given a dose of the "same medicine" that killed Jim Taylor.

Elizabeth was aware of the vicious campaign being waged against her, so she bought a shotgun and ammunition for protection. As she traveled about Clay and Adams counties, she told livestock dealers and livery men to pass the word that any cowboy drifting down toward Texas could find grub, bed, and tobacco at her ranch if he were willing to work. Soon after, a stream of Texans were bedding down at the Taylor ranch, some staying a few days, others staying several weeks. This gave Rees another chance to blacken Elizabeth's reputation. He hinted that the reason the Texans remained such a short time at Elizabeth's was because they refused an hour in bed with Mrs. Taylor instead of hard cash as wages.

Also, there was more trouble between the Taylor and Llewelyn boys. The Taylor boys were found guilty of wantonly and maliciously tearing down and destroying the fence enclosing the pasture land of John Llewelyn. Bail was set at $250 and they were released in their mother's custody.

Elizabeth owned a small tract of timber. Not long after her sons were released from jail, she discovered that some of her neighbors, in particular Edwin Roberts, were cutting her trees. In January of 1885, Roberts and Joseph Beyer were headed for her trees. She ran out and called for them to stop, but they drove their wagon on. She ordered a Texan who was working for her to hitch a team and go after the two men. She gave him her shotgun, but whether her instructions were to use it to frighten Roberts and Beyer, as she claimed, or to gun them down, as Rees T. Rees claimed, will remain unanswered. The Texan and the Taylor youngsters found Roberts and Beyer getting ready to leave, standing on the stolen logs which filled the wagon. Roberts was driving, and when he came abreast of the Taylor wagon, the shouting of the boys frightened his team so that it bolted. Beyer was pitched off. The fall stunned him, but as he lay on the ground he heard a gun being fired as the Taylor wagon raced off. Getting to his feet, Beyer ran after his wagon and team, and caught it as it reached the Rees place. By chance, Rees, J. F. Eller, Grant Bozarth, and another man were in the yard when the driverless wagon was bearing down on them. The situation was self-explanatory: Roberts was sprawled out dead on the logs, half his head blown off.

Rees made the most of this opportunity. By midnight, the two Taylor boys were behind bars, charged with murder. The Texan had disappeared. Rees claimed he had seen him walking along a fence with Elizabeth's brother, and the brother returned alone. Rees inferred from this that the cowboy had been killed and buried somewhere on the Taylor property. Deputy Sheriff Karnes, who was conducting the investigation, did not think the tip had enough merit to warrant digging. So Rees turned to more receptive ears, suggesting it was time something be done about those Taylors. G. W. Vangilder, John Llewelyn, David Bennett, and H. H. Hyde agreed with him. It was proposed that they ride to the house where Elizabeth and her brother, Tom Jones, were living, call them out, escort them to the county line, and forbid them to return under the penalty of death.

Rees and his fellow conspirators, accompanied by a score of other adherents, rode to the Taylor house, surrounded it, and demanded that the occupants come out. They were answered by a blast of hot gunfire from every window. Temporarily "in residence" were four Texans, identified later as Texas Bill Foster, Nat Clark, Bud Ferrell, and Nelson Cellery. They did the shooting, since Tom Jones did not have a gun; moreover, while Elizabeth was away, someone had made off with her stock of ammunition. No one was hit by the gunfire, for at the first blast, Rees' followers deserted him. Only he and his ringleaders were left, but they did not stay much longer.

The following night, John Llewelyn's barn was burned. He immediately accused Elizabeth of having the fire started. He was right, for she paid one of the Texans to burn the barn, but it was small satisfaction for all she suffered at the hands of her neighbors. She, her brother, and the others moved down to an old sod house to wait for the mob to return.

Shortly after midnight on March 15, she heard them coming. Rees' men stopped at the corrals and grabbed some rope mule halters, which they knotted together.

Horror stricken, Elizabeth heard Rees' booming voice ordering them out of the soddy, or else they would drop dynamite down the chimney.

The Texans, Cellery and Luther Wiggins, came out with hands raised. They were quickly tied and led off up the road to the Rees house. Tom Jones came out with Elizabeth, who was wearing only a nightgown. When she asked permission to get properly dressed, a man reached inside, grabbed a shawl, and threw it over her shoulders as her hands were tied down to her sides. The men wasted no time now in carrying out their plan.

Elizabeth Taylor and her brother, Tom Jones, were marched down the Spring Ranch Road to the bridge which spanned the shallow river. Their abductors fashioned nooses out of the halters, dropped them over their captives' heads, drew the nooses up tight around their throats, and led the two down to the sand bar beneath the bridge. Two men tied the loose ends of the ropes to a bridge stringer. Elizabeth and Tom were forced to mount two nervous horses, then with a blast of gunfire the animals leaped away, leaving the pair swinging back and forth.

On the morning of March 16, 1885, Elizabeth Taylor and Tom Jones were secretly buried in Spring Ranch Cemetery. But now the newspapers throughout the state were publishing the story of the double lynching, expressing shock and horror at the event. "The Shame of Nebraska," an Omaha paper called it. "This state can now claim the terrible distinction of being the first in this country to lynch a woman." It was a lynching totally unjustified by any evidence found against the victims. Yet nothing was done about it, even when Rees T. Rees, G. W. Vangilder, John Llewelyn, David Bennett, and H. H. Hyde were charged with murder in the first degree. They were brought to trial, acquitted, and allowed to walk away free men.

In the early days of the West, a woman might commit almost any sin, and not be ostracized by her community. However, as civilization advanced, so did austerity. The first two decades of the twentieth century proved to be mighty uncomfortable for the hell-raising ladies. Pearl Hart, as she called herself, was the last of the Western road agents and a lady of extremely doubtful virtue. She was born about 1871 in Lindsay, Ontario. At seventeen, she was seduced by a dapper gentleman named Hart, so several months later they eloped when she got in a family way. She went home to Mother for the birth of her son, then in 1893 went to the World's Colum-

Pearl Hart became a hero by robbing one of the last Western stagecoaches. A clever ruse gained her freedom from an Arizona jail. Always eager to confirm her notorious reputation, here Pearl poses as a gunslinger.

bian Exposition in Chicago. Pearl's husband, a small-time gambler and racing tout, took a job as a barker for a Western side show at the Exposition.

During the long hours that Hart spent luring customers inside the tent, Pearl was far from lonesome. She found the glamorous men of the Wild West Show compellingly attractive, so much more glamorous than her hubby that she walked out on him. Pearl went to Trinidad, Colorado, where she gave birth to a daughter. A year later, she sent the child to her mother back in Ontario, and drifted from town to town making her living as a cook, domestic, hotel maid, and dance-hall girl. There were enough men to provide excitement as well as money. Between periods of honest toil, she sold her favors to the men, who on sobering up the next day, found Pearl gone and their pockets empty. Some of Pearl's clients—especially miners on payday night—liked her so much that they refused to prosecute; others could afford the loss of money better than they could a dose of publicity.

In 1889, Pearl was working as a cook at the Mammoth Mining Camp in Arizona. While there, she struck up a relationship with a mustachioed miner named Joe Boot. Soon thereafter, the miners who staggered out of the saloons were slugged unconscious, to wake up in dark places with their pockets cleaned out. Becoming bolder with success, Pearl and Joe Boot started holding up lone men without knocking them cold first. One slammed a gun in the man's back while the other relieved him of his wallet. When Pearl learned her mother was seriously ill and in need of money, she sent her meager savings. Medicine and doctors were very high-priced, however, and her mother rapidly exhausted these funds.

Soon a request for more money arrived. Joe Boot suggested to Pearl that they hold up the stagecoach. One of the last stages in the Arizona Territory ran between Globe and Florence, a distance of sixty-five miles. There were usually some passengers with money in their pockets, and the days of the shotgun guard were long gone. It would be easy to rob the coach. Pearl cut her hair short, donned a white sombrero, and man's clothing. Armed with two pistols, each, the pair set out before dawn. At two o'clock the next day, they met the stage, rattling down the Globe highway.

Driver Orville Smith sighted the bandits standing in the road "with revolvers cocked and aim steady," and pulled up his horses so violently that the three passengers in the stage fell to the floor. The take from the robbery totaled $428. Pearl, playing the philanthropist, pulled three dollar bills from the roll and presented one to each passenger "for grub and lodging." The stage thundered into Florence, and Smith shouted out the news. A stagecoach was robbed by armed road agents in this modern year of 1899! The holdup might have been a success, had not Orville Smith recognized Pearl as one of the bandits.

Sheriff Truman quickly gathered a posse and took up the chase. He should not have hurried, for the fugitive pair were lost. When they found the Globe highway once more, they discovered they were less than a mile from the scene of their crime. Three days later, the posse caught up with the pair, and Sheriff Truman was dumbfounded to find them sleeping peacefully under a clump of trees.

The pair were prodded awake, and placed under arrest as Pearl blistered the ears of the posse with a string of expletives, then turned upon Joe Boot, calling him "a damn coward." On their arrival in Florence, Pearl was delighted to find she was now famous, for she represented to the citizens of Arizona all the romance of days gone by. Quickly forgetting that she had called Joe "a damn coward," she now swore her undying love for him. The outlaw career of the thirty-year-old, cigar-smoking Pearl Hart was over, but her fame was only beginning to spread.

After a fake suicide attempt, Pearl was shipped to Tucson. Sullen because she had to leave Joe Boot, the lady road agent was greatly pleased by the large crowd of admirers who greeted her on her arrival at the Tucson jail. Soon Pearl escaped the jail with a new lover, Ed Sherwood, a Phoenix bicycle thief. Pearl was recaptured in Deming, New Mexico, and returned to Tucson.

Putting on the airs of a celebrity, Pearl spoke at length

from her jail cell about a previous criminal career which existed only in her mind. The news reporters knew her stories to be a pack of lies, yet she made good copy, so her tales were printed as fact. Enjoying the notoriety, Pearl now revealed that she was an ardent feminist. She called on women everywhere to demand equal rights with their men. For herself, she insisted on wearing cowboy clothes in jail, complete with high-heeled boots and a Stetson.

In June 1899, Pearl and Joe Boot were once more united at the trial, where they swore their undying love for each other. Pearl was identified by the stage's passengers and driver, her attorney offered only a perfunctory defense; yet after ten minutes the jury acquitted her. The furious judge dismissed the jury and directed the prosecutor to rearraign Pearl on the charge of stealing the stage driver's revolver. Her second trial took about an hour, and the new jury deliberated for thirty seconds before returning a verdict of guilty. Pearl was sentenced to five years in the Territorial Prison at Yuma "to cure her of the habit of robbing stage coaches." Joe Boot was found guilty and sentenced to thirty years.

The part-time prostitute turned road agent was a real nuisance at Yuma Penitentiary, which had been built exclusively for male prisoners, and thus had no appropriate quarters for a female. To compound the problem, newsmen and tourists flocked to Yuma, begging to see the "famous lady highwayman."

The Arizona Territorial Prison was surrounded by a bleak, hot desert. The local Indians were promised a reward of fifty dollars for every escaped prisoner they caught. Many an innocent prospector found himself bound to a mule and carted off to Yuma in the hope that the trip might prove profitable to the Indian who captured him. Both Joe Boot and Pearl Hart managed to escape this grim fortress, each through his/her own efforts. Joe Boot simply vanished—one day he was there, the next day he was gone. Pearl left a few months later in a most extraordinary fashion which requires some explanation.

Pearl pulled the old gambit of "I have been made pregnant." She, of course, implied that she had been regularly raped at will by whoever came along. The none-too-subtle threat to the prison officials was that she would tell all the world of her treatment, and thus blacken the reputation of the institution and its director.

Warden Ingalls had never been happy about having a woman as a prisoner, since he had been compelled to rip the six tier bunks out of one cell and to cover the cell bars with boards to ensure Pearl's privacy. In addition, a dressmaker in Yuma had to be employed to make Pearl a special uniform. After Mrs. Ingalls escorted Pearl to her new cell, she supposedly said, "We'd better keep that woman far away from the other inmates. She'll shock them with her language and corrupt their morals."

Ingalls kept Pearl away from the men, but he could not keep her quiet. One of her favorite pastimes was to invite any man to come and join her, in the most explicit terms possible. Her descriptions of the treats she had in store upset most of the inmates, who "would howl like coyotes all during the night." Another six months passed, Pearl quit calling out lewd invitations to the male prisoners. She asked for books and began to write poetry. The prison chaplain told Warden Ingalls he thought justice would be served if Pearl were pardoned. Ingalls agreed, for the prison would be a lot better off without Pearl Hart around. The governor even visited Pearl and talked to her alone in her cell.

One day, a guard came to see the warden to say Pearl Hart was ill and would like to see the doctor. Ingalls sent for a nurse from Yuma who, upon examining Pearl, declared her to be pregnant. Ingalls shuddered. There were only two keys to Pearl's cell: he had one and his wife had the other. Only two persons had ever been alone with her in the cell: Yuma's leading clergyman and the Governor of the Arizona Territory.

The warden sent to Governor A. O. Brodie, who, to avoid a scandal, conditionally pardoned Pearl on December 19, 1902, on the condition that she leave Arizona and never return. The grounds for his action were "lack of accommodations for women prisoners." Pearl may have been pregnant, or she may have bribed the nurse. No doctor ever examined her.

Pearl next came into public view in May 1904, when she was arrested "for complicity with thieves" in Kansas City. At the age of thirty-three, Pearl Hart was a has-been. After her arrest, she disappeared. No one knows what became of her.

Now, after reading about a few of the women who broke the law for their paramours, let us go on to the more enterprising and commercial types.

The Girls of the Line

FOR MANY YEARS, the town of Pueblo, Colorado, boasted one of the most wide-open tenderloin districts of the West. The townspeople gave tacit if not explicit consent to the thriving business in flesh all the way into the twentieth century, until the bawds left their district to parade downtown on April 18, 1903. The invasion of sinners was described on page 1 of the *Pueblo Star-Journal* the next day:

SHAMELESSNESS RUNS RIOT
WITHOUT INTERFERENCE OF POLICE

Dissolute women raided the sidewalks of Sante Fe Avenue between First and Fourth Streets last evening and accosted passersby without let or hinderance from the police. No less than four complaints were made to the Star-Journal *by Sante Fe Avenue businessmen who protested the conditions were such that reputable people were being driven away from the neighborhood. Investigations showed that the complaints were to be well grounded and the state of things prevail such as would not be tolerated in any city where the police department was required by order from the executive, from whom it must come, to enforce even a reasonable degree of decency. Well-known businessmen informed the* Star-Journal *not*

135

Ladies of the night in an arm-waving, horn-blowing display that must have shocked the respectable folks of Denver.

only last night, but other nights, they have made specific complaints at police headquarters without result and without securing other reply than a mocking laugh. The Star-Journal *does not propose that such things shall continue and it now directs the personal attention of the Mayor to the matter and demands that he compel suppression of the evil.*

The girls worked either as individuals or in small groups, perhaps in the house of a madam. Such a house was often lavishly furnished and decorated, and generally conducted business with a more select clientele. At the other extreme, in the crib, a girl working on her own plied the same trade in conditions ranging from spareness to squalor. These cribs would be strung in a line along one street, thus giving the prostitution district the popular name "the line." It was also known as the red-light district after the red lights posted in the windows all along the line.

Myers Avenue, the line in Cripple Creek, Colorado, was lifted into national prominence after Julian Street, a famed writer of the day, took a horrified look at it and wrote an uncomplimentary article in *Collier's*. The town leaders were so incensed they bombarded the magazine's editors with telegrams. When these left the editors unmoved, the council sent out the following news bulletin: "Tonight the city council of Cripple Creek, Colorado approved unanimously changing the name of Myers Avenue to Julian Street." And Julian Street it is still called.

One author claims that after the Barbary Coast lost its glitter, the largest red-light district in the West could be found in Butte, Montana, which boasted more than a thousand girls hard at work in the oldest profession. One of the most notorious girls in the Butte district was Jew Jess, whom

The small building next to the gate is the last remnant of Pueblo, Colorado's crib row. It must have been hard just to lie down in such a tiny room, but cribs were the primary pleasure dens of many Western towns.

Cripple Creek, Colorado, once a city of 50,000, now almost a ghost town. The Myers Avenue "row" during the early 1900's.

police claimed to be the cleverest pickpocket around. Personable and smart as a whip, she was frequently arrested yet rarely convicted. Jess was a drug addict, and when "junked up," her crafty brain and nimble fingers were capable of just about anything. One story is told about Jess being hauled before a police judge on the charge of petty larceny and vagrancy. The evidence against her was vague, so the judge was forced to dismiss the case.

Apparently under the influence of a recent "shot," Jess, in gratitude, threw her arms around the broad shoulders of the surprised judge. Embarrassed, his honor disengaged her and blushingly rearranged his disheveled clothing. Later, he discovered his watch, wallet, tie pin, and lodge emblem were missing.

A police officer was sent to rearrest Jess, but there was not a trace of the missing articles. Indignantly, she pronounced her innocence. Again, the judge was forced to release Jess for lack of evidence. About a week later, a messenger delivered a package containing the missing articles to the judge's private chambers. No word of explanation followed.

Another girl of the Butte district was the much-publicized Mabel Ford, alleged to be the one-time wife of Robert Ford, the "dirty little coward" who shot "Thomas Howard," then the alias of Jesse James. Mabel delighted in recounting all the lurid details of the shooting, claiming she was present. The reason she was in Butte telling this story, she said, was that she deserted Ford because of this cowardly killing.

Wesley Davis, in his *Sketches of Butte*, described a typical Galena Street crib in the 1890's:

> *A bed in one corner, in another a stove, a coal hod and bundle of kindling. A small dresser with a wash basin against the wall. Permeating everything a mixed odor of disinfectant, hair oil and cheap perfume. On the walls, a few art pictures, oddly enough, usually of some pastoral or equally innocent scene, never a picture of a pornographic nature. A photograph or two, usually of other prostitutes or the favorite pimp of the moment.*

In another chapter of his book, Davis describes Galena Street itself:

> *It seemed like a street leading into hell. Young men, boys, old men; hundreds of them wandering about. Girls in the doors and windows soliciting in honeyed words. Young girls, some looking as though they should be in school. Beauty, withered hags, Indian squaws, mulattoes, Japanese, Chinese. Every face and color. Here and there a Chinaman with a wash basket. The shrill shrieks of a police whistle. The clang of the patrol wagon. Drunken cries. Maudlin tears. Bodies for sale.*

Although the newspapers initially took little notice of the evils of prostitution, many eventually were forced to the forefront of the mounting campaign against the institution. Usually by the time a town reached its second decade, attempts were being made to end the abomination. Comments like this began to appear in the papers:

> *The reckless manner in which the soiled doves settle around in various portions of our once moral village should at least suggest a herd law. Let the evil be concentrated or bounced.*

But the papers seemed to enjoy writing up stories of fights and duels between the ladies of the evening. And they usually had plenty of material, since the madams and the crib girls fought one another with the fury of female alley cats, over their pimps or over a matter as trivial as where they were born. They used any weapon they could lay their hands on, including sadirons, guns, and knives.

The *Pueblo Star-Journal* of February 10, 1902, printed the following story on page 2:

DUSKY FIGHTERS PAID FREIGHT

> *Mary Smith and Clara Brooks, two dusky denisons [sic] of the First Street region, "paid the freight" of a drunken fight in police court this morning, the tariff rate having been fixed by Judge Hogan at $10 each.*
>
> *Officer Green testified that each came after him to arrest the other, and remarked, "Both said they had been fighting; I knew both were drunk and supposed they wanted to be arrested. The Brooks woman said, 'We got into an argument and I ordered her out; she wouldn't go, so I struck her.'"*
>
> *Mary Smith declined to make a statement, because, she said, "De story's already don been tole, Judge."*

In the early days of San Francisco, a Creole spitfire from New Orleans was stabbed by a jealous Chileno. As she was being stitched up, she cursed both her assailant and her Adams revolver, which misfired. She left the doctor's office, grabbed a huge Bowie knife, then stabbed her Chilean enemy to death.

There is also on record the fight of two Mexican girls from a Barbary Coast fandango hall. At five on a cold morning, with their left arms wrapped with shawls, and their right hands flashing daggers, they made so many holes in each other that they were both dead by sunup.

In El Paso, Texas, competition was especially keen between two madams, Big Alice Abbott and quick-tempered Etta Clark across the street. The continuous argument finally erupted in a fight, the mention of which brought uproarious guffaws in the saloons for months to come. Around 9:30 on the warm spring evening of April 18, 1886, a police squad was sent to investigate a disturbance at one of the houses on Utah Street. The whole area was in an uproar as a huge woman lay shot and bleeding in the dusty street, while a petite redhead, cruelly beaten, sobbed hysterically in one of the houses.

The officers somehow pieced together the story. Bessie Colvin, one of Big Alice's in-residence girls, owed her $125 "back rent," but refused to pay up. Bessie, full of whiskey and false courage, stood firm as she and Alice put on a screaming and cursing match which awed all passersby. Bessie flounced out, dashed across to Etta Clark's brothel, and offered her services. Redheaded Etta promptly accepted, so Bessie tore back to her former home, told Big Alice she was leaving, then promptly took off again. Big Alice, with her girls Nina Ferrall and Josie Connaly at her heels, huffed and puffed across the street. Alice yelled and pounded on Etta's door until it was opened a crack. Big Alice flung herself against the door, ripping it from the hinges and mashing Etta's face in the process. At this moment, Alice spied her former girl walking out of Etta's sitting room.

Enraged, Alice stomped on through the broken door, shoving Etta violently aside. The redheaded Etta, deciding she needed protection, reached for a brass gas-lighter. (This

141

was a heavy wick-tipped rod 2½ feet long and ½ inch in diameter, used to light the gas burners.) The tiny Etta drew herself up and shook the lighter in Big Alice's face. Bessie was whimpering in the corner. Now Alice, blind with anger, raised her huge fist and hit Etta in the face as hard as she could. Bessie ran to help Etta, but was grabbed by Alice, who ran out the door, pulling Bessie along with her.

Etta ran to her room and came back with a Colt .45 in her hand. She pointed the weapon at Big Alice, who was facing her on the porch. The gun went off, enveloping both women in a cloud of smoke. Alice looked down in horror at the blood spreading from a spot between her thighs. She staggered to the center of the street as Etta fired again and missed.

It took six strong men to carry the big woman to her house. It made a dramatic scene: the helpless female, the girls weeping and wailing, and the men straining and stumbling under their mammoth burden. Doctor A. L. Justice was called and, upon arriving at the scene, reported that Big Alice was seriously wounded. Etta Clark was put in jail pending a hearing.

By April 27, nine days later, Big Alice was out of danger and the preliminary trial was held in her room. Justice L. H. Clark bound Etta over to the Grand Jury under $2,000 bond.

Nothing funny about this, you say? True enough—but it was the aftermath of this unfortunate incident that sent El Paso rocking with laughter. The *Herald*'s story was printed under a banner headline with all the details in typically turgid prose. The reporter, trying to be precise in pinpointing Alice's wound, wrote that Big Alice had been shot in the "public" arch. In Alice's case, this anatomical description was precise, indeed.

In a noncombative vein, one of the better tales about the shady ladies of the West is this one: A troupe of players came to a small saloon-theater in a far-off cowtown. One of the women in the case became acutely ill, so the manager of the group went out walking the dusty street and, on finding a well-dressed, fairly attractive woman, asked her if she would be willing to appear in the drama they were staging that evening. After he offered her $10, she agreed. He assured her all she would have to do was come out on the stage, wave her arms, scream, and fall down when the villain fired at her.

That night, just at the end of the first act, she appeared and died most promptly after being shot by the villain. As the curtain rang down, the villain stepped forward and shouted, "Oh, my God, what have I done?"

An angry voice shouted from the back of the room, You damn fool, you killed the only whore in town."

The story of Red Stockings is the shortest, and perhaps the happiest of such tales. In 1860, a girl known only as Red Stockings came to Colorado. Said to be born into a wealthy Boston family, she had been seduced in Paris. Humiliated and scorned upon her return to Boston, she headed West. There she was tagged with her nickname, which came from her habit of wearing bright stockings. Remembered as a fair beauty, bewitching, she left Colorado Territory in 1861 with several thousand dollars. According to the story, her departure marked the date of Red Stockings' return to respectability and marriage.

Mollie May reached the top of her profession by becoming madam of one of Leadville, Colorado's best-known brothels. Mollie, like so many in her trade, had been seduced by a suitor while still in her teens. Scorned and humiliated, she turned her back on "respectable society" and left for the frontier, appearing in the 1870's in Cheyenne and the Black Hills, and finally in 1878, in Leadville. Here Mollie remained until her death, becoming a well-known and almost respectable personage. Many citizens turned out for her funeral, and the local paper published a poem in her honor. It said in part:

> *Talk if you will of her*
> *But speak no ill of her—*
> *The sins of the living are not of the dead.*
>
> *Remember her charity,*
> *Forget all disparity,*
> *Let her judges be they whom she sheltered and fed.*

The exodus of Mollie May after her seduction was fairly typical, though there were some women who became prostitutes by choice. But the guardians of Victorian moralism preferred to believe that those unfortunates who turned from the virtuous path did so because they had been wronged.

On December 15, 1901, the *Pueblo Star-Journal* printed a real tearjerker on page one:

HE FOUND HIS SISTER
IN A QUESTIONABLE HOUSE

In his wanderings in search of the girl, Libblin, a day or two ago, came across the agent of the human[e] society who, upon hearing the story, recalled that she had during the years past received application for assistance from a Rose Libblin. She gave the young man a note to the keeper of one of the larger resorts of the city, and armed with this he visited the red light district and found his sister. He immediately recognized her though she was much changed in the appearance from the beautiful girl that Libblin had left when he went to Montana years ago.

She gladly consented to leave the life that she claims misfortune had forced her into, and Libblin will devote himself to providing a respectable living with himself and his sister. Till five years ago the Libblin family lived on a ranch between Rye and this city, and were well known to Pueblo people.

The poignant legend of the Silver Heels is set in South Park, Colorado. She was one of the girls in the mining camp called Buckskin Joe near Fairplay. Buckskin Joe was established in 1861 and was deserted by 1864, yet during its brief but flashy existence it was the county seat of Park County, had a courthouse, theater, dance halls, a post office, saloons, parlor house, two banks, and even a brass band. Silver Heels could have been a dance-hall girl or a prostitute—in either case, she was described as "beautiful of face" and could dance the fastest of all the girls. Also, she wore glittering silver slippers which gave rise to her name. Her good nature made her the idol of the camp. She fell in love with one of the miners, and they were engaged to be married.

Then tragedy struck Buckskin Joe in the form of a smallpox epidemic. The town was abandoned, but Silver Heels stayed on and nursed her lover, who had contracted the dread disease. After his death, Silver Heels still stayed on to nurse the miners and their families. She kept house for the sick, cooked meals, washed clothes, and helped them through the worst of the epidemic. When the town showed signs of life again, the grateful miners collected a sum of money to give to Silver Heels in appreciation. But when time came for the gift to be made, Silver Heels could not be found, for she had left Buckskin Joe without saying a word to a soul. The miners still wanted to do something. They decided to name the highest and most beautiful mountain in the area after the girl who nursed them back to health.

Several years later, a woman draped in heavy black veils to hide her smallpox scars visited the cemetery beneath Mt. Silver Heels. The miners insisted it was their Silver Heels, returned to visit her lover's grave.

Author Caroline Bancroft states this Silver Heels story is "all legend," yet there is a mountain named Silver Heels near Fairplay. Bancroft, when telling of the smallpox outbreak which occurred in Salida, Colorado, years later, offers another Silver Heels story. A Salida madam, Laura Evans, told a doctor to furnish uniforms for her girls so they could nurse the sick. One rather pretty girl, later called Silver Heels Jessie, was sent to nurse the minister's wife. The minister was so grateful to the young nurse that he wanted her to stay on as a housekeeper and companion for his wife. The pretty girl refused, saying, "Now that my job is done, I'll be on my way back to Miss Laura's on Front Street." The minister was flabbergasted, for he had been the most fanatical member of the crusade to shut down Front Street.

D Street, the crib row of Virginia City, Nevada, in the 1870's. Could Julia Bulette have entertained lavishly in a shack such as this?

The legend of all legends about the girls on the line concerns one Cyprian of the Comstock Lode, Julia Bulette. Some say that this dark-eyed, black-haired beauty was a Creole who came west to Virginia City, Nevada, when she became tired of the French Quarter of New Orleans. Legend also insists her house was a gourmet's delight, and before anyone snuggled between her satin sheets, he was offered perfectly prepared French dishes and the finest of wines and champagne.

Yet the fact was, her house stood on the corner of D and Union Streets and was not much more than a clapboard shack of two small rooms. Just before she died, Julia was not serving elegant dinners but was eating at the crib of Gertrude Homes, next door to her own. It was true that Julie served as a mascot to the fire company, and that she rode in a place of honor in a Fourth of July parade. But the story that she loved to ride around Virginia City in her own splendid carriage cannot be believed.

146

Whatever the veracity of other facts about Julia Bulette, one fact is certain: she was found murdered on her bed on Sunday, January 20, 1867. Her jewels and furs were stolen.

On January 22, the *Territorial Enterprise* printed:

> *The most cruel, outrageous and revolting murder ever committed in this city was that of Julia Bulette on Sunday morning. She lived in a little house by herself, near the corner of D and Union Streets, in a thickly settled neighborhood, and within a stone's throw of the station house. The murder was probably committed about five* A.M. *but it was not discovered until nearly noon, when the body was nearly cold and stiff in death. . . . She was found lying on her left side, with a pillow over her head and face, the bedclothes beneath her head being saturated with blood. Her throat was lacerated with the marks of finger nails, and the blood suffused and distorted countenance, together with the writhing position of the body, showed conclusive evidence of strangulation. . . . The murderer took a set of furs worth $400, two gold watches and chains, and several pieces of valuable jewelry, even taking the earrings from her ears. . . . His victim was known as Julia Bulette, and was a native of London, England, whence she emigrated when quite young, to New Orleans, and thence to California, in 1852 or 1853, where she lived in various cities and towns until April, 1863, when she came to Virginia. She is said to have married a man by the name of Smith—from whom she afterward separated—and has an uncle and a brother still living in the State of Louisiana. She was thirty-five years of age, belonging to that clan denominated "fair but frail" yet, being of a very kind disposition, few of her class had more friends. Julia Bulette was some time since elected honorary member of Virginia Engine Company No. 1 of this city. . . . She was still*

an honorary member of the company at the time of her death, therefore it was deemed eminently just and proper that she should be buried by the company.

Of Julia's funeral, the *Territorial Enterprise* reported:

Owing to the disagreeable storm prevailing, and the very muddy state of the streets, the procession was not so large as it would have been under more propitious conditions. Company No. 1 to the number of about 60, preceded by the Metropolitan Brass Band, marched on foot. The funeral was also attended by 18 carriages filled with friends of the deceased. She was taken to Flowery Hill Cemetery to the east of the city, where in her lonely grave her good and bad traits alike lie buried with her.

A year later, a man named John Millain was discovered to have some of Julia's stolen goods in his possession. He denied killing her, claiming he was only an accomplice in the robbery. Nevertheless, he was sentenced to be hanged on April 24, 1868. While Millain waited in jail, the respectable women of Virginia City began a crusade to free him. They brought wines and fine goods to his cell, but failed in their cause. On John Millain's hanging day, the mines, saloons, and schools closed, and the citizens gathered for the holiday. Shortly after noon, Millain and a priest arrived, then Millain mounted the gallows, kneeled for the blessing, bowed to the crowd, and made a flattering speech of farewell to the respectable ladies of the town: His last words before he was dropped through the trap door were a denial of his guilt.

The legend of Julia Bulette grew and grew. One of Virginia City's mines was named the "Julia" in her honor. The club car of the Virginia and Truckee Railroad bore the gold-plated name plate "Julia Bulette." And today there is a monument in Virginia City which reads:

Another story of a heroic fallen woman tells of Queenie, a dance-hall girl. When her pimp accused her of giving him a venereal disease, she was downcast and told the delivery boy, "You won't have to bring me any more groceries." Then she killed herself. Queenie was also considered a camp angel, and on the day of her funeral the camp declared a holiday. But Queenie's man did not attend her funeral.

We also have Molly B'Damn, who came to the Coeur d'Alene district in Idaho in March 1881 as an "uncommonly ravishing personality." She was a bundle of contradictions, for her blue eyes would melt with tenderness and sympathy one minute and in the next moment she would break out with the most monstrous profanities. She would rob the unwary, yet she would give to charity and nurse the sick.

Three months after her arrival in Coeur d'Alene, a bluff, red-shirted braggart came to camp with a thousand-dollar poke. He went from saloon to saloon showing off his dust. When he was drunk he visited Molly's place. Molly apparently rolled him. The next morning, the miner, no longer bragging, got a small outfit on credit and returned to the hills. Three months later, one of his friends came down to the camp to say Red-shirt was dying.

Molly insisted she be taken to his cabin. His friend consented, and for hours they trudged through forests and up mountains and down. When Molly found the sick man semiconscious, she doctored him with the only medicines available, whiskey and quinine. For several days and nights she nursed him until he was able to sit up and eat, then she returned to town. Within a year, Molly died. On the day of

149

her funeral, the miners left their diggin's and sluice boxes, the saloons closed, and a long procession followed her body to a burial ground on a sunny hillside.

Such tales occupy a permanent part of our Western lore, but are they true? Most likely not, if we are to believe a woman who grew up in Deadwood, South Dakota, and described how brief the prostitutes' span of glory really was. She told of seeing them, after only two or three years of whoring, slipping furtively down alleys in quest of a drink or some dope, then simply disappearing. Despite the elegant clothes and living quarters, the easy hours and gaiety, enjoyed by some, the life of the scarlet woman was usually drab and ugly. Whether working in a fancy house or a crib, she would have to succumb to the ravages of time. Only a very few women were able to leave their pasts behind and start a new life. For the rest . . . the frequent reports of attempted or successful suicide tell what kind of future these women had to look forward to.

The use of narcotics was common in the red-light district. Like alcohol, drugs may have made each day a little easier to get through, but offered no real escape. Many trollops used newsboys and messenger boys to act as runners. A girl would give a boy a Jack of Spades, or perhaps a Ten of Clubs, and a few dollars. He would rush to one of the drug stores where the code was understood, and then quickly return with the opiate. He could count on a good tip, for the girls of the line were a generous lot.

Closely associated with the red-light district were the hurdy-gurdy houses which were, strictly speaking, merely dance halls. Their popularity reached a peak in the 1860's in Colorado, Idaho, and Montana. In a few locales, the hurdy-gurdies were honest places where for a nominal fee plus the cost of a few drinks, a man could hire a dance partner. Next to the dance floor, a bar and a gambling area were available for the patrons, but the strong attraction remained the presence of the "gals that do so much toward making the nights lively."

A good stepper could make fair wages, but she had to be reasonably attractive. But many dressed in an eccentric manner, and many more were unreasonably unattractive. Alexander McClure had an interesting experience with one of the latter breed of hurdy-gurdy girl when he visited a Virginia City, Montana dance hall. Invited by one "not fair, but far and forty" to dance, he declined, saying that he never danced. Whereupon the lady replied with the "bewitching air" of her sex, "Damn it, don't tell me you don't, I've saw you dance forty times."

The hurdy-gurdies quickly declined in public view. Rowdiness, excessive drinking, and fights became common. As early as January, 1865, an editorial in the *Montana Post* criticized the halls as a useless waste of hard-earned money and a source of much mischief. As criticism mounted, attendance slumped. Soon, in order to attract patrons, the hurdy-gurdies became quasi-brothels. Now the worst fears of the dance-hall opponents were realized. Even before the big crusade against prostitution got started in this century, the hurdy-gurdies had succumbed to public censorship.

By the 1870's, the hurdy-gurdies were an integral part of the red-light district, where the name dropped from use. Yet the dance halls which now became popular were no different from the hurdy-gurdy. The hall contained a bar and dance floor, and frequently a small stage. The girls employed as dancers were as much a part of the red-light district as their sisters on the line. The prostitute, in fact, now utilized the dance hall for displaying her charms.

During the heyday of the hurdy-gurdy, when the dance halls were not fronts for prostitution, there was no need to sell anything but an innocuous dance. A girl could make money at this type of work alone. In fact, an occasional married woman in desperate need supported her family by becoming a dancer in a hurdy-gurdy hall, and was not considered a lost soul because of her occupation. If one of the girls spent the remaining hours of the night in bed with one of her dancing partners, it was strictly a free-lance proposition. Some of the dancing girls may have been whores when they first arrived in town, but after hours of being swung

For the price of a few drinks a man could hire a dance partner in a hurdy-gurdy dance hall. In many halls, a few dollars more could hire a partner for even longer, and for different purposes. This is an 1865 drawing of one of the hurdy-gurdies.

153

about by burly men, they wanted to go to bed only to go to sleep. Fifty quadrilles and four waltzes were very hard work.

The charge for a dance was a dollar, of which the girl took half, making her wages for a night, if she danced every dance, twenty-six dollars. The prettiest girls danced the most and had the best income, while the homeliest danced the least and most likely needed the extra wages of sin to boost their income. A beautiful girl might also collect thousands of dollars in gifts from her admirers, earning more in a week than a girl back east could make in two years.

Prostitution gained its foothold and flourished in the frontier because it was needed. The soiled doves comprised an accepted part of the community, indeed, a whorehouse was the sign of a town which had *arrived*. But the Western prostitutes did not confine themselves to any one town for long. The girls located themselves wherever their customers might be, as we shall see in the next chapter.

For Cowboys and Miners

THE WESTWARD EXPANSION of the railroads gave birth to some of the toughest frontier towns in history. Known as "rail-head" towns, each of these lawless communities in its turn marked the spot where the rails ended and the trail began. Consequently, many of these rail-head towns flourished as shipping points for the thousands of cattle driven north from Texas. As the Kansas Pacific Railroad built westward in the 1860's, Abilene and Hays City became the principal hell-roaring end towns. And Abilene was ready for the first flood of cows and cowboys in 1868—the women were waiting in the cribs on Texas Street. They were a tough, coarse lot in their paint and perfume; most of them were in Abilene because they could not meet the competition of the younger and more attractive whores back in St. Louis.

The Texas cowboys, denied the sight of a woman for three or four months, had money burning a hole in their pockets. By mid-July, there were about 1,500-2,000 cowboys camped on the prairie near Abilene, itching to get into the wild town. Abilene was completely lawless—no courthouse, no jail, a worthless Town Board, and a town marshal who himself had trouble keeping out of trouble. There was seldom a night which did not resound with gunfire, so it is strange that only a few killings were recorded. The first woman killed in Abilene was a whore by the name of Louisville Lou. She was shot by Jenny Lyons, another crib girl, in a fight over the affections of Quade Hill, a gambler.

Abilene boasted thirty-two licensed saloons, with the largest called The Alamo. Poker, faro, chuck-a-luck, and Spanish monte were popular at The Alamo, while an orchestra played day and night. The nude paintings covering its walls were imitations of the Venetian Renaissance painters, well-bosomed and hippy. The Alamo was the gathering place for the wealthy Texas cattlemen, who stayed at a hundred-room hotel called The Drovers' Cottage. The cowboys went to the Applejack Saloon, the Bull's Head, or one of the others. "Tanglefoot" whiskey sold for fifty cents a drink, but champagne brought twelve dollars a bottle.

The red-light district was a cluster of about twenty rambling wooden buildings a mile north of the railroad. Each of these contained ten or more rooms, making the total population of girls somewhere between 200 and 300. The chippies hustled in the saloons. But it was not long before the saloons were off-limits to the scarlet women. After Jenny Lyons shot up the Applejack Saloon trying to kill Quade Hill with the same pistol she had used on Louisville Lou, females were barred from all saloons in town.

In 1870, Abilene hired Tom Smith as marshal—a hard-fisted, burly, soft-spoken man from Kit Carson, Colorado. He was an efficient marshal who rarely used his gun, but he brought law and order to Abilene. His pay was $150 a month plus two dollars for each conviction. Smith was killed in his first year on the job, while attempting to make an arrest. His successor was six-foot, long-haired J. B. "Wild Bill" Hickok. Wild Bill also drew $150 a month, but he padded this with a take of twenty-five percent of all fines. He was overly quick on the trigger, played favorites, and tolerated lawlessness so long as it did not interfere with his own interests.

Mattie Silks also arrived in Abilene in 1870 to open the first parlor house. It was a large two-story yellow building, with its backyard screened by a high board fence. Her place was intended for the wealthy Texans, and her ten ladies were the youngest and most attractive in town. At the time, Mattie was perhaps twenty-three and was boasting even then as she did all her life, "I never was a prostitute. I was a madam from the time I was nineteen years old, in Springfield, Missouri.

I never worked for another madam. The girls who work for me are prostitutes, but I am and always have been a madam."

The Abilene boom burst in 1872, only four years after it had begun. Members of the Farmers' Protective Association, angry because the great Texas herds were swarming over and destroying their lands, adopted a resolution asking the Texans to kindly take their business somewhere else.

By this time, the railroads had advanced across Kansas, and the Cyprians advanced with them. Their next stop was Nauchville, Kansas, a half mile from Ellsworth. Nauchville built its own saloons, gambling palaces, and a race track. Mattie Silks had tried operating a bagnio on Ellsworth's South Main Street, but failed and built a house in Nauchville. Her place was too elegant for the trade, however, and before the summer was over, she packed up and went on to Dodge City. This left Lizzie Palmer as queen of the district. An aging, hard-bitten ex-St. Louis whore and madam, she bossed a hard-bitten lot of broads, not much better than the women in the cheapest cribs. In 1873, the economic panic that was sweeping the country hit Kansas hard. Cattle prices fell, and Ellsworth's boom was over.

Sixty miles to the south, the Sante Fe Railroad was building westward across Kansas, reaching Newton in 1871. This town was a cattle shipping point for only two years, yet "Bloody Newton" became famous for its red-light district a few blocks from the center of town. In "Hide Park," as it was aptly called, lived a collection of several hundred white, Negro, and Mexican bawds, all from the lowest strata of harlotry. When they hustled drinks in Ed Krum's dance hall or in Perry Tuttle's place, they received brass checks for the liquor they connived their male companions into buying. When the night was over, the checks were cashed in by the girls.

157

As Newton faded, Delano, another lawless settlement, sprang up across the Arkansas River from Wichita. Being on the south side of the river, where the bedding grounds for the herds coming up from Texas were located, gave Rowdy Joe Lowe and Red Beard, the vice lords of Delano, first crack at the constantly changing army of cowboys. Rowdy Kate, a small, good-looking woman, got her name from her husband.

Rowdy Joe Lowe and his rival, Red Beard, were such bitter enemies that only the death of the other man would bring peace of mind. Their dance-hall saloons were only a few yards apart, with their upper floors divided into small cubicles in which the bawds plied their trade. When one of Rowdy Joe's girls committed suicide with an overdose of morphine, he buried her without any ceremony in back of his dance hall. Months later, a girl died in Beard's place, and to shame Rowdy Joe, Red Beard had her buried in the Wichita cemetery.

Beard was educated and on the whole well behaved, while Lowe was a squat, ignorant tough. When Lowe was in his cups, the only person who could control his drunken rages was his wife, Kate. It was known that Lowe killed Jim

The westward-moving railroad made Wichita, Kansas, a thriving wide-open boomtown after 1872. This 1878 photo of Douglas Avenue shows one of Wichita's many saloons. Crib row ran nearby.

158

Sweet, a gambler, in Newton in the fall of 1871, and he was reputed to have killed others. The feud with Red Beard came to a finish on October 27, 1873, when Red Beard was killed during a shooting battle in Rowdy Joe's. Lowe gave himself up the next day, but was never prosecuted. After the killing, Rowdy Joe closed his place in Delano and took off for Denison, Texas, where hell was popping. Kate turned westward to Dodge City to build and operate a dance hall on the South Side. They reunited briefly in Dodge City before Lowe joined the gold rush to the Black Hills, where he was killed.

In 1872, the railroad came to Wichita, which soon had a half dozen hotels, two theaters, and several big general stores. The center of town was the corner of Main Street and Douglas Avenue, where Whitney Rupp, the Kansas City gambler, built his two-story Keno House. All games of chance were available while a brass band played from noon to midnight on the upper balcony. Wichita's line was located on Water Street, only two blocks away, with a score of brothels

to choose from. The toughest bawdy house in town belonged to the frequently arrested Mag Woods. Her man, George Woods, was a two-bit gambler who ran errands and handled the dirty work. Mag was coarse, pugnacious, hard as nails.

But Mag's reputation in Wichita was nothing compared to the stew she made later in Caldwell, the "Border Queen," which almost straddled the Kansas-Indian Territory line. There, her saloon-dance-hall-bordello named The Red Light became notorious for its violence. Two town marshals, one of Mag's bawds, and George Woods himself were killed in the Red Light. Close to Indian Territory, where the law did not follow, The Red Light was a gathering place for wanted men. Finally, the City Council took steps to close it. The Red Light's liquor license was canceled, and Marshal Hendry Brown boarded up the dive and stationed police at the door to stop anyone from entering. Mag screamed for justice, but Marshal Brown flatly told her that she and her tarts had just twenty-four hours to leave Caldwell. The next afternoon, as the 2:15 northbound stood at the depot, a hundred or so spectators gathered to watch Mag and her whores skedaddle. Shortly after two o'clock, the painted women came toward the depot carrying their suitcases, screaming a stream of obscenities as they boarded the train. But as the train pulled out, it was evident that Mag had exacted her revenge. Smoke billowed from the Red Light, which burned to the ground before nightfall.

After it became almost safe to walk on the streets of Denison, Texas, and to visit the saloons and gambling dens, Millie Hipps set up a stew on Skiddy Street, a block south of Main. There, among the rows of tents and shacks, the hurdy-gurdy joints, the cock-fighting pits, the gin mills, and the shameless whores from Joplin and Kansas City, Millie was the toughest and roughest of the lot. A hard-drinking, hatchet-faced woman, Millie first ran a bordello in Sedalia, Missouri, for the railroad gangs, before moving on to Joplin. When the Missouri, Kansas, and Texas began laying track south through the Indian Nations, she kept pace with the construction workers. At each rail head she was there with her tarts, ready for business.

The carnival air of Dodge City, Kansas, proved irresistible to many foolish young women from lonely farms and unhappy homes. To them the ramshackle camp was the most glamorous place on earth, with its railroad, its fine hotels, its music and dancing, its theaters, its free spenders and famous gunfighters. The Eastern newspapers called Dodge City "The Wickedest City in America." In a book entitled *Dodge City*, Robert M. Wright described the wild town as follows:

> *Her principal business is polygamy without the sanction of religion, her code of morals is the honor of thieves, and decency she knows not.*
>
> *Her virtue is prostitution and her beverage is whisky. She is a merry town and the only visible means of support of a great many of her citizens is jocularity. No restriction is placed on licentiousness. The town is full of prostitutes and every other place is a brothel.*

Dodge City, Kansas, was long known as the "wickedest city in America." This 1878 photograph is of the Varieties, one of Dodge's favorite dance halls and gambling places. The bartender is said to be the brother of Bat Masterson.

*Dutch Jake, a generous madam from the boom days of Dodge
City.*

Among the feminine contingent at Dodge City was
"Dutch Jake," a madam who provided riding horses and
baked delicious cookies for her girl "boarders." "Big Nose"
Kate, friend of Doc Holliday, the gunfighting dentist, was
also at Dodge for a time. Once, when Doc was under arrest
at Fort Griffin, Texas, she set fire to the hotel to distract the
town, went into the room where Doc was held, disarmed
the guard, then galloped out of town at Doc's side.

162

"Big Nose Kate" Fisher, sweetheart of Doc Holliday, the gunslinging Dodge City dentist. Kate was quite a hand with the sixgun herself.

This is Squirrel-tooth Alice, one of the popular girls of Dodge. Note her pet and namesake on her lap.

163

But the most famous and best-loved of all Dodge's shady ladies is Dora Hand, also known as Fannie Keenan. Dodge City knew her not only by two names, but also by two wholly different identities. Saint or sinner, Dora Hand was the most beautiful woman to grace Dodge in its heyday. Known as the Queen of the Fairy Belles, she was the most popular of the dance-hall girls. It was said she had been a singer in

"Timberline," the tallest of Dodge City's favorite "ladies of the shadows."

Dora Hand, the best-loved of all Dodge's shady ladies. Her murder was mourned with the finest funeral in Dodge's history.

grand opera, and she charmed the men of Dodge with her sentimental ballads. She was a kindly woman, always ready to help anyone in trouble. If some raw cowboy from Texas lost his pile at faro or drank too much redeye and was rolled south of the Deadline, Dora would grubstake him or redeem his saddle so he could ride home. She never asked for a security, nor even the names of the men she helped. When some-one fell sick, she was ready and able to play the part of a practical nurse. On Sunday, clad in simple black, she crossed the Deadline to a little church where she led the congregation in hymns and anthems. A quick change of attire after the Sunday evening service, and she was back at her trade in the dance hall.

Before Dodge City, other cow towns had known Dora Hand. She was in Abilene and Hays during their hell-roaring days, and inspired several men to fight to the death over her charms. All in all, Dora's beauty is said to have led to the deaths of twelve men.

In the summer of 1878, Dodge Mayor James H. "Dog" Kelley and James W. "Spike" Kennedy, errant son of a wealthy Texas cattleman, got into a fight. Kelley was a part-ner in the Alhambra Saloon and Gambling House, of which Dora Hand was the star attraction. Kelley threw Kennedy out of the saloon one night, apparently for lavishing his attentions on Dora. The Texan left for Kansas City, but he planned to come back and square up the account.

In October, Mayor Kelley became ill and was taken to the hospital at Fort Dodge for treatment. While Kelley was at the fort, Kennedy returned in the dark of night to wreak his vengeance. Not knowing that "Dog" Kelley was at the military camp five miles out of town, Kennedy stole up on Kelley's two-room frame house and fired two shots through the front door in the direction of the bedroom. The first slug passed over Fannie Barretson, one of the Alhambra girls, but the second passed through the thin partition and killed Dora Hand, asleep in the other room. Kennedy did not wait to find out the results of his murderous adventure, but instead rode madly out of town, believing he had killed the mayor of Dodge City.

Marshal Wyatt Earp, Bat Masterson, Charlie Bassett, and Bill Tilghman set out to bring Kennedy back to Dodge. The quartet pounded across seventy miles of prairie before sighting the fugitive at Cimarron Crossing. The Texan put the spurs to his horse and fled, but a slug from Masterson's rifle tore into his right arm, and Earp brought down his horse. When the posse members told Kennedy that he had shot Dora Hand instead of Mayor Kelly, he cursed them for not killing him. Back in Dodge, doctors took four inches of bone out of his shattered arm, leaving it useless. It was the only price he paid for his crime, as he was freed for lack of evidence.

The Dodge City *Globe* printed this tribute to Dora:

> *The deceased came to Dodge City this sum-*
> *mer and was engaged as vocalist in the Varie-*
> *ties and Comique shows. She was a prepos-*
> *sessing woman and her artful winning ways*
> *brought many admirers within her smile's*
> *blandishments. If we mistake not, Dora Hand*
> *has an eventful history. She had applied for*
> *a divorce from Theodore Hand. After a varied*
> *life the unexpected death messenger cuts her*
> *down in the full bloom of gayety and woman-*
> *hood. She was the innocent victim.*

Dora Hand, or Fannie Keenan, was put to rest in Prairie Grove Cemetery after the finest funeral in Dodge's history. A remarkable procession which accompanied her coffin included dance-hall girls, gamblers, gunslingers, saloonkeepers, cattlemen, and even some of the town's most respectable ladies. A minister who was wise to the ways of the frontier intoned the words for everyone to hear, "He that is without sin among you, let him first cast a stone at her."

The California gold rush of 1849 was followed by dozens of other gold rushes and the birth of a number of new frontiers. In the years between the two gold rushes to the north—the Fraser River strike of 1857-58 and the Klondike commotion of 1898—the miner, the gambler, the saloonkeeper, the prostitute, and the merchant opened up a good portion of the American West. From the discovery of Nevada's Comstock Lode in the fall of 1859 until the rush ended in 1880, millions in gold and silver poured over the Sierras into San Francisco. And it was a few pinches of gold dust discovered in Cherry

Creek, between Auraria and Denver City, which resulted in the great "Pikes Peak or Bust" migration of 1859, and which put Denver on the map as a major city of the West.

Denver's Holladay Street, the most wicked street in the West in the '70s and '80s, was the street of nobody's women and everybody's women. Approximately one thousand "brides of the multitude," as Forbes Parkhill called them, were available in the imposing parlor houses or lowly cribs which lines both sides of the street for three blocks. This red-light district was a metropolis, compared to Denver's first tenderloin, a cluster of log cabins on the south bank of Cherry Creek in the late 1850's. Then, in the '60s, the sin spots jumped the creek and moved north. Originally, this thoroughfare was named McGee Street after one of Denver's earliest settlers. Later, it was renamed for Ben Holladay, stagecoach operator. Denver's Chinatown, known as "Hop Alley," paralleled Holladay Street; the opium dens and Chinese gambling establishments had entrances on both Holladay and Hop Alley. In 1889, the unsavory reputation of

Freight wagons on a Denver street, 1866. A few pinches of gold dust brought about the "Pikes Peak or Bust" migration that put Denver on the map.

168

Holladay Street prompted the heirs of upright Ben Holladay to petition the Board of Aldermen to change the name Holladay Street to Market Street.

The Market Street cribs were just wide enough for a door and two narrow windows. Each crib contained two

Denver's Holladay Street was the most wicked street in the West in the 1870's and 1880's. Close to a thousand strumpets were available in the parlor houses and cribs that lined the street. This is Belle Bernard's place at 518 Holladay, one of the best houses in town.

Denver's "Hop Alley," home of opium and prostitution. This photo was probably taken in the early 1900's.

tiny rooms—a parlor in front, a boudoir in back. The rent, which ranged from fifteen to twenty-five dollars a week, was collected daily in cash. In the white section, the cribs were known as "dollar houses," while in the black belt they were called "two-bit houses." These two-bit houses could cost a man a lot more than two bits, as William Isas discovered in October 1891. Ardell Smith, whose crib was at 2235 Market, entertained the gentleman from Golden City, then, along with her friends, Blanche Morgan and Mattie Fisher, put morphine in Isas' beer. Isas kicked the bucket, and Ardell Smith was sentenced to one year in the county jail for involuntary manslaughter.

The 2000 block of Market Street, Denver, in 1905, when it was the heart of the red-light district. The two young ladies in the doorways on the left appear to be looking for work.

Ardel Smith was 35 when this photograph was taken for the 1891 Denver police blotter. That year, Ardel killed a Golden City man by putting too much morphine in his beer while he was visiting her crib on Market Street.

Unlike the denizens of the parlor houses, the girls of the cribs made no pretense of decorum. In a costume consisting of a low-necked, knee-length spangled dress and black silk stockings, the crib girl stood in her doorway and solicited the male shoppers who were strolling down the sidewalks, inspecting the merchandise. "Come on in, dearie," was the customary invitation, but if the prospect did not respond, the girl might grab his hat and pitch it inside her parlor. Some of the cribs displayed signs which shocked even the hardy residents of pioneer Denver. Finally, an ordinance was passed banning some of the overly zealous Market Street advertisers.

One sign complying with the new law read: MEN TAKEN IN AND DONE FOR. And that about summed it up, for while clasped in the arms of their gentlemen friends, the crib girls would bite the studs from their shirt fronts, or the tie pins from their cravats. One Denver dentist won a widespread underworld reputation for making steel biters which clamped to the rear of the girl's front teeth.

The parlor-house madams refused to tolerate any jewel-biting by their girls, for fear it would give the house a bad name. The madams liked to call their places "young ladies' boarding houses," which in a way they were, since the girls were required to pay for their room and board. But only two meals were served—breakfast at eleven-thirty in the morning and dinner at five in the afternoon—and the girl "boarders" split their earnings fifty-fifty with the madams. The girls were required to dress attractively, and were encouraged to charge clothing to the madams' accounts at the local stores. This kept the girls constantly in debt, thus giving the madam an additional means of keeping them in line. Many Denver merchants aided the madams—and, of course, themselves—by adding an additional twenty percent to the bills of these women of easy virtue. The madam squared the account, for she would get the sum back regardless of the cost.

Most parlor houses employed a male piano player who played for a small wage plus tips and drinks. It was customary for guests to tip "the professor" and to include him in a

172

A strange photograph of two young couples, taken around 1890. Are the girls real?

round of drinks. To encourage tips, a "kitty" was placed on the piano, usually bearing the sign, "Feed the kitty."

Very few of the parlor-house madams procured their girls through international white-slave rings. The exception was Macquereau Jack Maynard, owner of an infamous club and a string of cribs, who made an annual trip to French North Africa to acquire girls. He achieved some widespread

notoriety when he introduced the cash register into the oldest profession. The divorce courts provided a lucrative field for the madams, since alimony was rarely asked and even more rarely granted. A penniless young divorcee was certain to be propositioned by a procurer. His fee for each new girl ranged from five to ten dollars, depending upon her age, personality, and looks.

Besides putting Denver on the map, the rich gold strikes of the early '60s established the Colorado cities of Idaho Springs, Gold Run, Fairplay, Alma, California Gulch, Oro Gulch, Black Hawk, and Central City. Colorado's first true

This 1881 drawing was entitled "Saturday Night in a Denver, Colorado Bagnio." Or any night.

bonanza in silver extended from the 1860's well into the 1880's, and added the names of Georgetown, Ouray, Aspen, Creede, and in biggest letters of all—for a time rivaling even Denver for importance—Leadville. In 1890-91, it was gold again at Cripple Creek.

Georgetown's Brownell Street boasted five parlor houses in the '80s, with Mattie Estes, whose real name was Elizabeth C. Deyo, the pioneer madam. Mollie Dean, whose real name was Mary Ann Nephue, was another leading madam. Arden Shea, a miner, fell violently in love with Mollie; on catching her with another man, he killed her and blew out his own brains.

175

Other names in Georgetown made the news. Madam Jenny Aiken was burned to death in 1878; after a man was shot to death in her house, an angry mob set fire to her establishment. Madam Ada Lamont, one of Denver's top madams, ended her career here. But the most popular girl in town was Lottie White's star boarder, a girl known as Tid-bit.

Montana's golden era, from 1862 to 1876, gave birth to Bannock, Alder Gulch (Virginia City), Emigrant Gulch, Diamond City, Helena, and Butte, which enjoyed successive booms of gold, silver, and then, in 1893, a bonanza in copper. The Black Hills of South Dakota boomed with gold in 1876, at about the time deposits in Montana were exhausted, and the Black Hills boom was followed by the discovery of gold in Arizona and New Mexico.

This was the miner's West, dozens of new frontiers, widely separated in space, often overlapping in time, usually located in mountainous regions which normally would have been bypassed. Each boom had in common much the same pattern: the initial strike; the rush; the sudden growth of the makeshift town; and when the precious metal ran out, the quick desertion of the site. The booms had in common, too, some of the same miners, girls, and merchants, for all were a restless itinerant lot, moving from one strike to another, with an insatiable hunger for wealth.

The inevitable red-light district in each mining camp had a great deal to do with the camp's reputation—much of which came from the skillful pen of Eastern writers who visited the West and amused readers back home with their lusty accounts. In particular, four communities—Deadwood, Leadville, Tombstone, and Cripple Creek—were synonymous with the Wild West, for they pretty well lived up to the popular image of a mining camp. These four towns all became prominent between 1876 and 1900. Each had a roaring red-light district and a high crime rate. Deadwood mushroomed first in 1876, followed by Leadville in 1879. Two years later, Tombstone burst on the scene, and finally, in the 1890's, came the fourth, Cripple Creek. By the time one town was tamed,

A recent photograph of Bannock, Montana: on the right, Montana's first hotel; on the left, Skinner's Saloon; both built during the gold rush of the 1860's.

another boomed, and the circuit from boom to bust was repeated.

Of the four encampments, Deadwood probably least deserved its reputation. As the center of the Black Hills rush, Deadwood acquired more than the usual number of frontier characters, saloons, gambling dens, and prostitutes. While it cannot be denied that there was a certain amount of lawlessness, local newspaper accounts contradict the wild, weird stories that prevailed in the East.

Up in the Black Hills, Sunday was the miner's shopping day. The three thousand or so ragged, unwashed, and boisterous men who had established their sites crowded into Deadwood's narrow, muddy main street, all eager for excitement. All the stores were open, and only one or two curbside preachers reminded passersby of the Christian duties of the day. A prospector could find almost any type of entertainment he wanted in the saloons and bawdy houses. The first saloon in Deadwood was run by Ike Brown, who also owned the adjoining grocery store. Across both buildings was the sign "Zion's Cooperative Mercantile Institution," indicating that while he sold liquor, he was still a Mormon at heart.

Other saloons were quickly built, until by July 1877,

177

there were about seventy-five in town. Their owners practiced every form of skullduggery they could devise for the rapid separation of the miner and his dust. Along with the saloons were the gambling houses, where most of the professional gamblers put on a good, raucous show. One white-haired old fellow urged the miners, "Come on up, boys, and put your money down—everybody beats the old man—the girls all beat the old man—the boys all beat the old man—everybody beats the old man—forty years a gambler—the old

"Stud Horse Poker" at Jamestown, Colorado. Was this the way it really was? Yes, according to the Illustrated Police News *of 1883.*

178

fool—everybody beats the old man—put your money down, boys, and beat the old man." Of course, no one beat the old man.

Though women acted as dealers at many of the gaming tables, most of the prospectors preferred to have men as their adversaries, for the women were generally old hands, and unscrupulous ones at that. Most of the gambling games were said to be honest, but faro, a game at which the dealer has a very small percentage if honestly played, was the most

popular. The man who did not squander his dust on liquor or lose it gambling often managed to waste it on a loose woman. The hurdy-gurdy houses quickly sprang up to provide feminine company and collect the miners' gold.

Deadwood's first dance hall opened May 1, 1876, with only the owner's wife and daughter to entertain the customers; six women of more questionable virtue were soon added to the staff. Within a month, two more dance halls opened their doors. These were quickly joined by the variety theaters where a customer might be sensuously entertained by the woman of his choice in the privacy of a curtained box. The most notorious of the dance-hall owners was Al Swearingen, of the Gem Theater. Swearingen started out in Custer, then moved to the riper fields of Deadwood Gulch. He made frequent trips back east to recruit young women for his pleasure

The Gem Variety Theater, the most notorious dance hall in the heyday of Deadwood, South Dakota. Owner Al Swearingen filled his pleasure palace with young women he lured west with the promise of a theatrical career.

palace, promising them employment as waiter girls or actresses. When they reached Deadwood, however, he forced them into a life of shame. An ordinary night's take at the Gem amounted to $5,000—and on some occasions reached twice that amount—yet Swearingen died broke. He was killed in Denver while hitching a ride on a freight train. The Gem continued operations to the end of the gold rush, maintaining its notorious reputation as a "defiler of youth, a destroyer of homes, and a veritable abomination."

To keep order in places like the Gem, the *Deadwood Daily Times* proposed a monthly fine or license fee which would help replenish the city treasury, and would have "a most salutary effect in driving women of the street out of town or into the house of a responsible madam." These houses frequently made the headlines. For example, a woman named "Tricksie" was thoroughly beaten by her lover, so she snatched up a pistol and shot him in the head just behind the eyes. Fortunately, he had no brains, at least in that part of his skull, so he recovered in a few weeks. The newspaper also reported the story of another Deadwood girl who wore a special dress embroidered with the brands and initials of her lovers. Some of the initials caressed her rounded shoulders and ample bosom; others occupied the edges of this novel attire; then there were some she frequently sat on. Her affection for each man dictated where she placed his brand, thus a guy could tell just where he stood with her.

The murder of a young Charles Forbes by Bill Gay was headline news. Mrs. Gay was an especially attractive young woman whom Gay had picked from among professional ladies of Deadwood. He was naturally dubious about the constancy of her affections, and kept a close eye on her. Forbes was a rather stupid young man in his late teens when he sent Mrs. Gay a note, via Sam "Nigger General" Fields. The note asked her to "meet me this evening, my darling, by moonlight at 8:00 o'clock, at the corner of the big barn." Mrs. Gay, who did not care much about Forbes, used this opportunity to prove how faithful a wife she was and showed her husband, Gay, the letter. Gay cornered Sam Fields, found out who sent the note, then went out and killed Forbes. Tried and convicted, Gay spent three years in prison, but on his return to Deadwood he was met by a brass band. He later committed another murder in Montana and was greeted with a hangman's noose, not a brass band.

Like Mrs. Gay, a few of the scarlet ladies reformed. The poor girls who remained in harlotry did not live long. Within two or three years, drink, drugs, crime, and disease took them from their supposedly glamorous life. Many deaths reported as pneumonia or fever were actually due to laudanum or a lover's bullet, but this did not plague the conscience of Deadwood. The deaths of Emma Worth, from an overdose of morphine, or of Katie Smith—madam of the "Hidden Treasure Number Two"—from the same drug scarcely made a ripple among Deadwood's respectable citizens.

One of the most widely told stories about the Black Hills is about Phatty Thomas' load of cats. Thomas bought these in Cheyenne for two bits a piece, crated them, and loaded them on his wagon. On Spring Creek, near Sheridan, the wagon tipped over, but a group of friendly prospectors helped him recapture most of the cargo. According to the story, Thomas sold the cats to the town's painted women at sundry prices, depending on the quality of the cat. Thus we have the name "cat house."

Another favorite story is about the sidewalk loafer who watched a teamster unloading twenty barrels of whiskey and a sack of flour at a Deadwood store. Shaking his head in disbelief, he turned to his friend and asked, "What in hell do you suppose they want with all that flour?" Years later, the good people of South Dakota prohibited the sale of spirituous liquors, and the dens of immorality faded one by one. The proprietress of one of Rapid City's leading houses, when asked if she planned to reopen her brothel, said, "you can't run a sporting house on creek water!"

Leadville was born because of mining, and it promptly became the wealthiest, biggest, and wildest mining community of the times. The efforts of city government, the police, and the local citizenry were insufficient to control the awesome level of crime, so Leadville gained a national repu-

The interior of a dance hall on State Street, in Leadville, Colorado, the biggest, wealthiest, and wildest mining community of its time. This picture appeared in Leslie's, April 12, 1870.

tation for wickedness. Indeed, the town seemed to take real pride in its depravity. In no other town did the newspapers carry so many stories about the red-light district or appear to relish all the sordid details. Leadville, as the Queen, became the yardstick by which to measure other mining camps.

In Leadville, the Mollies, Sallies, Frankies, and Netties of the red-light district lived on the lower end of Harrison Avenue where variety theaters, dance halls, cribs, and parlor houses lined both sides of the street. Some of these girls, like the "Lop-Eared Kid" who blinded "Pioneer Pete" with a handful of pepper, attracted the attention of all Leadville while others, like the beautiful Josie Mansfield, simply attracted the men. The short-skirted, painted dance-hall girls earned plenty every night, but they envied the fancy ladies of the parlor houses. As the latter came into the dance halls or gambling houses, as they strolled down the streets or rode in their handsome carriages, they caused many a girl to try to join the scarlet sisterhood. Winnie Purdy's house at 115 West Fifth Avenue attracted many. Of her house, the *Herald Democrat* stated:

> *The most remarkable house of wickedness in Leadville was a dream of Oriental luxury. Paintings that would have sent Melvin Winstock's preacher into hysterics adorned the walls. Costly furniture, tapestries, velvet carpets, rich Oriental hangings and all the accessories of luxurious elegance were lavished in the interior adornment.*

When her guardian angel left town in haste, Winnie sold her elaborate house to Lillis Lovell, one of the most magnificent samples of womanhood to have "played the role of a succubus in the half world of the Cloud City." With such advertising, it is not surprising that girls under sixteen joined the boarders only to be "rescued" again and again. Robberies were committed in the houses, and murders were hushed up. Outstanding Leadville parlor houses were operated by Mollie May and Sallie Purple; other madams were Frankie Page, Carrie Linnell, and Mollie Price. Hundreds of girls operated from cribs in the tenderloin district, which included "Coon Row" and "French Row."

Madam Mattie Cook had a son, Alpha, who married a sporting girl named Etta Clark, a redhead who was so skinny she was called the "Grasshopper." Etta later opened a house of her own in El Paso, Texas, as described earlier. There she was killed in a fight not long after she shot Big Alice in her "public arch."

A hundred-fifty saloons, gambling houses, and dance halls flourished in Leadville, including such places as the Ice Palace or St. Anne's Rest, where one might play faro, chuck-a-luck, keno, the paddle wheel, and the shell game. "Pop" Wyman's Great Saloon was always crowded, even if Pop did not allow married men to gamble or drunks to be served. Wyman's was a combination saloon, gambling palace, dance hall and variety theater, with rooms for private parties in the upper stories of the three-story frame building. Just inside the swinging doors, a large Bible was chained to a mahogany pulpit; across the face of the clock was a sign reading, "Please don't swear," while a sign in the dance hall, above the orchestra, said, "Don't Shoot the Piano-player— He's Doing His Darndest."

The Texas House was resplendent with oil paintings, handsome furniture, rugs, and draperies. The Church Casino, so named because of its Gothic window, attracted the actors and actresses who came to town.

The Carbonate Concert Hall also boasted a Gothic window, and had living pine trees which formed "cozy arbors and grottos." It was run as a variety theater with such popular performers as Mollie Newton, "the most perfectly formed woman in America," who presented a series of beautiful tableaux representing Greek and Roman statuary. Here the patrons sat at tables on the main floor or in tiers of boxes flanking the stage on both sides. The men smoked and drank, watched the buffoonery, and listened to the broadly vulgar jokes. Of the "intermission," one *Leadville Chronicle* reporter wrote: "These long lapses are supposed to give the opportunity to the waiter girls to supply the occupants of the box gallery with drinks." Of course, there was an extra charge for the box seats and an extra charge for the drinks the waiter girls served.

Tombstone's descriptive name reflects its reputation, and a brief examination of the *Epitaph* or *Nugget* corroborates this impression. However, the lawlessness of Tombstone cannot be blamed entirely on the mining frontier, for Cochise County was a favorite rendezvous for cattle rustlers and border bandits as well. The Earp-Clanton feud, with its classic gunfight at the O. K. Corral, reflects this double source of trouble. As a mining center, Tombstone was of secondary importance; but the town did owe its existence to mining, and so its reputation reflected on the entire mining frontier.

Night was distinguished from day in Tombstone only by the stars. Saloons and gambling houses never closed, and the gambling tables circling the saloon walls were always surrounded by tense throngs. Gamblers played as the house's lookouts sat with their sixshooters or shotguns poised. The monte tables were stacked with gold and silver; faro was played in feverish silence; the roulette wheels spun; the dice in the chuck-a-luck boxes rattled noisily. When a player dropped out at the poker table another was waiting to grab his chair. Play at noon was as heavy as at midnight—a thousand dollars won or lost was nothing, for a loser today was a winner tomorrow.

Yet the saloons of Tombstone were not the boozing dens of old frontier tradition, for such places as the Crystal Palace, the Oriental, and the Alhambra were decorated with oil paintings, mirrors, and fancy brass and mahogany bars. Three bartenders were always on duty. Only a few rough men thumped on the bar and roared out an order for raw whiskey —the men of Tombstone displayed a preference for mixed drinks. The white-aproned dandies behind the bars were adept in concocting cocktails, mashes, sours, cobblers, flips, and sangarees. The blunderhead who botched a silver fizz or a pousse-café, or was so crude as to crush the sprig of mint in a julep, was promptly shipped to San Francisco, where the tippling was less elegant.

Nearby were the streets lined with cribs, palatial houses, rougher saloons, and dance halls where Mexican orchestras played as the men and women danced and caroused. In the wee hours of the morning, the sirens came in hansom cabs and carriages to the Crystal Palace, Oriental, or Alhambra and drank with the men at the bars or bucked the tiger— played against the faro bank—until dawn.

Nightly, the Bird Cage Opera House was packed to the doors. The bar was at the front and a horseshoe of private curtained boxes lined the walls. Seated on wooden benches, the general audience guzzled whiskey and beer and peered through the fog of tobacco smoke at the vaudeville show. Painted ladies in scanty costumes sang heartrending ballads of home and mother before hurrying to the boxes. Their voluptuous charms and soft graces sold many a bottle of wine, with its rake-off for the girl. When the performance ended, the benches were moved against the walls and the crowd whirled in a series of drunken dances until the sun climbed over the mountains.

Until 1893, shortly after Cripple Creek became the new miners' mecca, the town's saloons, gambling palaces, and dance halls stood along Bennett Avenue. Upstairs over the Anaconda, Buckhorn, and other saloons, the parlor houses operated by Minnie Smith, Molly King, Lolly Lee, and Blanche Barton—all old hands from Leadville, Aspen and Colorado City—were going strong. But alcohol and sex began to get so thoroughly mixed up into everything in Cripple Creek that a man could not enter a grocery store without being propositioned. Finally the town marshal, Hi Wilson, moved the girls and dance halls a block south to Myers Avenue. Wilson promised the girls nobody would bother them on Myers Avenue as long as they paid their tax, gave to the churches, and behaved demurely on the main street. The dance halls on Myers Avenue, such as the Bon-Ton, the Red Light, the Great View, the Topic, and the Casino, were basically taxi-dance halls. For a short quadrille, waltz, or schottische a miner paid two bits, which included a shot of rotgut and maybe a tiny quick kiss. The girl received half of the two bits and whatever else she could pry out of her temporary dance partner.

In 1900, Cripple Creek had seventy-three saloons, many of them facing Myers Avenue between Third and Fifth Streets. Some of the more popular bars were the Opera Club, the Combination, the Miners Exchange, and the Last Chance. To the east there was a long line of jerry-built dance halls with big, long bars where a man could buy a beer for five cents and get a free lunch. But food and drink were not the main attractions at the variety theaters. They all had eight- and ten-piece bands, lots of dance-hall girls, and racy burlesque shows. Before each performance, the management of the theater sent the band and show girls out to parade up and down the street to drum up interest—this was how the song "There'll Be a Hot Time in the Old Town Tonight" became popular.

Beyond Fourth Street one could see the racial progres-

A rather somber-looking crowd at a turn-of-the-century Cripple Creek saloon. Some historians claim this is a photograph of "Crapper Jack's" Dance Hall.

sion among the crib girls. First, the whites—French and Spanish—then the Japanese, and then the Negro as Myers Avenue neared the railroad trestle. Along the north side of the avenue were the fancy parlor houses with their prim curtains. Most of the cribs were flimsy two-room frame affairs, but a few were constructed of brick. They all fronted right on the street, showing a narrow door and a tiny window, and were identified not by street number, but by the girls' first names.

During the boom years around 1900, about 300 wanton women served the more than 40,000 men in the Cripple Creek district. The city fathers profited handsomely from the girls of the tenderloin, for every madam was taxed sixteen dollars a month, and her girls were taxed six dollars. Dance-hall and crib girls were taxed four dollars. These fees allowed

the women to work legally, and also made it possible to enforce a periodic physical examination of the girls.

Blanche Burton was Cripple Creek's first madam. Hazel Vernon, who reigned at The Old Homestead for years, was the best known. There were also Pearl DeVere, Laura Bell, Nell McClusky, Pearl Sevan, and Lola Livingston, all coming to the district from other Colorado mining towns.

In the alleys behind the Myers Avenue joints, there were several well-patronized opium dens. These two newspaper stories, printed in 1900, tell of this other life:

> *A "hop-joint" in the small brick building be-*
> *hind the Red Light dance hall was raided at*
> *noon today. The room was elaborately out-*
> *fitted. The accounts kept show that the den*

189

was well patronized by people of Myers Avenue.

Another opium den was raided yesterday. The police, for several days, have been watching the apartment of Lizzie Moore. Yesterday, the captain noticed three women go there at 6:00 A.M. After a quarter of an hour, the captain tip-toed in to find the women and the proprietress reclining on a Turkish rug hitting the pipe.

One of the girls of Cripple Creek was called Scarface Liz, once the most beautiful girl in the red lights of Leadville. At the peak of her popularity, she got involved in a brawl and had acid thrown in her face, disfiguring her forever. As soon as possible she left Leadville and set up shop in a tiny crib in Poverty Gulch. Another girl, named Liverlip, moved to Cripple Creek from Leadville after a man sliced her face with a razor. It happened again in Poverty Gulch, and again she survived and kept working. Later, during prohibition, Liverlip did a thriving business as a bootlegger.

The best-remembered crib girl was Leo the Lion, who once, at high noon, stood stark naked at the corner of Myers and Fourth Avenue crying, "I'm Leo the Lion, the queen of the row!" Some miners who knew her put her back in her crib to sleep off her mid-day binge. She was the same Madam Leo who later shocked Julian Street by telling him she was only making two or three dollars a day and would he please send her "some nice boys."

On the nights when she was "on the town," Grace Carlyle, an angel-faced platinum blonde, could always be found in Grant Crumley's Bennett Avenue Saloon, for she was Crumley's favorite tart. When Grace was attending to business, it was at Pearl Sevan's bagnio, Old Faithful, on Myers Avenue; but the time she spent in Crumley's was all for fun. As the night grew late and she became giddy with alcohol, she enjoyed being lifted to the top of the bar where she stripped naked and danced to the wild applause of the men in the saloon. The *Cripple Creek Crusher* said:

> *Such hilarious antics were nothing more than an expression of the natural ebullience of the world's richest mining camp and the increased potency of good Bourbon at high altitudes and not to be taken as proof of the town's depravity.*

Along about noon on Saturday, April 25, 1896, the sun was shining warmly when the bartender from the Topic Dance Hall strolled over to the Central Dance Hall and climbed the stairs to the second floor. Here his woman was ironing her frock in preparation for the afternoon's dance at the Topic. The two started to argue; she came at him with a Bowie knife; he slapped her face and grabbed her arm. Then the two of them knocked over the lighted gasoline stove, spreading its flames over the wood floor. Three minutes later, Cripple Creek residents heard Fire Chief Allen shoot off his revolver three times to call the volunteer firemen. The Central Dance Hall building burned so fast some of the girls on the third floor were trapped. They came down the ropes after dropping their cats, rabbits, and supplies of laudanum to their friends below. For thirty-five minutes, the hose companies kept the blaze under control, but this emptied the water out of the reservoir. The warm south wind blew harder until the embers floated across Myers Avenue, catching the Topic Dance Hall on fire, along with many other buildings.

Before long all of Cripple Creek was in flames. The fire lasted only three hours, but it wiped out the entire business district and thirty of the town's six hundred acres. The town rebuilt, but there were to be only five more years of boom-level mining. Though some mining continues to the present day, the population of Cripple Creek has diminished from 50,000 in its peak year of 1901, to less than 700 today.

191

Madams and Gamblers

THE PARLOR HOUSES and cribs were often on the same street, but there was a world of difference between the two. In the parlor houses, each girl was expected to dress in the latest fashion, which meant having several evening dresses and afternoon costumes. On the rough frontier, the warm house with its well-dressed women was the closest thing to a real home that most men knew. The brightly lit interiors contrasted sharply with the dismal hovels the men lived in by their mines or out on the range. The glittering chandeliers, the costly mirrors wreathed with inspiring banners, the inviting arrays of decanters, the carved woods, the music, the striking and often titillating paintings, the girls in their fine frills— all lent a bit of gentility to an otherwise harsh existence.

Some of the more enterprising madams advertised what they had to offer, in a little book so small that a gentleman could carry it in his vest pocket. Blanche Brown, for example, offered "Lots of Boarders. All the Comforts of Home." Minnie Hall told unhappy husbands she had "30 rooms, Music and Dance Hall, Five Parlors and Mikado Parlor, Finest Wines, Liquors and Cigars, 20 boarders, and a Cordial Welcome to Strangers." Belle Bernard welcomed strangers with boarders "Strictly First-class in Every Respect."

One of the many fabulous and colorful characters of the California gold rush was Eleanore Dumont, known as Madam Moustache, who made her headquarters in Nevada City, California, for a while. According to legend, Eleanore was a beautiful French woman who bore a slight growth of fuzz on her upper lip. One evening, a tired and thoroughly drunk miner made the trip to town to see the much-talked-of beauty. He took one look and yelled, "She's pretty, for sure, but look at her moustache." From that time on, Eleanore Dumont was laughingly called Madam Moustache.

The Nevada City establishment of Madam Moustache was a bit more plush than the average gold-camp bar. It contained a long, rough-boarded room which was fully fifty feet in length. The walls were draped with colored cloth and decorated with provocative canvases of nudes, which were imported from France. The Madam boasted the fanciest bar in California, behind which the gin slingers served fifty men at a time. At one end of the room was a cleared space for dancing and an orchestra of fifteen pieces. The rest of the space was taken up by twelve or more tables for poker, twenty-one, or monte.

When Nevada City's boom collapsed, so did Madam Moustache's parlor house. Eleanore began moving from one camp to another, her fortunes gradually declining. Her beauty faded, she drank too much, and a darker shadow of down was growing on her upper lip. The Madam's gaming skills began slipping too—ever so slightly, but an extra drink or two can make all the difference at cards. In 1859, with the discovery of the rich diggings of Nevada's Comstock Lode, she joined the Washoe rush. By 1860, it was common knowledge the Madam no longer deigned to make money other than at the vingt-et-un table.

Eleanore roamed across the West, following the new mining camps to Idaho and then the Black Hills. As her fortunes continued to plummet, she resumed the sale of her own flesh, offering her services in the construction camps along the route of the Union Pacific Railroad. In 1877, Madam Moustache was running a small-time brothel in Eureka,

(Overleaf) *A far cry from crib row: a parlor house in Leadville, Colorado, around the turn of the century. The elaborate furnishings and artwork must have made the house a palace in the eyes of the mountain-weary miners.*

193

La Fiesta de Los Angeles

SOUVENIR
SPORTING
GUIDE.....

THIS IS NOT THE REV. MAC.

Los
Angeles
California
1897...

Miss Ella Rorich

419 COMMERCIAL ST.

This popular young lady is oc-
cupying the mansion at 419 Commercial street where you will be
entertained in a royal manner.
She also has four beautiful young
ladies who assist in making it
pleasant to gentlemen callers.
Miss Ella is very popular among
the sporting fraternity and that
alone is recommendation enough.

Cover and page from a Los Angeles guidebook, 1897.

Nevada; two years later, the *Sacramento Union* of September
9, 1879, ran a brief dispatch from Bodie, California: "A woman
named Eleanore Dumont was found dead today about one
mile out of town, having committed suicide."

But no madam combined beauty and tragedy more poi-
gnantly than Ada Lamont, A dark-eyed beauty of nineteen,
she first arrived in Denver in the late summer of 1858, coming
from a solid Midwestern family. At seventeen, she had married a young minister, in a union which friends regarded as
perfect. The young bride took great pride in her duties as
a pastor's wife, so when the young preacher felt "the call"
to carry the gospel into the Rocky Mountain wilderness, Ada
happily went with him. The couple left from St. Joseph,
Missouri, on a wagon train; one dark night while en route,

196

Eleanore Dumont, a Frenchwoman who became a madam in Nevada City, California. A slight growth of hair on her upper lip gave her the nickname "Madame Moustache."

the youthful clergyman disappeared, and so did a young lady of relaxed reputation. The wagons halted for a full day while search parties fanned out, but no trace of the pair was found. The general assumption was that the pair were lovers who fled together.

As the wagon train pushed west, Ada maintained a stony silence until the train reached Cherry Creek. Here she said, "As a God-fearing woman, you see me for the last time. As of tomorrow, I start the first brothel in this settlement. Any of you men in need of a little fun will always find the flaps of my tent open."

Ada's debut in her new profession was delayed as a friendly band of Arapahoes met up with the wagon train. The young chief was so taken by the dark-eyed charmer in calico that he offered to swap five ponies for her. Ada, thinking the

197

PREFACE

"Honi Soit Qui Mal y Pense"

THIS Directory and Guide of the Sporting District has been before the people on many occasions, and has proven its authority as to what is doing in the "Queer Zone."

Anyone who knows to-day from yesterday will say that the Blue Book is the right book for the right people.

WHY NEW ORLEANS SHOULD HAVE THIS DIRECTORY

Because it is the only district of its kind in the States set aside for the fast women by law.

Because it puts the stranger on a proper and safe path as to where he may go and be free from "Hold-ups," and other games usually practiced upon the stranger.

It regulates the women so that they may live in one district to themselves instead of being scattered over the city and filling our thoroughfares with street walkers.

It also gives the names of women entertainers employed in the Dance Halls and Cabarets in the District.

Preface and five pages from the New Orleans Blue Book, 1915 edition—a guide to Storyville, the district centering around Basin Street which was set aside for free and lawful enjoyment of the sporting life. In many Western cities, a "blue book" could be found in the pocket of any sporting man.

MISS SPENCER has the distinction of conducting about one of the best establishments in the Tenderloin District, where swell men can be socially entertained by an array of swell ladies. As for beauty, her home has been pronounced extremely gorgeous by people who are in a position to know costly finery, cut glass and oil paintings, foreign draperies, etc.

Miss Spencer, while very young, is very charming, and, above all things a favorite with the boys—what one might say, those of the clubs.

May, as the club boys commonly call her, has never less than fifteen beautiful ladies—from all parts of this great and glorious country.

May is contemplating having an annex added to her present home, as her popularity has gained so in the past that she cannot accommodate her friends. You should see her girls.

PHONE 2927 MAIN

LETTER "A" (COLORED)

Adams, Tillie	229 N. Liberty
Allen, Patsy	324 N. Robertson
Allen, Florine	326 N. Robertson
Anthony, Marie	1504 Iberville
Allen, Rosie	1507 Iberville
Anderson, Elizabeth	1402 Bienville
Anderson, Bessie	1523 Bienville
Allen, Frances	1501 Conti
Alapender, Lula	1503 Conti
Anderson, Pauline	1571 Conti
Allen, Maude	1504 Conti

LETTER "B" (COLORED)

Bryant, Mary	227 N. Liberty
Bailey, Bertha	325 N. Liberty
Brown, Alice	322 N. Marais
Berry, Lillie	229 N. Villere
Breaux, Florena	226 N. Robertson
Brown, Mammie	320 N. Robertson
Brown, Bessie	324 N. Robertson
Brown, Mabel	1202 Iberville
Brown, Rosy	1428 Iberville
Burns, Albertha	1516 Iberville
Buce, Ruby	1503 Iberville
Bartholomew, Edna	1511 Iberville
Brants, Lillie	1531 Iberville
Bell, Mabel	1533 Iberville
Brown, Effie	1314 Bienville

102 RANCH CABARET, 206-208 N. Franklin Street
(White)

Annie Godfrey	Marie Lavigne	Lizzie Zimmer
Rosie Morgan	Gertrude Lenoire	Camille Gates
Daisy Wagner	Hattie Allen	Henrietta Penton
Sophie Smith	Gertie Garden	Josephine George

LALA CABARET, 135 N. Franklin Street
(Colored)

Safronice Carter	Jessie Burney	Jane Pinarba
Mandy Taylor	Alma Hughes	Viola Dalfrey

NEW MANHATTAN CABARET, 1500 Iberville St.
(Colored)

Carrie Robertson	Rosie Gibson	Grace Aunt
Carrie White	Anna Mitchell	Lena Leggett
Ella Williams	Rosie Cooper	Hattie Duffau
	Josephine Robertson	

Better known as the "Parisian Queen of America," needs little introduction in this country.

Emma's "Home of All Nations," as it is commonly called, is one place of amusement you can't very well afford to miss while in the District.

Everything goes here. Pleasure is the watchword.

Business has been on such an increase at the above place of late that Mme. Johnson had to occupy an "Annex." Emma never has less than twenty pretty women of all nations, who are clever entertainers.

Remember the name, Johnson's.

Aqui si hable Espanola.

Ici on parle francais.

PHONE CONNECTION

NOWHERE IN this country will you find a more complete and thorough sporting house than the ARLINGTON

Absolutely and unquestionably the most decorative and costly fitted out sporting palace ever placed before the American public.

The wonderful originality of everything that goes to fit out a mansion makes it the most attractive ever seen in this or the old country.

THE ARLINGTON

The Arlington, after suffering a loss of many thousand dollars through a fire, was refurnished and remodeled at an enormous expense, and the mansion is now a palace fit for a king.

Within the great walls of this mansion will be found the work of great artists from Europe and America. Many articles from various expositions will also be seen, and curios galore.

PHONE MAIN 1888

whole affair was a joke, nodded her acceptance to the chief, who rode off. When the chief returned with his warriors and the five ponies, Ada took refuge in a wagon until the chief finally gave up and left. But Ada kept her word about her new profession, for within a week she opened Denver's first house of prostitution. From that day on, every man who met Ada Lamont praised her charms as the most beautiful woman in the Colorado Territory. Her bagnio became known from St. Louis to San Francisco, and most of the new arrivals in town had at least one fling at her house.

Ada's business increased so rapidly that within a year she left her shack on Indian Row and moved into a two-story house on Arapahoe Street, where she could attract a higher-class trade. For ten years, she served the best liquor in Denver, operated a clean and honest house, and amassed a fortune.

But as Ada's career started in tragedy, so did it end. A decade after her husband disappeared, the silent prairie gave up his ghost. A friend of Ada's was returning to Denver from a trip to Kansas when he stumbled upon a human skeleton with a hole in the back of its head, and a bullet still lodged in its skull. In a clump of rotting rags was a small Bible with Ada's handwriting still legible. Ada's unthinking friend brought the Bible back to Denver and returned it to her. The shock was too much for Ada. Almost at once she began to drink. Her old charm rapidly deserted her, and she boarded up her house and moved on from mining camp to mining camp. Eventually she drifted to Georgetown, where in the midst of one of the West's biggest silver booms, she died of starvation.

A few years after Ada Lamont began her decline, wandering, blonde Mattie Silks began her reign as Queen of Denver's red-light section, at one time owning three imposing parlor houses. In March 1884, she paid A. H. Waters & Co. $14,000 cash for the premises on Holladay Street which she was to occupy for a quarter of a century, until she was dethroned as Queen by the dashing brunette, Jennie Rogers. According to historians Parkhill and Bancroft, Jennie was far and away the most beautiful madam in Denver, nearly

*For the dissatisfied customer: a brass "rain" check from
Mattie Silks' parlor house at 1942 Market Street, Denver. The check could also be used as a gift for the
discriminating gentleman.*

six feet tall and well proportioned. Since both Parkhill and
Bancroft write at great length about these two madams, and
a novel has been written about Mattie, we will only mention
them briefly.

Jennie's real name seems not to be known: Parkhill claims
her first name was Sara Jane, but according to one obit-
uary she was Leah J. Tehme, though she spelled it "Leeah."
She married a doctor, but soon found him dull company and
ran away with a steamboat captain named Rogers. In St.
Louis, one of her friends was the chief of police, who, after
Jennie set up her house in Denver, frequently made the long
train trip to spend a few wild nights with her. Jennie coveted
the plush establishment owned by Mattie Silks, and would
have given anything for such an elegant place. Parkhill says
the chief decided to take care of that for his paramour. The
story involves a politically ambitious millionaire, a female's
skull secretly buried in the millionaire's backyard, a rumor
of murder, blackmail, and the final payoff. Bancroft, however, discounts the rumors, and is probably correct in
doing so.

When old and sick with Bright's disease, Jennie went to
Chicago and fell for the blarneying of a young Irishman. She
thought their marriage was on the level, but on learning that
it was not, and that he was just a sharp operator after her
money, she returned to Denver and reopened her brothel.
But Jennie was deathly ill and soon died.

203

Jennie's rival, Mattie Silks, ran houses in the hell-roaring cow towns before she came to Denver in 1873, with her husband, George Silks. He found Denver uncongenial and soon took off for parts unknown. Cortez D. Thompson, a foot racer, was looking for a woman who would take care of him. He liked to spend large sums of money gambling, and was not averse to doing a little pimping, so Mattie took him to her plump bosom.

She loved Cortez fiercely, so fiercely that she fought Katie Fulton for him in the only known formal pistol duel between women. The *Denver News* reported:

> A most disgraceful row occurred late on Friday night at "Denver Park" in which two notorious women of the town, Mattie Silks and Katie Fulton, were principals, with two men, Thatcher and Thompson, seconds, and five or six participants on each side. There were some disfigured faces and broken noses, and Thompson received a pistol wound in the neck, not regarded as serious.

The next morning, Katie took off for Kansas City, but she was back in a few days. On September 7, the *News* reported:

> Katie Fulton felt terribly aggrieved yesterday. After being knocked down and kicked, and having her nose broken, she was yesterday brought before Justice Luthor on a charge of having on the occasion referred to, threatened the life of Mattie Silks. Some tall swearing was done to make the charge stick, but as a number of parties not connected with the crowd in any manner, denied the utterance of the threats on the drawing of the weapon, as alleged, the defendant was discharged, and went on her way rejoicing.

In 1886, madams Mattie Silks, Jennie Rogers, Rosa Lee,

and twelve others described in the *News* as "the giddy girls of Holladay Street" were arrested for conducting lewd houses. Indignant over what they considered an invasion of their constitutional rights, they formed a defense pool, employed a lawyer, and announced they would fight their cases up to the Supreme Court. When Jennie Rogers was brought to trial, the only evidence against her was from "stool pigeons." Her case was dismissed. The jury hearing the evidence against Minnie Clifford could not reach a verdict, so her case was dismissed. Jessie Sampson was found not guilty. Winnie Purdy, Laura Stevens, and Eva Lewis were all found guilty and appealed to the Supreme Court. When the Supreme Court failed to take prompt action, the trial judge dismissed their cases.

Later, after Jennie Rogers' house became more prominent than Mattie's, Mattie took Cortez on a vacation to Europe, after which they went up to the Klondike to see if the gold rush could use her talents. But the climate of the Yukon did not agree with Cortez, so the pair returned to Denver, where Cortez soon died. Mattie then took up with a saloon bouncer named Ready, who had a big diamond set in a front tooth, and married him in 1924, when she was seventy-six. Five years later, Mattie died and was buried in Fairmount Cemetery by the side of Cortez, under the name of Martha A. Ready.

Other noted madams of Denver's early days included May Smith, Belle Jewell, Lizzie Preston, Emma Nelson, Gussie Grant, Emma Lewis, Anna Guy, Marie Putnam, Clara Hayden, Lola Livingston, and Helen McEvoy. Latter-day madams, operating after Holladay Street was renamed Market, included Annie Ryan, Belle Bernard, Jennie Caylor, Clara and Emily Dumont, Lillian Dumont, Leona de Camp, Eva Lewis, Faye Stanley, Minnie Hall, Jennie Holmes, Annie Landeau, and Annie Wilson. The house at 2020 Market was operated for some years by the distinguished-looking, sloe-eyed Verona Baldwin, who figured in a scandal which made the headlines across the West. Verona claimed to be a cousin of the noted California millionaire "Lucky" Baldwin. On Jan-

"Sampling the Wares." A madam looks on as a sporting gentleman plants the kiss of approval on his choice for the night.

uary 4, 1883, she shot him through the left arm, afterwards declaring that he had seduced her and had ruined her "body and mind."

For pure pathos there is no tale like the story of Lois Lovell. Her older sister, Lil, was one of the finest and most magnificent women in the business. Lil showed up in Leadville in 1887, and two years later purchased the finest house of prostitution in the town—Winnie Purdy's. Lil ran the luxurious parlor houses until 1895, when she moved on to Denver. There her younger sister, Lois, joined her. But in the line of duty, Lois met a young Denver businessman and they fell in love. The young man asked her to marry him. Lois refused, knowing his future was bright and her reputation would ruin any career. He pleaded with her, but still she refused. The affair continued, with each party growing more desperate as time passed. The young man, about to leave on a business trip, made one last appeal to Lois, but Lois still felt there was no answer to their problem. After making sure her lover had left on his trip, she took poison and died.

The young man returned to Denver, and hastened to see Lois. He had come up with a solution—they would be married, move to California, and start a new life. At the door of Lil Lovell's parlor house, he was told of Lois' death. Stunned, he sat in the parlor for awhile, then asked the porter to take him to Riverside Cemetery and show him her grave. The young man stood looking at the fresh grave, pulled out a pistol, placed it against his head, pulled the trigger, and fell dead across Lois' grave.

From 1879 to 1887, when Leadville was in full swing with silver pouring out of the surrounding mountains, Mollie May reigned as one of the town's madams. Her house at 144 West Third Street was large and even had a telephone, one of the first in Leadville. The place was so classy that for $10,000 she sold it to the city, which used it as the City Hall. Mollie's former house provided offices for the mayor, city clerk, city council, and the police.

Now Mollie bought the property at 129-131 West Third Street, right next door to Sallie Purple's place of business. It was not long before Sallie and Mollie got into a midnight argument over the relative merits of Connaught and Tipperary as birthplaces. The two women barricaded themselves in their houses and fired round after round of ammunition at each other. The girls and guests from both houses joined in the shooting fray, madly pumping lead into the two houses. After an hour or so, the firing stopped as they waited for daylight. Tempers cooled, and business went on as usual, since miraculously no one was hurt.

In September 1880, Mollie and three other madams were raided by the police. The city collected money for their coffers by fining the houses from $25 to $100 a month, depending on the class of patronage the house received. Seventeen girls were arrested in the raid, and the *Leadville Daily Herald* reported that two young men, seeking to avoid arrest, leaped from the second floor of Mollie's house while the raid was in progress. The girls paid their fines, were released, and promptly went back to business. Then in April and May of 1882, Mollie again made headlines—this time with a baby-buying scandal. Word spread that Mollie was buying a nine-month-old baby girl from a Mr. and Mrs. Moore. On April 30, Mollie gave notice to the *Herald* that the parents of the child were not Mr. and Mrs. Moore, and that "if anyone attempts to interfere with the little one, the real mother will make herself known and show that it is not a subject for public comment." On May 11, Mollie gave an exclusive interview to the *Herald*. She told them she was adopting the baby until the mother, who was a decent but very poor woman, could contact her own mother, tell her of her marriage and the birth of the child, and receive financial assistance. Then the real mother would take the child.

On June 6, 1882, Mollie made the paper once more. She swore a warrant against Annie Layton for stealing a dress from her. Annie, in turn, got a warrant against Mollie for running a house of ill fame. Mollie retaliated with a warrant stating Annie was an inmate of a house of ill fame. The newspaper summed up the situation by saying, "It is likely these charges will be withdrawn, as both parties would be almost unable to prove their charges without incriminating themselves." On June 7, all charges were dropped and Mollie remained out of the papers until her death in 1887.

Cripple Creek, Colorado, created the legend of Pearl DeVere and was her final resting place. Pearl's first house in Cripple Creek was a small one on Myers Avenue, yet her business prospered. The fire of 1896 which swept through Cripple Creek destroyed most of the red-light district, Pearl's house included. But new buildings soon sprang up, and Pearl's place, The Old Homestead, started the whole town talking. The Old Homestead was a two-story brick building with all modern conveniences. The house had electric lights, running water, a telephone, and an intercom system. The bedrooms were heated with small coal stoves, and on the ground floor, the lavish parlor and the entertainment room were warmed with fireplaces. The rates at The Old Homestead were plenty steep, and only those known to Pearl could get in the door.

On June 4, 1897, a Friday night, a party was in full swing at The Old Homestead. Pearl was dressed in a gown imported from Paris that was reported to have cost eight hundred dollars; it was made of shell-pink chiffon encrusted with sequins and seed pearls. The party went on until morning, but Pearl had complained that her nerves were "unstrung" and retired early. The house was quiet until eleven the next morning, when Pearl was found lying on her face, breathing heavily. The doctor arrived and tried to save her, but Pearl had taken an overdose of morphine and died that afternoon at three o'clock.

Pearl DeVere's body, dressed in the exquisite ball gown she wore on the evening before her death, was escorted to Mt. Pisgah cemetery by policemen on horseback, the Elks

"Blind Man's Buff" in a Western bagnio. Later-night frivolities would most likely find the young ladies upstairs in the buff.

Club band, and buggies filled with the girls from the line. After the brief service, the band returned to town playing, "There'll Be a Hot Time in the Old Town Tonight."

While it was common knowledge that large quantities of champagne and wine were sold in the parlor houses, few people realize that this revenue often surpassed the profits from prostitution. It was not widely known that for many years, until the advent of Prohibition, many wine agents were the leading backers of the best houses. Often they supplied the initial costs of the first year's rent and furnishings, payment for the unofficial license to operate, and bail if the madam happened to be arrested. These funds were strictly a loan which had to be repaid, but the agents' only "interest" charge was that the house use their brand of wine and theirs only. This arrangement was common in El Paso in 1883, when the bordellos spruced up so much that they began advertising themselves as "Parlour Houses." The larger places were elaborately decorated with carved furniture, velvet drapes, full-length mirrors, and plush rugs. All of them employed full-time housekeeping staffs; some even hired an orchestra.

The first of the madams to arrive in El Paso was the aforementioned Big Alice Abbott. Said to be from a good family, well-educated, and the one-time wife of a Louisville lawyer, Alice never told why she became a madam. The six-foot beauty set up shop on Utah Street, where a blast from her whistle brought her quick protection from the police station a block away. Alice's house was comfortable, well staffed, and boasted a carriage house which held a fancy rig and a team of high-stepping white horses.

Four other madams followed Big Alice and settled nearby on Utah Street. Tillie Howard and her man, gambler Rufe Nemo, built a copper-roofed house which was regarded as one of El Paso's showplaces. Tillie was the most refined and considerate of the madams, for she gave her girls a regular salary instead of a commission. Redheaded, hot-tempered Etta "Grasshopper" Clark—Alice Abbott's adversary in the "public arch" shootout—settled on the corner of Utah and Second Streets in a $75,000, thirty-two room house with solid mahogany furniture. The other two madams, May Palmer and Gypsy Davenport, did not operate such fancy houses, but they supplied all the usual comforts.

These houses boarded anywhere from twenty to thirty girls of all nationalities, with the French beauties rated as the "pros." All were bedizened in fancy gowns, boas, heavy perfume, and make-up, "rats" in their hair, and "gay deceivers." These falsies were made of fine wire intricately woven into the proper shape, with small springs to give natural bounce and lifelike appearance and touch. Most of the girls smoked small cigars and drank as much as they could.

By 1905, open vice disappeared from the streets of El Paso as most of the gamblers went to Juarez. The red-light district was forced to move closer to the Rio Grande, at 8th and Chihuahua Streets. In the early '20s, the houses were closed for good, with many of the girls crossing to Juarez, which was still wide open.

In 1872, Annie McIntyre was twelve when her father's luck ran out and he was killed in a street brawl. Growing up an orphan in Rocky Bar, Idaho, dependent on charity, life was miserable, but Annie developed into a beautiful young woman. Before she was eighteen, she married Bill Morrow. By the time Annie was thirty-five, however, she was a widow with two sons. Despondent, Annie began drinking heavily, so her late husband's relatives took the boys away from her. Nearly destitute, she crossed Bald Mountain to the small town of Atlanta, where she opened a bordello in Red Light Alley.

Late in March 1898, she set out on snowshoes to cross back over Bald Mountain to Rocky Bar to attend a big spring dance. Emma Von Losch, a big German strumpet called Dutch Em, went with her. A blizzard was in the making when Mailman Tate passed them five miles out of Atlanta. When he met the Rocky Bar carrier at the summit, he was told a bad storm was brewing. Tate looked for Dutch Em and Annie on his return trip, but failed to find any sign of them as he hurried on to Atlanta in the storm. Three days later, when the storm was over, a search party was organized in Atlanta and a dozen Rocky Bar men set out to find the

211

two women. The rescue party from Atlanta was spread out across the northern slope, but it took the men a while before they found Annie crawling around on her hands and knees.

The warm, fur-trimmed coat she was wearing when she left Atlanta was gone, as were her woolen underskirts. A thin dress was all she wore against the icy blasts which swept the mountain. Annie had given her coat and underskirts to Dutch Em, who was freezing to death. The men roped Annie down to a sled and started for Atlanta at once, while others remained on the slope to search for Dutch Em. When the men reached Atlanta with Annie, they brought her immediately to the doctor, who was forced to amputate both her frostbitten feet just above the ankles. Before long, though, Annie was getting about on her own and could hop into a chair with the agility of a cat.

Dutch Em's lifeless body was found and buried in Atlanta's small cemetery. A fund was started by Annie's friend Henry Longheme, an Italian saloonkeeper, to provide her with a set of artificial feet. With his assistance, she opened a combination rooming house and restaurant where they lived together for twenty-two years. Annie managed to save between eleven and twelve thousand dollars which she gave Henry to deposit in her name in a San Francisco bank. Henry wrote her once from New York, but she never heard from him again. It was rather obvious that he had made off with her savings, but she refused to believe it. Peg-leg Annie Morrow died in Mountain Home in 1935.

Pearl Starr, daughter of Belle Starr and the famous outlaw Cole Younger, was born in Texas in 1867. She lived with her mother until Belle died in 1889, whereupon she married Will Harrison. Life with honest Will was too tame, and she soon deserted him. For a time, Pearl lived in Van Buren, Arkansas, across the river from Fort Smith, with her half-brother Eddie. In 1891, he was sentenced to the Ohio State Penitentiary for seven years. Shortly after that, Madame Van's bordello had a new "boarder," who called herself Rosa Reed. Pearl, now twenty-four, was far more attractive than her mother, and quickly became Van Buren's most popular tart.

212

"Peg Leg" Annie Morrow gained her epithet after losing both of her feet to frostbite during a blizzard. But her unselfish sacrifice during the storm moved the men of Atlanta, Idaho, to come to her aid.

But the big money was across the river in Fort Smith, so Pearl hoarded her earnings for the day when she could open her own house in the Border City's red-light district. A few months later, in November, Pearl leased the house at 25 Water Street, where she held forth as a prostitute and madam for twenty-three years. The first thing she did upon establishing her own house was to drop the pseudonym Rosa Reed and boldly state that she was Pearl Starr, daughter of Belle Starr. This certainly had commercial value, and she made the most of it. The long-established madams such as Maud McGrath, Dot Parker and Laura Ziegler would have resented the intrusion of anyone else into their territory. Instead, they helped her to recruit "boarders" from Hot Springs and Memphis. There was business enough for all, since Fort

213

Smith, a wild, lawless town situated on the edge of the frontier, attracted thousands of desperate men.

Fort Smith had ordinances against bawdy houses and streetwalkers, but instead, the madams and their "boarders" paid a weekly tax, and streetwalkers were fined five dollars whenever they were arrested for soliciting. As the outcry of respectable citizens mounted, new ordinances were passed, one of them making it a crime for prostitutes to loiter in the city cemetery, which was a favorite place for the streetwalker to take a man. The reform element demanded the removal of a garish star-shaped sign Pearl had put up on the front of her house. Outlined in red and white electric lights, the star could be seen from a block away, blazing its obscene welcome. Pearl refused to take it down.

The girl on the right is Pearl Starr, daughter of Belle Starr and the famed outlaw Cole Younger. For 23 years, Pearl was the gem of Fort Smith, Arkansas.

Pearl was a heavy drinker—she consumed a lot of liquor and she weighed two hundred pounds—yet on June 29, 1894, she gave birth to a girl, father unnamed, whom she named Ruth Reed. Four years later, at St. John's Hospital, Pearl gave birth to a son, Arthur E. Erbach. The birth certificate named E. Erbach, a German musician, as the father, and Rosa P. Reed as the mother. Three weeks after the birth of his son, "Count" Erbach died of typhoid-malaria. Pearl erected an eight-foot-high monument over his grave in Oak Cemetery, where in less than a year little Arthur was buried beside him.

Then on November 8, 1902, Pearl Starr became a mother again, calling the baby girl Jennette Andrews. Her father was Dell Andrews, a well-known Fort Smith gambler who left town with the arrival of the baby. No fault can be found with the way Pearl cared for her two little girls. When Jennette was old enough to begin school, Pearl took her and Ruth to St. Louis and placed them in a convent.

During the next five years in Fort Smith, Pearl was in and out of court so often and spent so much money for lawyers that she fell heavily into debt. During the last week of February 1916, she was arrested and put in jail. Now she was finished as a sporting-house madam in Fort Smith. She told her attorney she was willing to leave town if the charges against her were dropped. Now forty-nine years old and banished from Fort Smith, Pearl went to Hot Springs, then Denver, and then San Francisco. She died of a stroke on July 6, 1925, in Douglas, Arizona, where her daughter Ruth had been living with her. To avoid publicity, Ruth and Jennette buried their mother as Rosa Reed.

Laura Evans was one of the last scarlet women to join the ranks of Colorado's madams, and when she died in April of 1953 she was over nintey years old. According to Laura, she grew up in the South, married at age seventeen, deserted her husband and baby daughter, changed her name, and became a prostitute in St. Louis. Laura was about twenty-five when she hit Denver's Market Street like a bombshell, making caustic comments about the houses run by Jennie Rogers and Mattie Silks. After a few years, she graduated to Leadville where the silver was pouring out of the mines by the ton. She was popular, vital, vigorous, and determined to gain plenty of money to indulge her tastes.

Laura was flamboyant, and learned early in the game that it paid to advertise. She kept her name in the news by her wild escapades, and before long she was known from coast to coast. Leadville will never forget two of her capers. When the circus came to town she offered a circus worker a bucket of beer to lend her and her friend, Spuddy, a pair of brightly gilded Roman chariots. Each chariot was hitched to three of the circus' best horses, in Roman style, for the girls' chariot race. Laura and Spuddy raced with frantic speed down Harrison Street, banging the gongs on the front of the chariots and scattering people to safety. Laura turned a corner too sharply, smashed into a telephone pole, and lost a wheel, thus ending her brief career as a female Ben Hur. The law arrived, but released the pair with only a scolding.

Laura's enthusiasm for fast horses was still high. For the site of her next wild ride, she chose the famous Ice Palace, constructed in 1869 from blocks of beautifully carved ice by the proud citizens of Leadville. Laura hitched a nag called Broken Tail Charlie to a phaeton on runners, and then she and Spuddy plunged straight into the elaborate Norman structure, leaving a trail of cracked ice and destruction in their wake. Finally Broken Tail Charlie broke loose, headed back for the barn, and left Laura and Spuddy buried in the debris.

But Laura was good for more than a laugh. A strike occurred at the Maid of Erin mine, as a heavy guard of union sympathizers, armed with Winchesters, encircled the mine and stopped all traffic. The mine owners could not bring in the payroll, so they asked Laura if she could smuggle it in to the superintendent. Laura agreed, fastened the canvas bag with twenty-seven thousand dollars to the inside of her skirt, and rode off up Carbonate Hill. When a picket stopped her and asked where she was going, Laura answered, "The Maid of Erin mine. I want to see a friend that you fellows won't let come down to town."

Laura's part in the Maid of Erin strike led to her being

blacklisted by the miners' union, so toward the end of 1896, she left Leadville for Salida, Colorado, a bus rail center on the Rio Grande Railroad. She was an immediate success in her elaborate new house. Her girls were the best lookers in the West, and she "outfitted them in the prettiest silks and boarded them in the plushest rooms." Laura carried her money in a silk purse high on her left leg, while her girls "wore silk garters embellished with ten dollar gold pieces, locked on their thighs with gold lock and chain." Although Laura prided herself on her graduation from the ranks, she remained available—for a price—and hers was the last house to close in Colorado, lasting until 1950.

In addition to the glamourous madams of the Old West there were the female gamblers and card sharps. One rough-and-tumble woman typical of this period was Kitty Le Roy, who started as a jig dancer at the age of ten in Dallas, Texas. Kitty turned her talents to dealing faro, and in the 1870's she dealt the pasteboards in Dakota's Black Hills. She attracted her share of attention around Deadwood with her extravagant gypsylike costumes. Kitty was a starry beauty with her thick and curling brown hair and immense diamonds in her ears. She had five husbands, seven revolvers, a dozen Bowie knives, and always went around armed like a gun-fighter. More men were killed over her than over all the other women in the hills put together, and the question was whether her lovers killed off each other, or whether she herself had

During her heyday, Laura Evans rode a chariot down the main street of Leadville, Colorado, scattering pedestrians to safety. In 1950, she became the last Colorado madam to close up shop. This picture of Laura was taken near the end of her reign.

killed them. Kitty married her first husband because he had the nerve to let her shoot an apple off his head while she rode by on a horse at full speed. On one occasion, she dressed in male attire to fight a man who refused to duel with a woman. When he fell, she cried and married him just in time to become his widow.

Kitty's gambling hall in Deadwood was called "The Mint," which she used to attract husbands as well as money. One victim was a German prospector who struck an unusually rich vein. She made a play for him, took him for eight thousand dollars in gold, and when his claim failed, crowned his cranium with a bottle and sent him packing. But at the age of twenty-eight, Kitty met her doom in her last husband, for he beat her to the draw, shot her dead, then dramatically killed himself.

Belle Siddons came from Missouri, where during the first year of the Civil War she danced with and was escorted by officers of the Union Army. In the course of various social occasions, military secrets slipped out which she passed along to the Confederacy. In 1862, she was captured and sent to prison. After four months, Belle was released from prison, on her promise she would not return to Missouri until after the war. She held her end of the bargain, then returned to her hometown of Jefferson City, Missouri, and met Mr. Newton Hallett, an Army surgeon. They were married and moved to Texas, where the Yellow Fever epidemic of 1869 took the doctor's life. Belle was left to care for herself, but she had picked up some medicinal background from her husband, and she was a top-notch gambler. She began dealing twenty-one in Wichita, Kansas, and soon changed her name to Madame Vestal. Constantly moving from place to place, she ran a tented gambling hall in Denver in 1875-76, then followed the crowds to Deadwood, the new mecca.

Madame Vestal took her employees, her tent, and her gambling equipment with her in a luxurious omnibus. Once her tent was set up in the heart of Deadwood's red-light district, she changed her name to Lurline Monte Verde. Lurline soon met Archie McLaughlin, a stage robber, and fell in love with him. Archie and his gang prospered until 1878, when several of his men were wounded during a holdup. Lurline went to their hideout to help. They tried a getaway, but were captured. On the way back to Deadwood for trial, the stage carrying the prisoners was stopped, and the men were taken out and hanged.

Archie's death was Lurline's downfall, for she began drinking and drifting—first to Leadville in 1879, next to Las Vegas, then to Tombstone, and finally to San Francisco. In October, 1881, she was arrested and jailed in San Francisco. She was far from destitute, but her health had been destroyed by alcohol. In jail, the record of Belle Siddons—Mrs. Hallet— Madame Vestal—Lurline Monte Verde ended.

The old saying, "Lucky at cards, unlucky at love," held good for "Poker Alice," a young Suffolk, England, girl who became the acknowledged Queen of the Western gamblers. She smoked long black cheroots and packed a sixshooter she was not in the least reluctant to use. Alice Ivers was born on February 17, 1851, the daughter of a local schoolteacher. An intelligent and extremely likable girl, she was twelve when her family came to Richmond, Virginia, in 1863. Alice was educated in the exclusive Southern school where her father taught. When the Confederacy surrendered two years later, the Ivers family moved out west to Colorado.

In her early twenties, Alice married a young mining engineer named Duffield and settled in Lake City, Colorado. Here she first tasted gambling and started making money with her new-found hobby. Her good-looking husband was killed in a mine cave-in less than a year after their marriage, leaving Alice alone and destitute. Now she began devoting her full time to what she enjoyed most—gambling. She was a natural-born calculator, and her long slim fingers manipulated the cards deftly and surely. Night after night, she sat playing faro with the best. For a few years, she drifted from one Colorado mining town to another—Alamosa, Leadville, Georgetown, Central City—and then to Clifton, Arizona, during its heyday.

After a successful stay in Deadwood, Alice moved on to Silver City, New Mexico, where new mines were producing large amounts of bullion. She arrived with only $10.00 in her pocket and went into the first saloon she came to. Walking up to the faro table, she risked the gold piece. She won! So she bet again. Almost every time she bet, she won. Soon the other players dropped out, leaving only Alice and the dealer. Eventually he lost his nerve and declared the faro bank closed. She had made $10,000 in less than three hours of play. From Silver City she went to Leadville, where she lost all her money, but in Central City she won it back.

A dealer in a Pecos, Texas, saloon once thought he had found an easy mark in the little blonde woman with the English accent. Alice caught him dealing off the bottom of the deck. For a few hands she watched him closely as he cheated. Suddenly Alice pushed back her chair, raked in the "pot" with her left hand and pulled out her gun with her right. Alice hauled in about $5,000, which was enough for a week-long spending spree in New York. She bought clothes and jewelry and dined in the fancy restaurants until she had only enough money for a return ticket West. She came back broke, but happy. "Easy come, easy go" soon became the pattern of her life: a big win in the West followed by a big binge in the East.

The little woman with the neat blonde hair, blue eyes and deadpan expression became a familiar figure in every boomtown between St. Louis and San Francisco, and from Canada to the Rio Grande. She always carried her Colt and stuck a long black cheroot in the side of her mouth.

When Alice was forty-two and back in Deadwood, she worked in a saloon alongside the other "house gambler," William G. Tubbs. One day a drunken miner accused the unarmed Tubbs of cheating and drew his Bowie knife. As the miner lunged, a single shot rang out. The prospector dropped the knife and grabbed his arm, cursing wildly. Poker Alice was standing at her table, a wisp of smoke curling from the barrel of her sixgun. Alice married Tubbs and they retired to a small homestead forty-eight miles west of Sturgis, South Dakota. There they adopted seven children who had been orphaned, and raised chickens on their land.

During the blizzard of 1910, Tubbs died of pneumonia,

With a Colt at her side and a black cheroot in her mouth, "Poker Alice" Tubbs was the acknowledged queen of Western gamblers. This picture shows Alice shortly before her death in 1930.

so Alice put the body on a sleigh and dragged it through the snow drifts into Sturgis. She pawned her engagement ring for twenty-five dollars to pay for his burial. After Tubbs was interred, Alice went to the local saloon where she earned back her $25.00. Soon she was back on her farm with her gold ring back on her finger. Alice decided to hire a man named George Huckert to manage the tiny ranch. Times were hard and money was scarce. Huckert's wages piled up and up, until it became cheaper to marry him than to pay him off. They soon separated, however, and Alice went back to the gaming tables. She began playing poker more than faro, and acquired the nickname of "Poker Alice."

After coming out of retirement, Poker Alice set up a place of her own where men could gamble and have some female companionship afterward. She closed her house on Sundays, being a very religious person, and made the girls in her establishment attend the Sunday School lessons she taught. In her long career as a gambler, she had never worked on Sundays, and did not plan to change now. The soldiers at Fort Meade visited Poker Alice's place in droves the other six days of the week. One night, a bunch of drunken troopers

221

demanded to be let in after closing time. Poker Alice got her gun and told them to go away and then fired through the door. She heard a dull thud as a trooper from Company K, Fourth Cavalry, fell dead in the doorway. At her trial Alice was found guilty, but she was released by a judge who could not find it in his heart to send a white-haired old lady to jail.

Not too long after this, the reformers in the town had Alice arrested for running a disorderly house. She was found guilty and convicted, but her friends petitioned the governor and she was released. At last, she closed her place, and bought a small house in Sturgis.

She became more religious and read the Bible even more. She loved to reminisce about the past. At seventy-four she said, "I would rather play poker with five or six experts than eat." It was a tourist who found the little old lady bedridden and dying early in 1930. Poker Alice was rushed to the local hospital and died on the operating table at seventy-nine.

Among Poker Alice's contemporaries, were Kitty the Schemer, Air-ship Annie, China Mary, Haltershanks Eve, Bow-legged Mary, Faro Nell, Prairie Rose, and the Iowa Bull. As gamblers they were never too successful, for as Poker Alice claimed, they could not control their emotions. But Prairie Rose could always win a bet when she had to. She was well endowed with natural assets which she freely displayed after laying down a bet that she could walk stark naked down the main street of a Kansas cow town. And she made certain the loser paid off, for though she was undraped, she carried a loaded pistol in each hand.

Northern Lights

In 1898, DAWSON CITY in the Yukon Territory was the heart of the richest gold country on the continent. To its theaters and dance halls the miners came for relief from the long, lonely hours spent working on their claims. They laughed, drank, and threw their gold dust recklessly about. The amenities offered in Dawson City were few, but basic: drink, a woman, and a place to unload his gold dust. Every other building carried the sign, "Gold Dust Bought," while the rest catered to his sensual needs.

Mattie Silks, the notorious Denver courtesan, was on board the *Susie* on the last down-river trip of the 1898 season. She was leaving Dawson because her gambler-lover, Cortez Thompson, could not stand the bitter rain and snow of the Klondike. Mattie and Cortez had come to Dawson City figuring that the special merchandise Mattie offered was in far greater demand in the northern reaches than in Denver. The Dawson City Mattie found looked much the same as the towns of the American prairie and Rockies. Built on a flat in a bend of the river, Dawson was a collection of hastily erected log and frame shanties, a little larger than its neighbor, Lousetown.

Jenkins, proprietor of the Sour Dough saloon, rented Mattie a good-sized frame building on Second Street for $350.00 a month. Her leading competitor was Beatrice Larne. Mattie's expenses were high, but her total receipts were enormous. Each of her girls was earning about fifty dollars a day,

Off to the gold fields! Women joined the men in the frenzied march to the Klondike in 1898. This trio posed in Dyea for a photograph before taking foot on the Chilkoot Pass. Once in Dawson, the young lady would find easier ways to dig gold than panning the creeks.

This tent-and-cabin mudhole was Dawson City, Yukon, in 1897. A year later, Dawson was the heart of the richest gold country on the continent.

even after paying Mattie her fifty per cent of the take plus board. Mattie's sales of liquid refreshments brought huge profits, for she sold champagne for thirty dollars a quart with the boarder's cut on each being only five dollars. Whiskey was fifty cents a shot, but there was no beer or gin in Dawson. Most of the whiskey was made from grain alcohol which cost sixty dollars a gallon; when diluted and colored and sold by the drink, the gallon brought in over $130.

Mattie brought along the old gold scales she once used at

Georgetown and a little square of thick carpet to catch the dust which spilled from the scales. As usual, Cortez was no help with the business, because he spent most of his time playing faro at Joe Cooper's Dominion Saloon. Late in the summer, Cortez developed a heavy cold and treated it with his favorite remedy, whiskey. Mattie, too, couldn't stand the constant downpour which left Dawson's streets ankle-deep in mud. All around her, Mattie saw evidence of colds which developed into pneumonia, and she dreaded the approach of the long Arctic winter. She wanted to go home to Denver, so she squared up Cortez's gambling debts and booked passage on the *Susie,* taking back a net profit of $38,000 for her ninety days at Dawson City.

In *High Jinks on the Klondike,* Richard O'Connor tells of the Alaska-bound voyage of the steamer *Amur* in 1897 when, crowded among the 500 passengers, were fifty sporting women. Some of them were young and comely, but most were experienced, hardhearted harpies. When warned not to ply their trade onboard ship, the "fractious and unhappy" bawds railed at the officer and crew and snarled their curses at the passengers. One of the loudest complainers, Big Annie, was calmed down by one of the clergymen aboard who told her: "Indeed it's shameful, the conditions aboard this ship. But try to bear it. We'll all be in Skagway in little more than a week, and once there you'll see that things will be a whole lot better for you and the other girls." Big Annie was flabbergasted to hear a man of the cloth say that a licentious life ashore would be "better" than a continent life aboard ship, and she shut up for the rest of the voyage.

By the end of the summer of the following year, all the paddlewheel steamers on the Yukon River were overloaded with soiled doves, dance-hall queens, and whiskey from the Barbary Coast. Among the more curious feminine specimens in the far North was Calamity Jane, by this time a living ghost who could not reconcile herself to the closing of the Western frontier. Age and disillusion had caught up with her, but she still wanted someplace where the churchgoers, the grocers, the mining companies, and the women's clubs had not ruined the frontier spirit. So Jane came to the Klondike, took a quick look around, and decided the Yukon was not for her; perhaps the Arctic cold got into her aging bones, or perhaps Dawson City just wasn't wild enough for a veteran of Deadwood.

Susie Bluenose, on the other hand, found the Yukon gold rush too wild for her taste. When Susie showed up at the mission at Golovin Bar near Nome to take over the secretarial work, she noticed Nelly Page's roadhouse nearby. It soon became the object of Susie's reforming urge. A thirtyish spinster who dressed in black, the aptly named Miss Bluenose came every night to deliver a temperance lecture. Nelly Page, realizing that Susie was driving away the paying customers, ordered her Indian boys to guard the door and bar Susie's entry. It worked quite well until the night Rex Beach, his partner, Federal Commissioner Nudd and U.S. Marshal Lamont dropped in for a drinking and singing session. Nelly's sentinels had fallen asleep at their post, and Susie managed to breach the defenses. She burst into the barroom and screamed, "Stop that music!" Rex Beach was playing his mandolin. Nelly told him to play louder, and she resumed dancing with Marshal Lamont.

Susie jumped up on a chair and shouted, "You blackguards, you roistering scoundrels, you're all going to roast in hell. Do you know that?" Then she jumped down off the chair and shouldered her way over to Nelly. "Young woman," Susie yelled, "if this racket is not stopped at once I'm going to have this den of iniquity closed immediately. I am going to report you to the United States Marshal!"

The music and dancing stopped. There was a deathly silence as Marshal Lamont disengaged himself from Nelly, marched over to Susie, and bowed gallantly. "I am at your service, Madame. Would you care to dance?"

She fled into the cold Arctic night and never again visited Nelly Page's roadhouse.

In the spring rush of 1897, Gussie Lamore, a comely dance-hall girl of nineteen, came to Dawson City from Circle

City. Gussie happened to love fresh eggs, possibly because they were both expensive and scarce. One day her gambler friend, Swiftwater Bill, was seated in a restaurant when, to his surprise and chagrin, he saw Gussie enter, clutching the arm of another well-known gambler. The pair ordered fried eggs. In a jealous fury, Swiftwater achieved legendary immortality by going out and buying up every egg in Dawson to frustrate Gussie. There are several versions of the conclusion to the tale. One says that Swiftwater returned to the cafe, had the eggs fried one at a time, and flipped them through the window to a pack of dogs, all the while commenting to the gathering crowd on the mutts' cleverness in catching the eggs on the fly. In other versions, Swiftwater either presented the eggs to Gussie as a grand gesture of his true emotions, or invited the other dance-hall girls to share the eggs with him.

In Dawson dance halls, the miners paid a dollar for a drink and a dance. They danced in their dirty mackinaws, muddy boots, and mukluks, and the music never stopped, day or night. The wages for common labor were from ten to twenty dollars a day—a lot of money in that era. But the cost of living insured that no laborer would become rich: lumber cost $250 a thousand board feet; eggs were ten dollars a dozen; oysters cost a dollar each; potatoes from the Stewart River nearby were fifty dollars a sack; condensed milk was four dollars a quart! Moose meat, dark and coarse, was reasonable in price while caribou, sweet and tender, was very dear. When a fella was able to save up a few dollars, after months of arduous work on a creek, he might blow the whole poke of dust for the pleasures of a night or two with a Dawson City girl. Marriage was virtually out of the question, for if the girl was young, she was a more valuable piece of property than any gold mine. Once in a while, however, the tables were nicely turned. Such was the case with a Klondiker nicknamed Dog-tooth Harry.

Harry was truly ugly, even by Yukon standards, and a girl had to be very drunk or very broke before she would look a second time at him. But Harry was a serious-minded man who wanted more than a quick tumble—he wanted to get married. He had been rebuffed by countless girls whom he had approached with the suggestion.

One day, he fell head over heels in love with a Dawson dance-hall girl who was better looking than most. Her prices for after-hours fun were high—so high that she scared away far more men than she hooked. Dog-tooth Harry's proposal of marriage made her laugh. He offered her a home, comfort, security, and a change from her present life. She continued to reject him, sparing no conceivable insult to his looks.

One day, after she had dismissed Harry from her thoughts, she publicly announced she was worth her weight in gold dust and would sell herself for such a price and not an ounce less. Hearing this, Dog-tooth Harry snatched the bawd off the dance-hall floor and carried her to the nearest store bearing the sign, "Gold dust bought." Dropping her onto one pan, he slung weights onto the other, finding she tipped

"Snake Hips Lulu" in her working clothes. No, she didn't work on the stage, but graced a Klondike dance hall in her rather theatrical garb.

229

the scale at 142 pounds or $24,424. She was still spitting and screaming as he left her to climb off the scales. Harry ran back to his shack, pulled out his pokes from their secret hiding place, and returned to the store. He had the proprietor weigh out 142 pounds, and exchange it for $24,424 in bills. Cash in hand, he returned to the dance hall and the girl.

Now, as expected, she swiftly changed her tune. $24,424 was a lot of money, even in Dawson. Dog-tooth was now her hero, for he accepted her on her own statement of worth. She declared that she had never meant to insult him, that she had been joking with him all along. She threw her arms around Harry's neck and offered him her painted lips to seal the bargain. Dog-tooth threw off her clutching hands and looking her full in the eye, he thrust the wad of bills into his inner pocket, spat contemptuously between her feet, and walked out.

Altercations between dance-hall girls and their patrons were nowhere as frequent as spats within the ranks of the charmers. A clawing, eye-scratching, hair-pulling fight between the entertainers was itself one of the more cherished forms of entertainment in the streets of Dawson. One memorable tiff involved Bertha the Adder and Seattle Emily. Bertha was so incensed that she tore off all Emily's clothes in the brawl on the riverfront, then chased her through town, pelting her naked hide with rocks.

Another celebrated encounter "starred" Nellie the Pig, an attractive young dance-hall girl whose sobriquet was conferred on her by the Klondikers in honor of her turned-up nose. Nellie's opponents were "The Petite Sisters Pickering," who specialized in toe dancing and ballads. In passing Nellie on the street, the sisters twitched their skirts aside with such a disdainful flourish that Nellie became enraged. Angry words were exchanged, and the Pickerings advanced to attack Nellie from both flanks. However, the sisters ran into such a furious buzzsaw that they were unable to manage even a clumsy pirouette for a month.

230

Lusty, brawling Dawson City was the mecca of the sourdoughs swarming over the Yukon in search of gold, but many

A Klondike dance-hall
beauty.

Klondike dance-hall girls during one of their more peaceful moments, a
"drinking party." On other occasions, they were known to engage in eye-
scratching, hair-pulling brawls in the streets of Dawson City.

a man is said to have come north only for a glimpse of the fabulous Klondike Kate. Kate, née Kathleen Rockwell, with her sweet heart-shaped face and vivacious smile, was a girl to make the gold-rushers forget the lonely creeks and the empty pans. When she did her famous Flame Dance, swathed in chiffon and floating through colored lights, the cheering miners literally paved the stage of the Savoy Theater with gold dust.

Kate was a dancing girl with a heart, for if a sourdough grew careless with drink, she guarded his nugget-filled poke and saw that he got it back reasonably full. Many a miner down on his luck got a grubstake and a fresh start from her earnings. Kate took in as much as $750 in gold in a single night, and amassed a fortune of $100,000 in just a few years. But she lost it all, in a way that was typical of her romantic temperament: she lavished her love and her money on a slick-haired man who left her in the lurch.

In 1905, Alexander Pantages, the theater magnate who got his start as a waiter in Dawson, found himself sued for breach of promise by Kate Rockwell. Though Pantages, a Greek immigrant, could hardly speak the language when he arrived in Dawson, it was not long before he was operating the Orpheum Theater. In 1900 he became enamored of Kate, who was a vision in her $1,500 Parisian gown, belt of twenty-dollar gold pieces, and headdress of lighted candles. According to Kate's sworn testimony, she bought Pantages seventy-five cent cigars and fifteen dollar silk shirts, and when they left Dawson together in 1901, she paid all the traveling expenses. In the 1905 suit, Kate asked for $25,000, but the theater magnate settled out of court for less than $5,000. Pantages went on to build his theater chain into a $15,000,000 asset, but died a broken man in 1936 after two lengthy courtroom bouts. He was found guilty of attempted rape, and in an unrelated case, his wife was convicted of second-degree murder, the result of an auto accident. Both verdicts were ultimately reversed by higher courts, but Pantages was ruined.

Once, when Kate was doing her dance at the Savoy, she spied a blond young miner watching her intently from a position against the wall. She asked him for a dance, but he

232

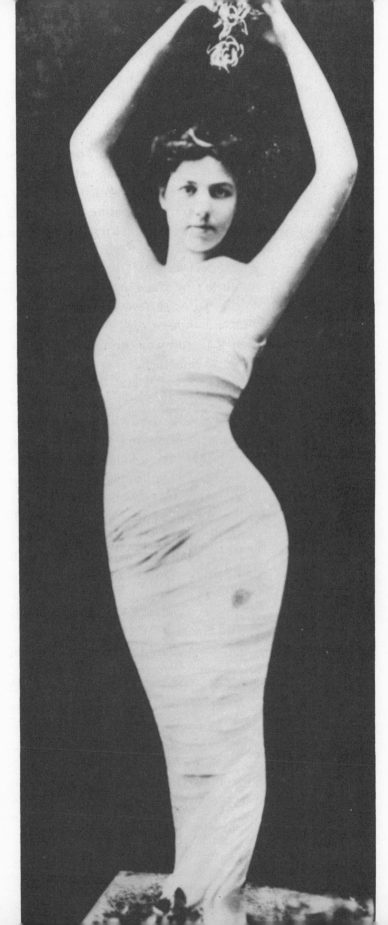

Many a man was said to have come north to Dawson only for a glimpse of Klondike Kate, one of the most famous Klondike dance-hall girls. Her death in 1957 was noted in both News-week and Time.

was shy, and after a while he disappeared. Thirty-three years later, long after Kate had retired and settled in Oregon, she received a letter from the blond miner, whose name was John Matson, telling her he had loved her from the first moment he saw her. The two were married, though Matson remained in the Klondike until he died. After the Pantages scandal, Kate capitalized on the publicity and became a favorite of newsmen and feature writers as Klondike Kate.

Some years ago, at a reunion of Yukon sourdoughs in Portland, the toastmaster introduced Kate as the guest of honor with these words: "She was the girl we young miners dreamed of, sitting by the fire in our lonely cabins on the frozen creeks. To us she was laughter and beauty and song. She was forgetfulness of hardship and homesickness. But more than that, she was our friend—a square shooter." In 1957, Klondike Kate died in her sleep; her passing was duly noted by both *Newsweek* and *Time*.

Two of the really ferocious dance-hall girls were called the Oregon Mare and the Grizzly Bear. Neither could be described as pretty; the Grizzly's appearance was really fearsome because she had had one eye gouged out in a fight. The continued presence of these two in the dance halls was due to the simple fact that men were afraid to turn them down for a drink and dance. When annoyed, the Oregon Mare kicked her antagonist repeatedly on the shins with sharp pointed shoes. The Grizzly Bear's technique was even more painful. A "mountain of a woman," with arms and shoulders like a stevedore, she would grab and hug her victim until his ribs cracked.

It wasn't hard to understand why these two terrors were so determined to hold onto their jobs, for a dance-hall girl raked in a lot of loot for swinging around the floor with the bearded, sweaty, and odiferous men. The lusty polkas, quadrilles, and waltzes were exhausting, but most of the girls were brawny amazons who could take the punishment. The dance halls paid the girls a salary of about $50 a week, in addition to which the dancers received twenty-five cents out of every dollar spent by their partners. Thus, most girls col-

234

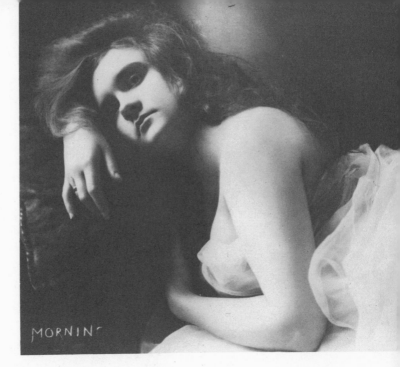

"Morning" for this Klondike girl meant the end of the day, not the beginning.

MORNIN'

lected about $200 a week. Besides, since the dance-hall girls had the first crack at the sourdough, there was always the possibility of marrying one who had struck it rich out on the creeks. One prospector from Chicago became so enthused by the charms of one of the girls that he hurled a poke of nuggets at her as she spun around the dance floor. Unfortunately, the gold-filled sack broke her cheekbone. The contrite prospector lolled around his loved one during her traumatic illness and, when she recovered, found himself taking vows before a preacher.

The Klondikers were starved for entertainment of any kind, after the long hard months on the trail north. The actresses, dancers, and singers of Dawson were accorded all the respect they deserved or demanded. Female performers could be divided roughly into three classifications: the dramatic actresses, the flashier girls who simply sang and danced, and the variety girls who worked in the lowest-class music halls and visited with the customers after their turns on stage. The same men who made lewd suggestions to the skimpily clad girls of the rougher establishments would sit like obedient children for a sentimental act, then empty their pockets

An 1899 photograph of Klondike Belle, one of the Dawson girls who dug gold from the gold-diggers.

in appreciation. At one performance, Monte Snow and his sister picked up $142 thrown on the stage for their dancing and singing. Nine-year-old Little Margie Newman, "The Princess of the Klondike," invariably stood heel-deep in nuggets after she rendered a sentimental ballad. One man was so moved by her performance that he wrote a poem about her which ended:

God bless you, Little Margie, for you made better men.
God bless you, Little Margie, for you take us home again.

On the day Margie left town, Frank Conrad of the claim Eleven Eldorado tore off his solid gold watch and nugget chain and tossed them to her on the steamer's deck. She smiled, so he pulled out a fifty-dollar bill, wrapped it around a silver dollar, and threw it to her. She smiled again, and he produced a hundred-dollar bill, wrapped a silver dollar in it, and heaved it to the deck for the reward of a third smile.

Cad Wilson was no beauty, and she could not sing. Yet her personality was such that the miners threw nuggets and gold watches onto the stage as she ran about laughing and picking up the loot, all the while holding her dress up to display her skinny legs. Eddie Dolan, the stage-manager at the Tivoli, would close her act by pretending he was reading a letter from Cad's mother which said in part; "Be sure and be a good girl and pick nice clean friends." Then he would cry out, "I leave it to you, fellers, if she don't pick 'em clean!" Cad wore the largest nugget belt in the Klondike, given to her on July 4 by a group of Klondikers who had argued for months as to who found the biggest nuggets. Each put his biggest nugget into Cad's belt and it was so large it went around her waist one and a half times. Cad Wilson's theme song, "Such a Nice Girl, Too," was a byword until one enamored miner filled her bathtub full of wine. Not only did Cad not allow the fellow to scrub her back or watch her splash about in the grape—Cad had the wine rebottled and sold!

Though the dance halls were of differing levels of morality, in outward appearance they were all the same—hastily erected two-story buildings with large plate-glass windows in front. Upon entering, one found oneself in a small dark room dominated by a sheet-iron stove, a long polished bar, and a mirrored backbar. Several bartenders—in their starched shirts, white aprons and waistcoats, and diamond stickpins—served the thirsty men. Behind the saloon was a smaller room for faro, poker, dice, and roulette. Further back was the crude theater, with its ground floor, balcony and small stage. Part of the second floor contained a dozen bedrooms which could be rented, by the day or by the hour.

A large sign on the balcony of the theater section reminded, "Gentlemen in private boxes are expected to order refreshments." This bit of barroom etiquette was never breached, for it was a mark of a man's affluence to be seen in a box with a bevy of girls, drinking wine at sixty dollars a bottle. A private box in a Dawson dance hall became *the* status symbol of the miners. One night at the Monte Carlo,

During the Klondike gold rush, the Palace Grand Theater in Dawson was the territory's most lavish entertainment center. Arizona Charlie Meadows built the emporium in 1899, using lumber from two dismantled steamships.

a miner had $1,700 worth of wine sent to his private box. (It was in Skagway, Alaska, however, that the art of dance-hall box-rushing was developed to its greatest efficiency. After the stage show, the female singers and dancers rushed up to the boxes like a gaggle of vultures, shrieking, laughing, and demanding drinks. Without any invitation from the man who would have to pick up the tab, they would ring the bell for the waiter and order wine at twenty dollars and upward a pint.)

Before the scoundrels arrived in Dawson to adulterate whiskey with water and knockout drops, the saloonkeepers of the Yukon were regarded as men of integrity. They served as bankers, arbiters of disputes, and much-needed friends of those who were on the verge of cracking up from the Arctic solitude. The decent and generous saloonkeepers could always be relied on for "a meal and a flop" when a man was down on his luck.

Then with the arrival of the stampeders, Dawson's saloons multiplied, became fancier, and showed more interest in a customer's money and less concern about the customer. A man was expected to come in and start spreading his gold dust or stay out. The home-away-from-home atmosphere was gone—no longer could a miner, hungry for human companionship, linger in the warmth of a potbellied stove and a drink of honest whiskey.

A good saloon could pull in close to $15,000 a night. This spic-and-span establishment is the Office Saloon in Nelson, British Columbia.

The traditional barroom nudes battle for prominence with whiskey ads in this Nelson, British Columbia, saloon.

The exterior of the "Wake-Up-Jake" Saloon at Barkerville, British Columbia, decorated for Christmas. Everyone posed but the horses.

The Canadian authorities' only concern with the Dawson saloons was to insist on the collection of license fees. Colonel Steele, head of the Mounties in Dawson, felt some qualms about allowing any scoundrel with enough money to buy a license to open a saloon, but his government maintained only that "fees must be collected, the rum seller take care of himself, the dram drinker take his chances, regardless of the consequences to his morals." In the winter of 1898-1899 a total of $90,000 was collected in saloon license fees to fatten the territorial treasury. Yet this was only a dribble compared to the gold dust pouring into the coffers of the saloonkeepers. One elaborate saloon which opened in Dawson the summer of 1898 took in $15,000 on opening night! Despite Colonel Steele's undercover force in plain clothes, the gold rushers had little protection against the sharpers, drunk-rollers, short-change artists, and unscrupulous women.

Before gold-hungry girls rushed to the Yukon towns with their available charms, the early Klondike prospectors often had to content themselves with Eskimo squaws.

242

Frequently, wealthy miners who could not leave their claims had their favorite dance-hall girls brought out by dog sled. One such owner of a rich claim fell hard for a Dawson dance-hall favorite and suggested she accompany him to his cabin for the spring cleanup. Not in the least affronted by the proposal, her only objection was that business got awfully good in the spring, and she'd be giving up a lot of money. He promised to compensate the girl for her lost profits, but was taken aback by her demand for $1,000 a day and all the nuggets she could pick up on his claim in her spare time. Still, it was cheaper than marrying her, so he agreed to her demands. She stayed a month, returning to Dawson with $30,000 and enough big nuggets for a belt.

A Dawson City showgirl being given the whirl by a free-spending lover could really enjoy herself. French champagne flowed freely, and gowns from the fashion houses of Paris were available. Some of the fancier restaurants offered menus to please the most jaded palate. In the winter of 1899, one menu offered: Baltimore oysters, Consommé Impérial, Klondike grayling, Salade Homard, Paté Poulet, roast beef, ptarmigan with mushrooms, Omelette au rhum, Fromage Roquefort, with the appropriate wines and liquors.

When the music stopped, the men were expected to quench their thirst and that of their partners expensively. Champagne at thirty dollars a pint was the favorite order, since a girl got a cut of five dollars for each bottle her partner bought. A few hours' work in a dance hall paid the girl well, for she had no time to waste on anyone without a full poke. When she finished with a miner, most of his gold had found its way to the house's till and to the girl's stocking bank. What really hurt the morning after was the knowledge that the girls turned over most of their earnings to their pimp—particularly if they were veterans of the Barbary Coast. The dance-hall girls vied with each other to see whose "mac" was dressed the most expensively. And no sourdough had a ghost of a chance, no matter how much he spent, of coming between the girl and her entrepreneur.

The only official interference with the common prostitutes of Dawson was imposed when Captain Constantine of the Mounties ordered them to stop wearing bloomers, though they were permitted to keep their scarlet curtains and their red lampshades. The whores protested violently against this archaic prejudice, and strange tales were told about the sometimes forcible means employed to "debloomer" the protesting harlots. It would have been more just of the Mounties to do something about the prostitutes of Paradise Alley, or "Hell's Half Acre," who were more white slaves than prostitutes.

243

Most of them were in bondage for their passage money to the pimps who had brought them north. Paradise Alley ran behind dance-hall row, and from a double line of identical frame shacks approximately 70 girls sold their wares.

The girls who laughed and sang in the dance halls were not much happier than the wretches of Paradise Alley, for many were involved in tawdry love affairs with gamblers, saloonkeepers, and dance-hall owners. In the winter of 1898-99, the *Nugget* reported several suicides and murders among their number. Stella Hill, a nineteen-year-old from Oregon, swallowed strychnine four days before Christmas after she learned that her boy friend, the bartender at the Palmer, had another woman. Libby White was shot to death in the Monte Carlo. Helen Holden tried to kill herself with chloroform because she was jealous of a saloonkeeper's affections. The most pathetic story of all was the death of Myrtle Brocee, who danced and sang at the Tivoli. She shot herself to death in a room over Sam Bonnifield's gambling house. The coroner's inquest was unusually gallant. Several men testified that they had slept with Miss Brocee, but each swore under oath that she had remained absolutely virtuous. The man she was actually living with was Harry Woolrich, a Klondike gambler, and he testified with a straight face that his companion was a virgin. Thus, Myrtle Brocee, her honor unstained, went to her rest in a coffin with silver-plated handles and a silken interior of baby blue and white.

The results of a fight between two Paradise Alley bawds on the night of October 13, 1898, bring to mind the tale of Cripple Creek. One girl hurled a lamp at the other; within hours, the house they both worked in burned down. Wind carried the sparks to the tightly packed stores of Front Street, and soon the business district of Dawson was a mass of flames. Forty buildings were destroyed and the total loss amounted to more than half a million dollars. This aroused the citizens, who compelled the police to order all prostitutes to move to

245

There's no mistaking this girl's profession.

Lousetown. But six months later, on the evening of April 26, 1899, another fire roared through the business section of Dawson. This time the damage was twice as great. Banks, hotels, stores, and warehouses were destroyed before the fire was brought under control. This fire had started in the room of a young lady living over the Bodega Saloon. She was closely questioned as to whether she had left a cigarette or a curling iron burning in her room. In Dawson, a woman who smoked or curled her hair was deemed to belong with the ladies of Lousetown. The board of inquiry could not determine whether the girl's negligence had started the fire, but they recommended that "women-of-the-town" be henceforth excluded from all public buildings other than licensed hotels.

As late as 1901, Dawson still had only a hundred women, though it boasted a population of 5,000. It was a seller's market with a vengeance. Rumors of the shortage reached un-

As this photo of Dawson's Paradise Alley shows, the girls of "Hell's Half Acre" were white slaves in more ways than one. The cribs appear barely larger than outhouses.

The members of this gruesome crew look more like Chicago hoods than Yukon prospectors. The stark facade of the Whitehorse Hotel needed no more decoration than the faces of the three girls in the window.

married women in all parts of the United States. It was not long before various newspapers carried advertisements such as the one below, which appeared in the Marysville, California, paper:

A HUSBAND WANTED—*by a lady who can wash, cook, scour, sew, milk, spin, weave, hoe (can't plow), cut wood, make fires, feed the pigs, raise chickens, rock the cradle (but not gold-rocker, I thank you, Sir!), saw a plank, drive a nail, etc. These are a few of her solid accomplishments. Now for the Ornamental ones. She has read Murray's* Geography *and can find 6 states on the Atlas. Can read—and you can see that she can write! Could paint roses, butterflies, etc., but will paint houses, white-wash fences, etc. Could once dance. Can ride a horse, a donkey or ox. I hear you ask, Can she scold? No, she can't! As for her terms: her age is none of your business. She is neither handsome nor a fright; yet an old man need not apply, nor without any education. Gold? There must be 20,000 dollars settled on her before she will bind herself to perform all the above. Address your reply to Dorothy Scraggs, P.O. Marysville, giving your* real *name.*

Unmarried girls were so anxious to get to Dawson City and find a husband with some prospects that they would go to any lengths to find a passage for themselves. When one Klondiker returned to his hometown for a brief visit, he was approached by a hostess who asked when he would be going back to the Yukon, and could she go along. He told her he was leaving in a few days. She begged to accompany him, promising to give him her life's savings of a thousand dollars to buy the necessary mining equipment. She would cook, sew, darn and wash for him, and sleep with him as often as he wished en route. When they reached Dawson City and she started making money at her profession, she would hand

248

over a percentage of her earnings until she married. She even offered to go into harness with his huskies, provided he would "go easy on the whip."

One New York girl was more subtle, for the editor of the *Dawson City Nugget* received a letter saying:

> *Kindly place this photograph in a prominent*
> *place in your window. The first man who calls*
> *to ask about it, tell him he is to give you the*
> *money for this advertisement before you give*
> *him my address.*

The photo was enclosed, as were her vital statistics. She was twenty and honest enough to state bluntly that she wanted a rich husband. Within half an hour of the notice being put on view, a long queue of applicants were waiting with their gold dust.

By 1902, Dawson's heyday was past. The benches were worked to a vanishing point; the influx of Klondike-bound gold seekers dwindled; the swarm of men already there thinned out. Some of the miners headed north-by-west over the Yukon frontier into Alaska, to try their luck in Nome. The lucky minority departed, perhaps satisfied—if any man is ever satisfied—with the gold they had acquired. Others left, their strength and health eroded by the hostile climate and terrain. The gold diggers were leaving Dawson City by the thousands, as fast as they had come only a couple of years before. Its swift descent into a "ghost town" began, and a ghost town it has remained.

Red Liquor

JUST BEHIND THE SETTLERS and ranchers and fortune hunters came the whiskey wagons. They bounced west, crossed the deserts, and threaded the passes of the Rockies and Sierras to the Pacific Ocean, for whiskey helped make life endurable for the men who lived with loneliness, ate beans and salt meat, and worked eighteen hours a day. After the evening meal of fried beef and a biscuit, the stopper came out of the happiness jug, and the tin cup was passed around the campfire. In the flickering light of the fire, a bit of booze softened the edges of the harsh environment and gave an emotional lift to the booted and buckskinned men. Ranchers, railroad contractors, U.S. Marshals, and mountain men all shared the faith that whiskey was an elixir of immense medicinal value. It strengthened the heart, improved respiration, cured hydrophobia, eased chills, cooled fevers, helped general debility, and cured kidney ailments, snake bite, malaria, and palpitation.

This much is certainly sure: after a good long pull on the jug, the patient was feeling better. If the keg was empty or the patient had scruples about taking his liquor straight, Paine's Celery Compound offered an agreeable and respectable substitute. So did Dr. Simmon's Liver Regulator, "the cowboy's friend." The Indian braves thought highly of Dr. Sweet's Infallible Liniment. Rubbed on externally, it was said to grow hair, especially if followed by internal applicatons to clinch the roots. The actual medication in Hostetter's

Bitters was so minimal and the cutting edge of the alcohol so keen that the bitters were being sold by the drink.

Luke Short, the famous gambler, got his start when he filled his wagon with "Old Pine Top" and set up business in a thicket near the Red Cloud Indian Reservation. One reason why the Indian went crazy when drinking—to the extent that until recently Federal law prohibited him from drinking—was due to the contents of "Indian Whiskey." One old recipe called for: one barrel of creek water; two gallons of alcohol; two ounces of strychnine for a "kick"; three plugs of tobacco to make the Indians sick (they thought that whiskey had to make them sick or it wasn't any good); red pepper for the bite; and soap for the bead. Stir well and strain into another barrel. Sell one bottle for at least one buffalo robe.

As mentioned earlier, the apex of Western masculine society and the epitome of local culture was the saloon. There the working man relaxed amid the companionship of his friends. He could play cards, have a drink, have a free lunch, conduct business. A small number of these strongholds of manhood had special mixed drinks for which they became

The photographer seems to be the center of attention in this shot of Phil Kuhn's Bar, at the corner of 17th and Custer in Denver. The whiskey is there, but the wild women are conspicuous by their absence.

Four bartenders and an elaborate free lunch added prestige to this saloon in Cheyenne, Wyoming, during the early 1900's.

famed, but all served basic beer and whiskey—by which was meant bourbon. Clear, ice-cold mountain streams were diverted into the ditches between the tents and cabins. Thus bourbon and ditch water became inseparable.

When a Westerner asked the bartender for "whiskey" and he got what he asked for, which was mighty doubtful, it was barrel whiskey. All the drinker had to rely on was his own taste and experience, plus whatever faith he had in the integrity of the saloonkeeper, since "pure" whiskey could be easily doctored. In southern California, tequila masqueraded

under the trade name of many a fine old bourbon. Raw and fiery, it burned the bellies of the men who painted their tonsils with it, leaving the drinker "so shaky he couldn't pour a drink of whiskey into a barrel with the head out." Most of the potions available deserved the vile names given them—skull varnish, tarantula juice, Taos Lightning, snake water, bug juice, and dynamite. It may have been terrible whiskey, or not even whiskey at all, but one thing you could count on was that it would pack a powerful punch.

The Wells Fargo Saloon in Junction City, Kansas, truth-

Many patrons overshot the well-placed spitoon in this Central City, Colorado, saloon. The chairs seem to be for leaning only.

255

fully announced, "The Worst Liquors, the Poorest Cigars, and a Miserable Billiard Table." Robert Ford, "the dirty little coward," operated Ford's Exchange at Creede, Colorado, and served the worst drinks in the Rocky Mountains. Much of the "overnight" whiskey produced in the cellar by the locals was as deficient in proof as it was in the aroma of genuine bourbon. It was common in the whiskey mills of the West for a customer to request a drink of "sink-taller whiskey." For it was generally believed that a piece of tallow floats in weak whiskey but sinks in high-proof alcoholic spirits.

Despite all the difficulties in getting an honest glass of whiskey, everyone was willing to take his chances. When an Army detachment happened to cross trails with a whiskey wagon, a crude bar was often set up across a pair of barrels. Whiskey also followed the rail-heads—first dispensed in tents, then in prefabricated shacks moved on flatcars, with the barman often setting out the drinks before the roof was raised. For example, when Forsythe, Montana, was the "end of the track" on the Northern Pacific, twelve saloons were moved in, with bar, tables, piano, and chairs in place. In a matter of hours, the professors were spanking the ivories and one man was shot in an argument over a dance-hall girl.

At one time or another, almost all the men of any community took their pleasures in the saloons, gambling houses or brothels. The miner, the freighter, the clerk, the cowboy, and the businessman mingled as equals in the saloon, since the only limit on one's enjoyment was the size of one's purse. The personalities of the proprietor and the bartender were important, as business was boosted if they were philosophers or comics. A good bartender was a craftsman, even an artist; a philosopher; an encyclopedia of sporting information; a belle-lettrist; and a great humanitarian. He used oil to slick down his hair, wore his lodge emblem on his jacket of white, or once white, duck. A glittering rock sparkled on his ring finger and another flashy stone was screwed into the middle of his stiff-bosomed shirt.

256   It was a matter of professional pride with Western bartenders to be able to run up on order some 150 different cocktails, rickeys, fizzes, cobblers, punches, and cups. But

An ample display of "Saturday Night Art" welcomes prospective imbibers in the Manhattan Saloon on Josephine Street, Nelson, British Columbia. The cigar case is to the left of the bartender, and, for the real tenderfoot, a "fresh milk" sign hangs nearby.

always the staples were beer and red liquor. Mostly, the bartender's job consisted of turning the beer taps or reaching for the bottle of bar whiskey and setting out a glass of water as a chaser. And only the poltroon touched the water. In the 1890's, the average saloon served two kinds of whiskey which were ordered as rye or bourbon. The liquors were stored in barrels in the cellar, and brought upstairs in jugs for decanting into the bar bottles. If a rube came in, the mixologist might serve him what was known as the "cops' bottle," the cheapest cut whiskey in the house. The patrons poured their own. If the customer was a gentleman he took about an ounce and a half. It was unwritten etiquette that the dram never reached the glass rim, for if it did, the bartender threw the pilgrim a hard look, or asked, "Will you need a towel, too?"

In general, the work involved in keeping bar was to see that the walking board behind the bar was dry, use a chamois cloth on the woodwork, shine the brass, keep the money

A shot of good rotgut would leave the drinker's hands so shaky he "couldn't pour a drink of whiskey into a barrel with the head out." The ornate Brown Jug Saloon in Victoria, British Columbia, provided towels for the trembling barflies to wipe their hands on.

straight, and say to any quarrelsome drinker, "Yes, sir, ain't it the truth?" A good bartender did not drink while on duty. If urged, he would say, "But I will take a mild cigar." This five cent "Ultra-Colorado" is known in the history of bars as "the saloon cigar." At the end of the day, it went back into the box and the barman took credit for it from the cash drawer. If pushed hard by a special friend to take a drink,

As evidenced by the signs, the Hoffman House in Rossland, British Columbia, served as check casher and laundry pickup as well as saloon. A large mural hangs above the bar in place of the customary mirror.

258

the bartender would draw what was known as a "snit" of beer in his private glass. It was about the size of an eyecup and he filled it with foam and could put down a hundred or more if necessary and still not receive a message. Yet the customer paid each time for a full glass.

A truly colorful figure of the saloon world was the touring liquor drummer who was out on the road as early as 1869. Not all whiskey salesmen were gentlemen. One dirty trick used in the days of bulk whiskey was to slip a nail into the barrels of a competitor. Whiskey just cannot tolerate iron, and turns a repulsive black color in the presence of even a slight amount of the metal. Another stunt was the comparative test. The drummer would pour out his own liquor first, then divert the customer with sporting stories so that the drink stood quietly for a while. While the whiskey stood in the glass, the drummer talked on and on. He pointed out the long-lasting bead and the delightful color. If sales were lagging, he bragged that his whiskey was so good that consumers in the state the distillery was located in would not let the liquor get far from home. When sales were booming, he declared that his label was known from coast to coast. When the distillery had ample inventories of old mellow whiskey, he talked up aging as a most desirable feature. At other times he never mentioned the subject. Finally, he poured the rival brand into a glass and invited comparison. His own whiskey always won the test. Why? Because the higher alcohols, the undesirable flavors, and the aldehydes evaporated first, leaving only a smooth drink. Oldtime distillers sometimes left the bung out of the barrel to get rid of these "pig tracks."

Whiskey drummers were generous spenders. Treating in a bar was a way of winning customers for their brand, and hopefully of earning the loyalty of the saloon proprietor. Old Roy Bean, in his "Jersey Lily," had a dodge for collecting on far more drinks than he actually served. He would line up his old empties on the bar and insist upon payment from the salesman based on the empty-bottle count. One traveler complained about a bottle which did not look to him as though it had been emptied during the "drinks for the house."

Judge Bean agreed, saying," it does look fairly dry, but

it's the way of drinkin' that some of the boys has. They not only drink the bottle dry, but they sop it out."

Before Kansas went dry, and long before Carry Nation smashed the bar of the Carey Hotel in Wichita, six indignant young women converged in the saloon run by Bradley & Hildreth in Mound City, Kansas. They were armed with axes and hatchets and hit the bar just as Jim Tomlinson was taking his early morning eye-opener. Miss Sarah Wattles stood behind the bar and broke up all the glassware while a whiskey drummer from Leavenworth stood outside to watch the fun. His wagon was equipped with barrels and faucets so that samples of his spirits could be drawn off for his potential customers. While he looked in at what was happening inside, one of the ladies quietly slipped up to his wagon and opened all the spigots. Someone called the salesman's attention to the fact that now he had troubles of his own. Mad as a hornet, he threatened the young woman. Now Amelia Botkin stepped out of the saloon with her ax in hand and proposed to split his head open. A small town in Kansas was not the place to go threatening a woman. The liquor drummer just barely escaped from Miss Botkin's wrath, only to find a rope draped around his neck while the citizens made plans for a lynching at the rear of the saloon. Their better judgment prevailed, however, and he was released and ordered to make tracks. Though one of his horses fell dead before he was ten minutes out of town, he still made it to Fort Scott, riding bareback, never to return to Mound City.

Liquor represented a large percentage of all the goods shipped west, and it was one of the most sought-after items. A dearth of liquor was considered by some almost as serious as a shortage of food. Many communities supported their own breweries and distilleries, and took great pride in the local products. A good indication of a town's prosperity was to be found in the number of saloons operating, for more than any other business, a saloon served as a gauge of the flow of money. A business census conducted by the *Daily Chronicle* in Leadville, Colorado, in June 1879, reported ten dry-goods stores, four banks, thirty-one restaurants, and four churches. In con-

"But I will take a mild cigar"—that's what the bartender was supposed to have replied to offers of a free drink. This Pocatello, Idaho, bartender looks slightly under the weather as he pours himself another beer. And that's no "snit" glass, either.

trast, there were 120 saloons, nineteen beer halls, and 228 gambling houses and private-club rooms. No other town of its size could approach these figures, but they indicate the economic impact of the saloon on the Western community. Only a high-class parlor house was a more lucrative enterprise than a saloon.

Naturally, competition was keen among the rival grog shops, and some minor distinctions developed between the bit and two-bit saloons and their clientele. In order to attract more customers, the owners resorted to various lures such as bands, pretty waiter girls, and dance halls. Price wars developed between competitors, much to the delight of the drinking men. Some saloons encouraged bar girls and prosti-

261

tutes to ply their trade on the premises. Yet all of these were frills which detracted from the essentially male atmosphere of the true saloon. A saloon was predominantly a men's social club; only occasionally would a woman own and tend her own bar.

The saloon in the West was even more of a social institution than its Eastern counterpart. When a man lost his lodge pin, it was only natural for an advertisement to appear directing the finder to return the pin to the loser's favorite watering place. Bat Masterson, ordering a new nickel-plated .45 caliber revolver from the Colt factory in Hartford, Connecticut, requested that future correspondence be sent to him in care

There was no dancing permitted in the all-male Long Branch Saloon in Dodge City, Kansas, and there was no "Miss Kitty." The bar was owned by Dodge's first sheriff, Charles Bassett, and served only top-grade liquor.

of the Opera House Saloon in Dodge City. And in Butte, when Molly Demurska, queen of the red-light district, married the town marshal, Jack Jolly, the knot was tied in the Clipper Shades Saloon.

In Dodge City, Kansas, the important men made their headquarters at the Long Branch Saloon, opened in 1883 by Charles Bassett, Ford County's first Sheriff, and A. J. Peacock. The Long Branch offered a high-toned sporting atmosphere, with only top-grade liquor served at the bar. Its customers included railroad men, cattle kings, buffalo hunters, and travelers. The saloon took its name from the celebrated sporting resort on the Atlantic seaboard, since many of the men in Dodge came from the Eastern states. There was no "Miss Kitty" and no dancing in the original Long Branch. In 1876, there were nineteen places licensed to sell liquor in Dodge. Other well-known saloons on Front Street were Beatty and Kelley's Alhambra; A. B. Webster's Alamo; Muellar and Straeter's Old House Saloon; the Opera House Saloon; the Junction Saloon; and the Green Front. Of course, all the dance halls and most of the hotels had bars, and no one in Dodge was more than one hundred yards from some place of liquid refreshment, open seven days a week, twenty-four hours a day. When a new saloon was opened or a new management took over, a magnificent free lunch was laid out and the men were expected to come to the joint to celebrate.

As railroad service improved and Dodge became more prosperous, carload after carload of beer rolled in every summer. In July 1879, a facetious note appeared in the *Dodge City Times:*

> *A young lady, Miss An Heiser, is stopping in the city at present. A great many gentlemen have called upon her and express themselves well pleased with her general appearance. The only criticism we have heard made is that the length of her neck is a little out of proportion to that of her body.*
> *The "out of proportion" is to enable the*

263

fellows to embrace the neck. An Heiser is a
delusion too many persons hug. It brings them
to their beer.

The movies and television to the contrary, "shootouts" were not encouraged in the saloons. When the Masterson brothers, Jim and Bat, plugged the bartender of the Lady Gay Saloon in Dodge City, they were promptly arrested and fined ten dollars and costs. There was also a complaint that some of the bullets went through the Long Branch Saloon next door, while other bullets disturbed the conduct of business in G. M. Hoover's wholesale liquor warehouse. Hoover's was lucky that the kegs of genuine Kentucky Club were only put in jeopardy and not punctured by the gunplay.

Uncle Dick Wootton, Denver's first saloonkeeper, arrived in December 1858 with a wagonload of Taos Lightning. Immediately upon setting up, one barrel was tapped and a bar counter made of the other barrels. The awful watered-down whiskey—beefed up by the addition of pepper, tobacco, and gunpowder—was served in tin cups and everyone in town was invited to help himself. It was a memorable Christmas party—for those who could remember it afterwards. The enthusiastic city fathers promised Uncle Dick a free city lot if he would settle down and open up shop. Wootton, already a frontier oldtimer with a wife and two daughters, accepted. Soon his Western Saloon became the headquarters for many a Pike's Peaker. But Wootton's restaurant-saloon was doomed in a town where thousands of immigrants were discovering that gold nuggets could not be picked up in the streets and that food was scarce. For those who came to Colorado to gamble with cards and dice rather than with a pick and a pan, Wootton's place was their first stop. Uncle Dick advanced them $25, taking their ox or mule teams as collateral for the loan. These sports set up their tables, and generally returned the next day with the $30 to repay him. Uncle Dick did a thriving business as Cherry Creek's pioneer banker, for his Taos Lightning was a straight cash commodity, and as a saloonkeeper he was the most readily available source of funds.

In June 1859, Denver saw the opening of Apollo Hall, a billiard parlor and saloon. This ramshackle two-story tavern on Larimer Street got around to a Grand Opening Ball in September, when the town's elite feasted on a five-dollar dinner and danced to "the best music the country affords." A month later, candles were stuck into the plank walls and rude benches were placed in the large upstairs room for Denver's first theatrical performance. Four hundred pioneers squeezed into the hall to applaud the actors.

The interior of the average nineteenth-century saloon was dimly lighted, with the bar running lengthwise down the left side as one entered. The bar was ornately hand-carved, in oak, mahogany, cherrywood or hollywood. The floor was covered with sawdust to absorb the beer drip and foam. The poorest saloons handled hard stuff only, and were known as barrelhouses. Along the wall were lined up fifty-gallon barrels of whiskey lying in racks on the floor, with a second tier

The Arcadia Dance Hall, Denver, as shown in Harper's Weekly, *Feb. 19, 1866.*

This elegant saloon in Buffalo, Wyoming, boasted a Tiffany lampshade behind the bar. A stuffed eagle is mounted on the pedestal to the right.

The barroom nude has been moved to make way for festive decorations in this early-day saloon in Van Wyck, Idaho. As much a part of the Western saloon as the whiskey itself, the large nude painting traditionally hung over the bar.

on top of the first, each with its spigot. Bulk sales, by the quart or gallon, were made direct from the barrel to the customer. Single drinks were tapped directly from the barrel to the glass over a plain, unvarnished plank counter. These cheap barrelhouses specialized in rectified whiskey, flavored with a little bourbon and a squirt of glycerine to take out the scratch.

At the other end of the spectrum were the fancy places, which all gloried in having "the longest bar in the world." Erickson's Saloon in Portland, Oregon, boasted a bar which measured 84 feet and a $5,000 pipe organ and ladies' orchestra, judiciously surrounded by an electrically charged railing. If the license fee was low, the bars offered many more comforts, but if the license fee was high, the saloon had a plainer character because there were fewer competitors and plenty of customers. In the corner, there often stood a one-armed bandit, or perhaps the John L. Sullivan Athletic Punching Machine with its sign: "How Hard Can You Hit at the Great John L.?" Behind the bar was the backbar or mantel, as well as the huge mirror decorated with mottoes. Some were serious, such as "Don't Ask for Credit," while some were in a lighter vein: "If you spit on the floor at home, spit on the floor here: we want you to feel at home." Bartenders often bought up the men's temperance pledge cards at an agreed price of from five to ten free drinks. The cards were then displayed on the mirror as trophies. The central section of the backbar was a carefully arranged high altar of shining glassware. On its flanks lay a bung-starter, assorted lemons, bottles of muscatel, port, catawba, and that sovereign remedy, rock and rye. No one called for these esoteric articles, yet they gave an air of elegance.

The standard exhibit was always the barroom nude. There was a large and appreciative audience of art lovers for these scenes in which elegant but somewhat overweight sirens, shaped like dray horses, by some inadvertence displayed an expanse of flesh. Outright indecent pictures were not common: the barroom nude combined the allegedly classical with the spicy. "Venus in the Bath" or "Diana Surprised" were two favorites. These pictures and others of their type

270

The Buckhorn Saloon in San Antonio was almost a museum with its collection of antlers and rattlesnake skins. The signs on the tables were meant to be heeded; a blasphemous parrot was shot to death here for profanity.

were known collectively as "Saturday Night" paintings. The other dominant form of saloon ornamentation was that of wildlife—a motif still somewhat in vogue today. The Buckhorn Saloon in San Antonio was almost a museum with its collection of antlers, rattlesnake skins and a much too clever parrot which greeted all comers in a sing-song parody of the litany. Until it was finally shot for blasphemy, the parrot intoned, "Ora pro nobis (pray for us)—god-dam it!"

The pictorial advertisements supplied by brewers, distillers, and rectifying houses also gave life to the saloon interior. The subject matter was either patriotic, classical, pugi-

271

listic, or spicy. Some were elaborate, such as the huge color lithograph of Cassily Adams' gory but fascinating "Custer's Last Fight" which was handed out for years by Anheuser-Busch to advertise Budweiser beer. Telling a powerful, melodramatic, nightmarish story of the 1876 massacre on the Little Big Horn, the picture is myth masquerading as history. Saloon statisticians proudly assert that there have been more casualties as a result of barroom arguments over the picture than resulted from the massacre itself.

Fort Worth's fabulous White Elephant Saloon outdid every other establishment for elegance with its rich woodwork, dazzling chandeliers, and imported furnishings. Opposite the decorative bar and running parallel to it was a lunch counter stocked with "the best on this or any other market, conducted by a chef de cuisine whose knowledge of pleasing the palate has been acquired by years of experience." Historians seem to agree that the advertising was borne out by the facts. Of course, the White Elephant and other big saloons could afford to be generous with the free lunch, for their gambling halls were usually among the leading local industries. The saloon apologists claimed that gambling kept money in circulation. And it did, though most of the money wound up in the house's coffers.

There never was any shortage of saloons in Butte, Montana, and they vied with each other for the patronage of the thirsty copper miners. Ever more enormous scoops of five-cent beer together with platter upon platter of every imaginable variety of luncheon delicacy was the saloons' answer to competition. The larger the scoop, and the bigger the lunch, the greater the ring-up on the cash register. The Council Bar, an enormous, barn-sized saloon which sold thousands of schooners of beer each day, is a good example. At one end of its half-block-long bar, behind which six or seven bartenders toiled, a twenty-foot section contained an array of food that might tempt any gourmet.

Great platters of bologna, liverwurst, anchovies, summer sausages, pickled tripe, pig's snout, sliced corn beef, frankfurters, and a half dozen other varieties of cold cuts gleamed beside platters of a dozen kinds of smoked, pickled, and kippered fish. Domestic and imported cheeses of every variety were cut into appetizing cubes and slices. Five varieties of bread were stacked on large trays—rye, white, whole wheat, graham, and pumpernickel, with added plates of salted and plain crackers. Pickles were grouped with whole and sliced beets, radishes, tiny green onions and sliced Bermudas. A white-coated attendant kept the miners' plates filled and saw to it that all comers had enough. It was a help-yourself arrangement and everything was free. The only requisite was the purchase of a glass of beer before helping yourself.

No story about Butte would be complete without some mention of a "Shawn O'Farrell," that potent drink as old as the city itself. A sacred tradition in the town, the Shawn O'Farrell consisted of two drinks for the price of one—a full ounce glass of whiskey washed down with a pint-sized scoop of beer, both for one thin dime. Shawn O'Farrells were not served at any hour of the day or night, but were reserved for the hour after the miners changed shifts. To be eligible to purchase the combo for a dime, the buyer needed a lunch bucket on his arm to prove he had spent the day in the mines. The whiskey cut the copper dust from a miner's lungs, and the cooling beer slaked the thirst of eight hours spent in the "hotboxes." The modern-day Shawn O' is now referred to as a "boilermaker."

The Bank Exchange Saloon of Silver City, New Mexico, ran the following advertisement in the local paper:

> *The belligerent portion of the community can find a particularly rampant specimen of the Feline species, usually denominated the "Tiger," ready to engage them at all times.*

This tiger was the faro bank. The lure of liquid refreshments was frequently rivaled by that of the gambling offered by the saloon. The gambling hall was often one of the fanciest structures in the community. Granville Stuart described one he visited in California during the 1850's.

Magnificently decorated with plate glass mir-
rors and brilliantly lighted chandeliers, it con-
tained at one end a balcony where a string
band performed. Situated on the floor were
numerous gaming tables and a bar. All man-
ner of games were provided, but faro, roulette
and poker remained the favorite standbys.
Professionals, amateurs, and the curious min-
gled together, wagering large and small sums
on the whims of Lady Luck.

How honestly the games were run was always a matter
of conjecture. The square gambler and his associate, the law-
abiding saloon keeper, were not much in evidence in any
boomtown. (Nonetheless, gambling was most prevalent in
the early years of a town, and seemed to taper only after the
first boom waned.) The odds always favored the house and
were, no doubt, frequently improved by skillful manipulation.
Those caught redhanded in the act of cheating were pun-
ished immediately and usually fatally. Occasionally, a local
editor spoke out against the evils of gambling, but some
observers seemed to regard gambling as a male prerogative
and necessity. According to the *Butte Miner* of December 4,
1877, a husband became irate at his wife and caused a scene
because she scolded him for his visiting the tables. The edi-
torialist concluded, "What sensible man wants a wife if she
refused to support him, and even goes so far as to discourage
his little recreations, such as faro, poker, etc.?" The *Silver Reef
Miner* of March 27, 1882, stated that draw poker was a game
in which you always found a player much better than yourself. This results in the loss of money and some conceit, until
"You will never think as much of yourself after it is over as
you did before, but you will be worth more to society."
Faro was the most popular game in the Western gambling
house since it offered the player his greatest chance of winning. The percentage in favor of the house was only one and
three-fourths, while the house cut in other games ranged up
to and sometimes over six. The sharp players preferred faro
because it was commonly believed to be impossible to operate

a crooked game. Their belief was an illusion, for any game operated by the house could be rigged. A clever dealer at faro or twenty-one can make his own odds in favor of the house, even today. "Readers" or marked cards appeared in faro as much as in any other game. Also, cards trimmed slightly along the edges, known as "strippers," were often used. Sometimes cards were "sanded," making them stick together. Even a new deck could be marked in a few deals, by means of a tiny needle set in the dealer's ring. Also a horsehair set in the dealer's box would hold back any special card until the moment came for a killing.

A number of poker superstitions started out West, such as, it was bad luck to count one's chips or to play with a kibitzer looking over one's shoulder; and everyone knew a player who drew a pat hand of jacks full on red sevens would not leave the game alive. It was a lifetime of bad luck to play with a one-eyed gambler, which gave rise to the expression, "There's a one-eyed man in the game." The easiest way to change your bad luck was to walk three times around your chair.

Roulette was always a favorite in the larger houses. The

"The Tiger"—a faro game at full blast in Bisbee, Arizona, 1903. The man standing near the wall in a soft hat is Charlie Bassett, Dodge City's first sheriff.

house percentage was about six in a square game, but few roulette wheels were spun squarely. Stud poker was far more popular than draw. Keno, similar to bingo, was a dice game operated by means of a "goose," and appealed to those who played for small stakes. In the Mexican border states, Spanish monte, a game similar to short faro, was favored above all others, with the Mexicans calling the gringo players "los God dammes."

Spanish monte must not be confused with three-card monte, a variation of the shell game in which three cards are used in place of the three walnut shells and pea. While Spanish monte is a gambling game, three-card monte is essentially a swindle in which the operator of the "pitch" cheats the sucker with his dexterity in palming and manipulating the cards. The operator of three-card monte was never called a dealer; instead, since he threw his three cards face down on the table, he was known as a "thrower." Most card and dice games were played indoors, but the monte thrower usually set up his pitch on a street corner.

Hieronymus, a dice game very similar to chuck-a-luck, was also popular in the West. It was played with three dice and two wooden bowls which were connected bottom-to-bottom by a tube. Bets were placed on a numbered layout, then the dice were placed in the upper bowl and allowed to fall through the tube onto a tambourine covered by the lower bowl. The operator paid according to how many figures on the dice corresponded to those on which the bets were made. The house percentage was enormous.

"Policy" was the poor man's gambling game. Like its modern offspring, the numbers racket, it made the poor much poorer and the operators richer. The Western towns of the last quarter of the nineteenth century all abounded with policy shops. Originally, the winning numbers were those drawn in the Colorado State Lottery, established in 1867; later, the basis for paying off was the Kentucky State Lottery, or the Frankfort Lottery.

A saloon-gambling house in Pueblo, Colorado, which operated in the '80s and '90s was famous for its Hieronymous bowl, six faro banks, four roulette wheels, four tables for

The back room of a saloon in Leadville in the early 1900's, with roulette wheel in the foreground and a faro bank to the rear.

hazard and craps, two tables for stud poker, two for draw poker, one for short faro, and one for twenty-one. Keno games and policy drawings were held daily in the two back rooms. The games were run wide open twenty-four hours a day, and fifty men worked in three eight-hour shifts. Instead of giving a little money to a big loser, the house gave him a brass check, not honored at the tables, which was good for drinks at the bar, a night's lodgings, or a meal.

The West attracted many professional gamblers from the Mississippi steamboats, from New Orleans, from Natchez-under-the-hill, from Vicksburg, and from Chicago. And for years paper money was viewed with suspicion, with gold dust the prevailing medium of exchange in the mining camps. Every saloon, gambling hall, and sporting house contained a pair of gold scales which always rested on a small square of carpet. A cashier with a quick hand could always manage to drop a few grains into the carpeting, for an extra profit of ten to twenty dollars per night. For years, the twenty-five-cent piece was the smallest denomination of hard money in circulation—making two bits the price of the morning paper, of a loaf of bread, or a shot of Taos Lightning. By the '80s, gold dust no longer was current, but the West liked the feel of "hard money," and silver dollars were always preferred to paper until they disappeared from circulation.

In March 1885, copies of the *Topeka Capital* containing the official proclamation of the new Kansas dry law arrived in Dodge City. Three or four of the leading saloons actually closed their doors that same day. On the next Thursday, several saloonkeepers announced that "temperance drinks" could be purchased at their bars. George M. Hoover offered his stock of cigars at wholesale; his bartender, the only occupant of the house, had nothing to do but scratch his chin.

Yet Dodge was only apparently dry—liquor continued to flow, dry law or no. It would not be long before all of the U.S. would be apparently dry.

278

How Times Have Changed

THE OLDTIME SALOONS provided their customers with a wide variety of services—a bath, a cigar, a card game, a fund of the latest jokes, as well as a shot of whiskey. The saloon was the place where the stranger could check his grip. In a country which has never provided public comfort stations, the saloon took care of that as well. At the end of the century, it was a place to find a pool table, a gramophone, a "Hand Kineto-scope" for viewing a sexy midway dance, the Corbett-Fitz-simmons fight, or a picture of a steam express train going sixty miles an hour. There was a need for social expression, for a feeling of belonging, and for warmth and companion-ship. The saloon met those needs, with no time limit, because the clock over the bar was covered with a sign which said, "This clock is always out of order." Critics of the saloon gave little thought to the contribution it made to male society. Perhaps that is why Alvin Hulteen of Evanston, Illinois, when sentenced to attend Salvation Army services for three succes-sive Sundays or go to jail, chose to go to jail. Or why a patient in St. Ann's Hospital in Butte, Montana, leaped from a second-story window in the dead of winter and made his way, clad only in his nightshirt, to the comradeship of a barrelhouse.

The gamblers and saloonkeepers arrived in a new area with the first men, and the girls soon followed. No matter how short a town's life span, the saloon stayed to the end. Often the saloon housed other forms of entertainment—vari-ety theater, dance hall, billiard parlor, whoring rooms. Not

Prostitutes were in the vanguard of every Western settlement. This unnamed woman is said to have been the first prostitute in Lincoln, Nebraska.

all of these diversions can be characterized as vice, but when the respectable ladies started reforming the town, a guilt-by-association rule resulted in an assault on the institution of the saloon, that seat of temptations to the wavering husband.

The 1890's was the period of double beds and double standards, and there were only two kinds of women, one sort to be revered and the other to be frankly enjoyed. The first, until married, wore cotton stockings no matter how rich her father. To these conventional women, virtue was as tangible as the whalebone that bound their straining middles. Many of them bathed while wearing their nightgowns, and not a single one had been completely naked since the day she was born. These women boasted that no matter how many children they had borne, their doctors had never beheld their bodies.

For the male, there were two distinct and separate worlds: the home and the life outside. This does not mean that the wives were not aware of what their men did outside the home; they knew all too well. But nice people did not divorce; they arranged and evaded. They slept in the same beds and never spoke. They forgave grimly or not at all. But they did not divorce.

Gradually, as law and order came into a new town, various practices were classified as misdemeanors, nuisances, and offenses. Over a period of time, a multitude of regulations covering a multitude of sins were passed by the all-wise city fathers. At the top of the list stood the bawdy house. Prostitutes and lewd women were strictly forbidden from plying their trade openly within the town.

Then saloon reform came with a vengeance, led by a one-woman riot named Carry Nation whose crusade doomed the water hole for years to come. Carry Nation was the fearless foe of anyone who made, sold, or consumed any kind of spirits. With her trusty axe, she busted up more drinking joints than all the land's rowdy drunks put together. Carry

While Carry Nation crusaded, these two young ladies enjoyed some liquid refreshment in a Kansas bordello.

was born in Kentucky in 1846 and lived the life of a "Southern belle" as a girl. At twenty-one, she married Dr. Gloyd and settled down to what she thought was going to be a career as a doctor's wife. But because Dr. Gloyd was a heavy drinker, her married life was a trial until he died in 1870. Four years later, Carry married David Nation, and joined him in his anti-saloon crusading. In 1889, she launched her own crusade against alcohol and saloons by demolishing the bars of Medicine Lodge, Kansas. It is said she destroyed the nude over the bar first, then the glasses, and finally the bottles of whiskey.

The sale of liquor violated the 1885 dry law in Kansas, and Carry was determined to make things so hot for any saloonkeeper that he would close shop. With each success, her confidence increased and her attacks became more violent. She started with an umbrella, then moved up to bricks and billiard balls, and finally a hatchet. At first, she merely destroyed the spirits, glasses, and "filthy" pictures, but soon she set her sights on the saloons themselves with all their fixtures. Finally, she attacked the people who ran or patronized these establishments. Carry Nation became a symbol of the temperance movement in her black alpaca dress with the white ribbon, and her block pole bonnet. She gathered supporters wherever she went, and operated with the complete conviction that God was on her side.

The self-appointed guardian of public morality once turned her destructive talents on the old curved bar in the basement of the Hotel Carey in Wichita, the most elegant saloon in all of Kansas. The enormous oil painting by John Noble, "Cleopatra at the Bath," which delineated the Maid of the Nile disporting herself with her maids and eunuchs, was slashed and riddled, and for good measure she broke the huge mirror which cost $1,500. In Chicago, Mrs. Nation ordered a nude statue to be covered with a Mother Hubbard and a poke bonnet. The old agitator's last battle with the pictorial side of salooning occurred in Butte, where she denounced the pictures on the walls of the Windsor dance hall. But this was one battle she lost; in a hair-pulling fight with May Malloy, Carry was given a black eye and kicked out into Galen Street.

Carry's conviction made it possible for her to endure insults and attacks which would have discouraged any old-time Federal Marshal. After one of her attacks in Wichita, she was thrown in jail by the police. First she sang, "Am I a Soldier at the Cross?" then she cried, then she told her jailers she would emerge from jail "a roaring lion and . . . make all hell roar." As Carry languished behind bars, public opinion

283

began to mount both for her and against her. The *Kansas City Journal* warned her that "if she keeps on, she is going to get hurt." William Allen White, the famed editor of the *Emporia Gazette*, wrote, "She has aroused the law-abiding people of Kansas to the disgrace of the law breakers—partly by her lawlessness."

For weeks, the city officials tried to keep Carry Nation out of circulation by imposing a quarantine for smallpox on the jail where she was being held. Instantly the jail became a national shrine for those who shared her views on alcohol. Women's Temperance groups held "prayer vigils" outside the jail, and letters and telegrams reached Carry from all over the country. On January 12, 1901, she was finally released on $200 bail.

With every event, Carry Nation's fame and her campaign grew. In 1901, a Chicago theater offered her seventy-five dollars a night to appear in the drama, *Ten Nights in a Bar Room*. Carry needed money for her campaign, but she declined the offer, telling the manager she could visit and wreck ten barrooms in the time it would take her to put on one performance.

Carry's husband, David, tried to discourage her from the more violent, lawless parts of her campaign. At one meeting of her Hatchet Brigade, Carry noticed that David, then seventy-three years old, was in the audience. She called him up on the platform and introduced him to the crowd. "Ladies, this is my husband. He's a lawyer and he's going home today to prosecute a druggist that's been selling liquor," she promised. But then he addressed the audience with less zeal, telling what a hard time he had getting his wife out of jail after her saloon raids.

In 1901, Carry started her newspaper, *The Smasher's Mail*, which printed all letters to the editor that were critical of her under the heading "Letters from Hell." Throughout that year, she was in and out of jail three times in Wichita, seven times in Topeka, and in places far distant from Kansas, such as San Francisco and Philadelphia. Each arrest and release gave fuel to her campaign, and she started selling small replicas of her hatchet for souvenirs. In Kansas, her campaign

An unknown prostitute of Las Vegas, New Mexico, 1915, a denizen of the vanishing red-light district.

was a complete success, for the state became as dry in fact as it was in law. Now Carry was ready to take on the whole United States.

College students from anti-prohibitionist institutions invited her to their campuses to tell them about the "evils" of drink. Sometimes Carry was made the butt of a joke; at Yale, for example, the Jolly Eight, composed of the most notorious drinkers on campus, served as her escort. At odd points in her speech they cheered her lustily, until it was obvious that their cheering had little to do with her words. When Carry was later told her escorts were drunk, she rushed to report the outrage to President Arthur H. Hadley. Dr. Hadley tried to escape, but his flowing academic robes got caught in an umbrella stand. The good doctor was less than sympathetic, and Carry subsequently wrote that she had detected the odor of "the grape" on his breath.

In November 1901, David divorced Carry for neglect and nearly two years later he died. David's death did not dim Carry's conviction that if America would ban alcohol and give women the vote the nation's troubles would be over.

285

*Two of the very special ladies of Las Vegas, New Mexico,
posing with a friend, about 1915.*

286

*Two more of the Las Vegas ladies. The cross-eyed rasc
is more likely a customer than a mac.*

From 1903 until her death in 1911, she became more and more a national institution and less and less a hellraising crusader. Still, she managed to stir up trouble and create news. In 1906, her newspaper, *The Hatchet,* was banned from the mails because the postal authorities found her editorial against the "vice of self-abuse" to be entirely too graphic in its description. In 1907, when she was living in Washington, D.C., she tried to storm the Senate but was thrown out. In 1908, she visited Ireland, Scotland, and England and was physically assaulted when she tried to reform Dundee, Scotland, the home of the most conscientious, hard-working, two-fisted drinkers in the world.

As the Temperance and Women's Rights movements grew, the parlor house slipped from its place as the epitome of luxury. The Kansas bagnio of Madame Sperber, who is shown here with some of her girls, was a far cry from the sumptuous parlors that had earlier graced the Western boomtown.

On January 3, 1911, while lecturing at Eureka Springs, Arkansas, against the evils of drink, she collapsed. Taken back to Leavenworth, Kansas, the scene of some of her early victories, she died. Her body was taken to Belton, Missouri, and in 1924, the Carry A. Nation Monument Association of Belton erected a monument over her grave. The inscription reads: "Faithful to the Cause of Prohibition, 'She Hath Done What She Could.'"

Although her campaign failed to outlaw liquor in her lifetime, Carry's cause was culminated in 1919 with the Volstead Act and Prohibition. The Roaring Twenties, with its speakeasies, bootleg whiskey, and bathtub gin served to kill off the last of the oldtime saloons.

Like the saloons, one by one the red-light districts of the United States toppled and fell. At the dawn of the twentieth century there were an estimated 141 recognized red-light districts in the major cities of the country. In the second decade of the century, they met their demise. Chicago's Everleigh Club was shuttered on October 25, 1911, and the rest of the South Side Levee closed soon after. St. Louis, Minneapolis, Portland, and Los Angeles closed their districts before 1913; Denver's Line was shut down in 1915. On September 12, 1915, the last of Baltimore's brothels closed; 1917 brought the demise of San Francisco's Barbary Coast and its Uptown Tenderloin, Seattle's Skid Road, and New Orleans' Storyville.

The abolition of these long-tolerated houses was primarily a side effect of the movement for female emancipation. Politicians were no longer willing to allow such houses to function when an aroused womanhood would soon be able to vote them out of their offices. Once prostitution became an object of political attack, it was no longer possible to maintain the kind of investment necessary for the better class of houses. Increasingly, the surviving brothels became a low kind of place where customers could be serviced and turned out in a hurry. Those few men who earlier had visited the expensive bordello turned to call girls. Birth control also contributed to the decline of the brothel: wives who previously viewed their husband's commerce with prostitutes as the only alternative to more and more children for themselves now found they could keep their husbands satisfied at home.

One holdout against change was Jackson, California, a town in the center of the Mother Lode Country. Jackson did not turn its scarlet ladies out into the street until 1956, when Attorney General Edmund G. (Pat) Brown closed the parlor houses down. Yet Brown did not have an easy time carrying out his moral crusade in Jackson. In 1951, he sent plainclothesmen from his office to check on the reports that the bordellos were operating openly. They asked directions from a local policeman, who freely complied. Then Brown complained to the chief of police, who closed the houses. The next day, the city council fired the chief and immediately replaced him. Thus the houses lost only one day of business. Brown complained to the new chief, who declared that he had looked around and couldn't find any open prostitution going on in Jackson. Finally, in the spring of 1956, Brown sent in some state police who visited the four operating houses and arrested about fifty people. This raid shut the houses down for good, after wide-open operation for more than a century— ever since Jackson was called Botilleas because of the numerous empty whiskey bottles abandoned by Forty-niners.

Several years later, a group of Jackson businessmen were discussing the numerous historical plaques which had been placed around the Mother Lode Country as markers for tourists. One man commented on the injustice that no recognition had ever been given to the last of the California whorehouses. The group decided to rectify this oversight, and immediately they formed a committee known as the "Environmental Resources Enabling Committee to Investigate Our Necessary Services." Its purpose was to place a bronze historical marker in front of the old bordellos. The mayor and chief of police both thought the idea an excellent one. The plaque was cast, mounted on a cement foundation, and unveiled a few weeks later before television cameras from Los Angeles and San Francisco. The bronze plaque was cast in the shape of a heart. In the upper left was a red lantern and on the right was a dollar sign. The inscription read:

---

*World's Oldest Profession
flourished 50 yards east of
this plaque for many years
until this most perfect
example of free enterprise
was padlocked by
unsympathetic
politicians.*

E.R.E.C.T.I.O.N.S.

The plaque was installed on Valentine's Day, and on the very next Sunday, Reverend Long of Jackson's Methodist Church began his attack, charging that the monument was a crack in the door and would bring back prostitution. His initial thrust was followed by a plethora of telephone calls from elderly ladies demanding that the offending plaque be taken down. The city council refused, and wax casts were made of the inscription and small replicas appeared in the bars around town. Reverend Long increased the pace of his crusade, and more and more indignant ladies made anonymous telephone calls to councilmen and police. A few days later, someone dumped a basket of red paint over the marker, covering the inscription. Sometime during the dark hours of the sixth day after the unveiling, the plaque was ripped from its cement foundation. The whores with hearts of gold had made their last stand, wiped out by the respectable women.

Today the call girl has replaced the boarder, and the madam, once garbed in suggestive mystery, is now nearly invisible. The advantages for her in running a call operation are numerous. It is movable, and very little money is spent for rent, utilities, decorations, laundry, upkeep, and furnishings. Graft payments are smaller, as are the risks of a raid, for an arrest only nets one or two young ladies. Two or three girls—with a few friendly bartenders, taxi drivers, and desk clerks as friends—can operate profitably at minimum risk. The disadvantages of this system are largely the customer's, since the call girl is "a pig in a poke." What is more, the girl's rates are high and her time limited. The old time parlor house offered something more than plain sex, but that extra something has vanished.

There are still a number of extant brothels—particularly in Nevada, where prostitution is legal—but they lack the glamor of the early West. One such establishment just across the Nevada State line from California is nothing more than a set of mobile homes, a depressing comedown from the golden age of the parlor houses.

The modern drinkerie, done up in red leather and indirect fluorescent lighting, is a far cry from the plain old men's club and refuge. A modern bartender has no choice but to allow unescorted women to sit and drink at the railless bar.

Times have certainly changed.

Selected Bibliography

Bancroft, Caroline: *Denver's Lively Past. From a Wild and Woolly Camp to Queen City of the Plains.* Boulder, Colorado: Johnson, 1952.

———: *Six Racy Madams.* Boulder, Colorado: Johnson, 1965.

Barsness, Larry: *Gold Camp.* New York: Hastings House, 1962.

Beebe, Lucius and Charles Clegg: *U. S. West, The Saga of Wells Fargo.* New York: E. P. Dutton, 1949.

———: *Legends of the Comstock Lode.* Oakland, California: Graham H. Hardy, 1950.

———: *The American West.* New York: E. P. Dutton, 1955.

Benjamin, Harry and R. E. L. Masters: *Prostitution and Morality. A report on the prostitute in contemporary society and analysis of causes and effects of suppression.* New York: Julian, 1964.

Berry, Don: *A Majority of Scoundrels. The Western Frontier 1822-1834.* New York: Ballantine, 1971.

Berton, Pierre: *The Klondike Fever.* New York: Knopf, 1958.

Blair, Kay R.: *Ladies of the Lamplight.* Denver: Timberline Den ver, 1971.

Brown, Dee: *The Gentle Tamers. Women of the Old Wild West.* New York: Putnam, 1958.

Bullough, Vern L.: "The American Brothel." *Medical Aspects of Human Sexuality,* Vol. VII, No. 4, April, 1973, pp. 198-211.

Burk, Mrs. Clinton: *Life and Adventures of Calamity Jane by Herself*. Self-published, ca. 1896.

Carson, Gerald: *The Social History of Bourbon*. New York: Dodd, Mead, 1963.

Cox, Ross: *Adventures on the Columbia River*. London, 1831.

Davidson, Levette J. and Forrester Blake (Eds.): *Rocky Mountain Tales*. Norman, Okla.: University of Oklahoma, 1947.

Drago, Harry Sinclair: *Wild Woolly & Wicked*. New York: Clarkson N. Potter, 1960.

———: *Notorious Ladies of the Frontier*. New York: Dodd, Mead, 1969.

Feitz, Leland: *Myers Avenue*. Denver: The Golden Bell Press, 1967.

Fisher, Vardis and Opal Laurel Holmes: *Gold Rushes and Mining Camps of the Early American West*. Caldwell, Idaho: Caxton, 1968.

Gentry, Curt: *The Madams of San Francisco*. New York: Doubleday, 1964.

Hogg, Garry: *Lust for Gold*. New York: A. S. Barnes, 1962.

Horan, James D.: *Desperate Women*. New York: Putnam, 1953.

Hunt, Inez and Wanetta W. Draper: *To Colorado's Restless Ghosts*. Denver: Sage, 1960.

Lewis, Oscar: *High Sierra Country, American Folkways Series*, New York: Duell, Sloan and Pearce, 1955.

Lucia, Ellis: *Klondike Kate. The Life and Legend of Kitty Rockwell, the Queen of the Yukon*. New York: Hastings House, 1962.

Lyman, George D.: *The Saga of the Comstock Lode*. New York: Charles Scribner's Sons, 1937.

Marks, Edward B.: *They All Had Glamour. From the Swedish Nightingale to the Naked Lady*. New York: Messner, 1944.

Miller, Max: *Holladay Street*. New York: Ballantine, 1971.

Miller, Ronald Dean: *Shady Ladies of the West*. Los Angeles: Westernlore, 1964.

O'Connor, Richard: *High Jinks on the Klondike*. New York: Bobbs-Merrill, 1954.

Parker, Watson: *Gold in the Black Hills*. Norman, Oklahoma: University of Oklahoma, 1966.

Parkhill, Forbes: *The Wildest of the West*. New York: Holt, 1951.

Porter, Kenneth W.: "Jane Barnes, First White Woman in Oregon." *Oregon Historical Quarterly*, Vol. XXXI, 1930, pp. 123-135.

Rascoe, Burton: *Belle Starr, "The Bandit Queen."* New York: Random House, 1941.

Ray, Grace Ernestine: *Wily Women of the West*. San Antonio, Texas: Naylor, 1972.

Sanger, William W.: *The History of Prostitution: Its Extent, Causes, and Effects Throughout the World. Being an official report to the board of Alms House Governors of the City of New York*. First published in 1859. Reprint edition: New York: Arno, 1972.

Smith, Duane A.: *Rocky Mountain Mining Camps. The Urban Frontier*. Bloomington, Indiana: Indiana University, 1967.

Vestal, Stanley: *Queen of Cowtowns, Dodge City*. New York: Harper, 1952.

Wellman, Paul J.: *A Dynasty of Western Outlaws*. New York: Doubleday, 1961.

Williams, Brad and Choral Pepper: *Lost Legends of the West*. New York: Ballantine, 1970.

Wilson, Georges F.: *Here They Dug the Gold*. New York: Readers Union, 1952.

Winick, Charles and Paul M. Kinsie: *The Lively Commerce*. Chicago: Quadrangle, 1971.

Works Project Administration: *Copper Camp*. New York: Hastings House, 1943.

Zamonski, Stanley W. and Teddy Keller: *The Fifty-Niners. A Denver Diary*. Denver: Sage, 1961.

Picture Credits

PICTURES APPEAR by courtesy of the:

Alaska Travel Bureau (224, 225).
California State Library (65, 78, 100).
Cy Martin Collection (16, 60, 137).
Division of Manuscripts, Library, University of Oklahoma
    (104B).
Fort Union National Monument, National Park Service (54).
Graham Hardy Collection (96, 146).
History Room, Wells Fargo Bank (83, 88).
Idaho Historical Society (106, 261, 269).
Kansas State Historical Society (112, 159, 161, 162, 163A,
    164, 165, 262, 283).
McBride Museum, Whitehorse, Yukon Territory (231, 233,
    236, 242, 246).
Montana Highway Commission (177).
Nebraska State Historical Society (280).
New York Public Library Picture Collection (63).
Pennell Collection, University of Kansas, Lawrence (281,
    288).
Provincial Archives, Victoria, British Columbia, Canada (239,
    240, 241–G. W. Miller Photo, 247, 257, 258A, 258B).
Public Archives of Canada (229, 230, 235, 238, 244).
San Francisco Maritime Museum (23).
South Dakota State Historical Society (180).
State Historical Society of Colorado (171B, 183, 251, 265).
State of Nevada, Publicity Photo (93).
Western History Collections, University of Oklahoma (104A,
    114, 116, 117, 120, 129, 214, 221, 271, 275).

Western History Department, Denver Public Library (25, 27,
   32, 41, 43, 97, 105, 109, 111, 122, 136, 138, 152,
   163B, 168, 169, 170, 171A, 173, 174, 180, 189, 194,
   213, 217—Fred and Jo Mazzulla Collection, 254, 277,
   285, 286, 287).
Wyoming State Archives and Historical Department (252,
   266).

Index

References to illustrations are indicated by boldface numbers

301